UNTOLD STORIES

Untold Stories

MEMORIES AND LIVES OF
VICTORIAN KOORIS

JAN CRITCHETT

MELBOURNE UNIVERSITY PRESS

MELBOURNE UNIVERSITY PRESS
PO Box 278, Carlton South, Victoria 3053, Australia
info@mup.unimelb.edu.au
www.mup.com.au

First published 1998

Designed by Liz Nicholson, Design Bite
Typeset by Clinton Ellicott, MoBros, in 10.5 point Utopia
Printed in Australia by RossCo Print

National Library of Australia Cataloguing-in-Publication entry

Critchett, Jan. Untold Stories: memories and lives of Victorian Kooris

 Bibliography.
 Includes index.
 ISBN 0 522 84818 4.

 1. Aborigines, Australian—Victoria—Western District—History.
 2. Aborigines, Australian—Victoria—Western District—Interviews.
 3. Western District (Vic.)—Colonization. I. Title.

994.570049915

DEDICATED TO TWO KOORI ELDERS,
MRS CONNIE HART AND MRS AMY LOWE, WHO
BOTH PASSED AWAY IN 1993. WITHOUT THEIR
FRIENDSHIP, SUPPORT AND ENCOURAGEMENT
OVER TWO DECADES I WOULD NOT HAVE FELT
ABLE TO BEGIN THE RESEARCH THAT LED TO
THIS BOOK.

Contents

Contents

Illustrations

Acknowledgements

I especially would like to thank the descendants of those about whom I have written. Without their help this book would not exist. Some have passed away, and I mention them first: Mary Clarke in 1984, Connie Hart and Amy Lowe in 1993, and Euphemia Mullett in 1997. Others include Regina Rose, Terry Hood, Flo Finn, Pauline Mullett, Valda Mullett, Russell Mullett, Daryl Tonkin, Merle Rose, Lynette Hayes, Natalie Finn, Melita Simpson, Kylie Simpson, Gloria Hood, Rita and Kevin Hood, Lindsay Mobourne, Lillian Paine (née Mobourne) and her husband Tom Paine, Russell Mobourne, Banjo Clarke, Maisie Clarke, Roslyn Britton, Henry Alberts, Don Alberts, Mark Rose, Maureen Pugh (née Austin), Elizabeth (Libby) Clarke, Bernice Clarke, Patricia Clarke, Geoff Clark, Lionel Harradine, Kath and Bill Edwards, Brian Nelson, Edna Brown and Ivan Couzens.

I also thank the many others who have contributed in a major way: Jill Gallagher, Sandra Smith and the Museum of Victoria Aboriginal Cultural Heritage Advisory Committee for their support, the Australian Institute of Aboriginal and Torres Strait Islander Studies and the Faculty of Arts at Deakin University for small grants of research funding, Ian MacFarlane and others of Public Records Victoria for their help, Australian Archives (Victoria) for access to their collection, Jim Berg and the Koorie Heritage Trust for their valued assistance, Helen D. Harris OAM for her research assistance, John Scarce and Gary Pearson of the Registry of Births, Deaths and Marriages for their co-operation and support, Allan Willingham for generously providing pre-publication access to his list of newspaper references in *Camperdown: A Heritage Documentation of Historic Places*, and Reg Grauer for sharing information about Wilmot Abraham. John Manifold's poem 'The Land' and his account of Pompey Austin's story of the flatfish in the Milky Way appear by permission of Miranda Manifold, who generously allowed their publication without the payment of a fee. Publication was made possible by financial support from Deakin University's Faculty of Arts Research Directorate, School of Australian and International Studies and Centre for Australian Studies. I wish to express my heartfelt appreciation of Jenny Lee's contribution as editor.

The list of those who helped and are not already mentioned is far too long to name every person but, at the risk of overlooking someone who should be publicly thanked, I thank Gary Presland, Mary Hamilton, Phillip Ritchie, Mary Eagle, John Jones, Muriel Clampett, Ann Wilkinson, Betty Huf, Rex Lucas, Robert Hood, William Weatherly, John Cooper, Josie Black, Linda Wilkinson, Colin Lane, Robert Moloney, Rex Mathieson, Shane Howard, Helene Jedwab, Jill Heathcote, Ellena Biggs, Les O'Callaghan (Warrnambool Historical Society), Norma Wynd (Camperdown and District Historical Society) and Marie Boyce of the Warrnambool branch of the Australian Institute of Genealogical Studies.

Finally I must express my gratitude to my friend, Kirrae wurrung Elder Banjo Clarke, to whom I am deeply indebted. I began my work with the help of Mrs Connie Hart and Mrs Amy Lowe, but it was Banjo who saw the project to completion, reading almost all the biographies and adding his stories. In this way the oral tradition joined the evidence from the written sources to make a much richer and more inclusive account.

Introduction

This book is a series of short biographies of Aboriginal men and women from the Western District of Victoria. It draws partly on oral histories, including the memories of Koori Elders, and partly on official records created by the invading culture. It tells the stories of individuals negotiating, each in his or her own way, the circumstances imposed upon them by European occupation of their land and the dispossession that followed.

When I began these biographies, as a gubba (white) historian living in the Western District, I doubted that I would find enough material. Nothing could be further from the truth. On the one hand, local Elders generously shared with me an oral tradition stretching back to the establishment of the Western District Aboriginal stations at Framlingham (1865) and Lake Condah (1867) and to the poisonings and violence of the earlier contact period in the 1830s and 1840s. On the other, I was first impressed and then appalled at the quantity and detail of the information that survived in official records. Perhaps it was my new preoccupation with individuals that opened my eyes. The truth was well put by Commissioner Elliott Johnston, QC, in the *National Report* of the Royal Commission into Aboriginal Deaths in Custody:

> *Aboriginal people have a unique history of being ordered, controlled and monitored by the State. For each individual there are files maintained by agents of the State; schools, community welfare, adoption, medical, police, prison, probation and parole and, finally, coroners' files document each life to a degree that few non-Aboriginal peoples lives would be recorded. Not infrequently the files contain false or misleading information; all too often the files disclose not merely the recorded life history of the Aboriginal person but also the prejudices, ignorance and paternalism of those making the record.*

... The files start from birth; perhaps recording a child adopted out, perhaps its birth merely noted as a costly additional burden; through childhood, perhaps forcibly removed from parents after having been categorized as having mixed racial origins and therefore being denied a loving upbringing by parents and family; through encounters at school, probably to be described as truant, intractable and unteachable; to juvenile courts, magistrates courts, possibly Supreme Court; through the dismissive entries in medical records ('drunk again'), and in the standard entries in the note books of police investigating death in a cell ('no suspicious circumstances').[1]

I have not chosen the subjects of these biographies because they are representative of the life of the average Koori, though their experiences say a lot about what it has meant to be Aboriginal. Some are here because memories of them were alive in the oral tradition of Koori communities. Others, in a sense, chose themselves by living a life in the written records of the past. Some provided information to nineteenth-century ethnographers such as James Dawson, Brough Smyth and A. W. Howitt; others acted as leaders in making the views of their community felt, or were local identities who attracted regular press comment, or repeatedly came to the attention of the authorities, so that they built up fat files in various archives.

Weaving through these Koori biographies are the stories of several influential Europeans, who exercised their power for good or for ill. Among them are a number of individuals who were prepared to speak up on behalf of Aboriginal interests at the risk of being ostracised by their fellow settlers—James Dawson, author of one of the few sustained studies of the language and customs of the Western District Aboriginal people, and his daughter Isabella; John Murray, MLA for Warrnambool and later Chief Secretary and Premier of Victoria, who tirelessly defended Aboriginal interests inside and outside Parliament; William Goodall, manager of the Framlingham Aboriginal Station, whose affection for the people under his charge put him at odds with his employers; and a number of landowners and townspeople who at various times supported local Aboriginal people against the dictates of an unfeeling administration. Other Europeans emerge from these stories in a less flattering light. Foremost among these is a missionary, the Reverend John Heinrich Stähle, manager of the Lake Condah Aboriginal Station. For this I make no apology. Stähle's power and the way in which he used it were central to the lives of many of the people mentioned in these biographies. It is difficult to be objective about the missionaries. In *Mr Maloga*, Nancy Cato admits that when she was young she was deeply prejudiced against them, believing them to be 'interfering busy-bodies who destroyed local cultures and customs ... in order to enforce their Christian beliefs and moral standards'. More recently she reached the conclusion that men such as John Green at Coranderrk and Daniel Matthews at Maloga did 'valuable work', providing practical help to Aboriginals and speaking out against abuses when no one else was prepared to do so. The Reverend Dr Keith Cole takes a similar view in his brief history of the Lake Condah Aboriginal Station.

Whether one views the missionaries with condemnation or approval, there is no denying that running an Aboriginal station was extremely difficult. It was precisely those who showed most independence of spirit, who stood up for their rights, that the missionaries felt impelled to force to obedience. At Lake Condah, Stähle repeatedly invoked the ultimate weapon, the passing by the government of an Order in Council requiring an Aboriginal to reside where ordered, always distant from country and kin. In this crushing way the power of the state, and of the Board and its local representative, the mission manager, was demonstrated to all who might be considering some independent thought—something it was officially stated that Aboriginals lacked.

Life is a complicated business and human behaviour wonder-fully varied, making the truth about an individual life hard to know. This is particularly so when the main sources have been created largely by another culture, which at the time either was dispossessing or had dispossessed those about whom the records were being created. I have worked hard to overcome this. As much as possible I have sought to present the voice of the Koori ancestor, using his or her own words. What you have here is not the truth so much as the truth seen from a number of different vantage points. It is easy to identify the values and vested interests that led a mission manager to describe certain behaviour and incidents as he did. The same is true of all the people whose views appear here. The ultimate truth may be elusive, but enough information survives for us to experience the dimensions of these individual Koori lives.

I wanted particularly to find out what survived about individuals in the contact period—to seek out records of names and births and parentage surviving in official documents and local history. Over the years many Kooris, knowing of my interest in such things, have approached me hoping that I had come across their ancestors' tribal names so that they could bring these names back into use. I watched out for such information. I am interested not only in the impact of European arrival and culture but also in the evidence of the survival and adaptation of traditional customs—largely missing from the Board records, where the emphasis was on the degree to which Aboriginals were being successfully 'civilised'.

I also visited Koori descendants seeking any help they could give—family stories, genealogical details, photos, suggestions as to where to look for information. As a result the project changed shape, growing and transforming itself over time. As I added their questions to mine and listened to their comments and stories, I gained a new understanding of the way information from the past shapes the present. This was no distant past, but a past that had the power to confirm identity, to provide proof of Aboriginality, of tribal background and of changes to kinship links brought about by European intervention—all of increasing importance in the post-Mabo era.

Stories from the Koori oral tradition show how differently the shared experience is perceived by indigenous and settler Australians. The account of events from the Koori side, so long ignored in conventional histories, allows non-Kooris to appreciate the effect of European colonisation as Kooris felt it. Stories from the oral tradition help non-Kooris to understand 'the true history of the past', as Kirrae wurrung Elder Banjo Clarke would say—that is, a history that includes what Kooris know happened to their people. As well as providing evidence of how incidents appeared from 'the other side of the frontier', these stories indicate which aspects of the past were seen as valuable to keep alive for the next generation. When Banjo Clarke tells the story of young Pompey Austin's death, for example, it doesn't matter to him whether it was Pompey's brother or nephews who were in jail with him at the time. What matters is that there was family with him, for that's how Banjo knows what Pompey did in the last hours before his death. The reason he was in jail isn't important, either—rabbit stealing, drunkenness, vagrancy or whatever—all minor offences for which almost all the local Koori men were jailed at one time or another. What matters is that he was in jail when he died—many Western District Aboriginals know the jail well, though few have died in custody—and how the human spirit triumphs in adversity. The story of how Pompey lived in those last few hours of his life is something to be remembered and proudly told.

Most of the people about whom I have written lived in the Warrnambool–Framlingham area for at least part of their lives. For those who are unfamiliar with the area, it is important to know that there are two Framlinghams—in the words of a Koori friend, 'a white one and a black one'—a few kilometres apart. In this book all references are to the black one, the Framlingham Aboriginal community.

In the past I would have taken care to explain that Framlingham was not a mission station like Lake Condah, where a missionary employed by the Church of England Mission managed the station while receiving food and clothing for the residents from the Board for the Protection of the Aborigines (BPA). Framlingham was solely a Board station, and for most of the time it had a non-clerical manager appointed by the Board. I would also have explained that it ceased to be an Aboriginal station as early as 1889–90. Now I have come to understand that the Framlingham Aboriginal community has been a living and evolving entity ever since 1865. To those involved, the dates that mark the end of one government-imposed policy and the beginning of another blur and are often relatively unimportant compared with the continuing life of the community. Now, like everyone else, I call Framlingham 'the mission'. For most of its history the Framlingham community has been subjected to what can be quite accurately termed missionary activities of one kind or another.

Concern is sometimes raised that in writing Aboriginal history it is best to avoid matters that might make non-Aboriginal people feel guilty. My aim is not to make people feel guilty but to state what happened. This needs to be known, whether it makes people feel guilty or not. Otherwise white people's history remains different from what Aboriginal people know to be the truth. There can be no expectation of good relations between Aboriginal and non-Aboriginal Australians until we accept our shared history.

This is not to suggest that more Aboriginals died in the south as a result of violence than from the effects of introduced diseases to which the Aboriginals had no immunity. Measles, whooping cough, diphtheria, tuberculosis, influenza and even the common cold could kill people who had no immunity to them. But does the fact that more Aboriginal people died in the frontier period from introduced disease than from violence mean that we should edit out any mention of the killing of Aboriginals from our history? And should the fact that Aboriginals killed Aboriginals be used to excuse the actions of Europeans? We live among community members who tell of war against their people, here on the Western

District plains and in the distant mountains and around many of the waterholes. It is impossible to sit and listen to the accounts and not feel their anger and pain as they recall the treatment meted out to their people in the past and recount stories of the discrimination they continue to experience in the present.

Untold Stories is an exploration of the way the past lives in the present, shaping how we see ourselves and constantly reminding us of who we are. Justifying his inclusion of a chapter on history in the *Report* of the Royal Commission into Aboriginal Deaths in Custody, Commissioner Elliott Johnston stated that he had done so 'not because the chapter adds to what is known but because what is known is known to historians and Aboriginal people; it is little known to non-Aboriginal people and . . . it must become more known'.[2] In a similar vein, I have written these biographies in the hope that the circumstances of individual lives will touch the hearts of people in the general community as well as making the archival information more accessible to Kooris.

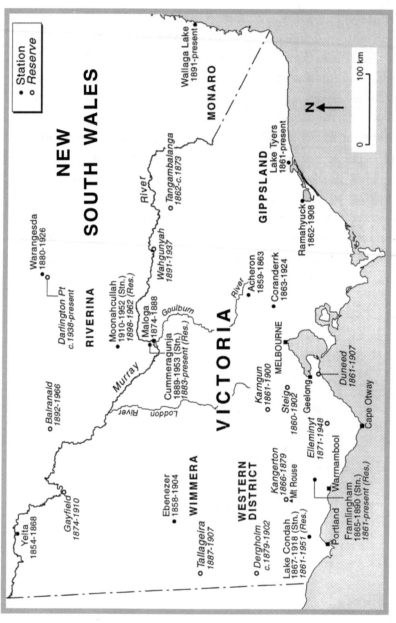

LOCATIONS OF VICTORIAN STATIONS AND RESERVES, 1860–1966.

SINCE 1966 SOME LAND FROM THE MAIN ABORIGINAL STATIONS HAS BEEN RETURNED TO ABORIGINAL COMMUNITIES THROUGH LAND ACTS, INCLUDING THE VICTORIAN ABORIGINAL LANDS ACTS 1970 AND 1991 AND THE COMMONWEALTH ABORIGINAL LAND (LAKE CONDAH AND FRAMLINGHAM FOREST) ACT 1987. WHILE LAKE CONDAH, EBENEZER, RAMAHYUCK AND CORANDERRK GAINED VERY SMALL AREAS, LARGELY THE CEMETERY AND ACCESS ROAD, FRAMLINGHAM AND LAKE TYERS GAINED LARGE PORTIONS OF THE PREVIOUSLY RESERVED LAND. RECENTLY, MORE LAND (AT LAKE CONDAH, FRAMLINGHAM AND CORANDERRK) HAS BEEN PURCHASED WITH FUNDS FROM COMMONWEALTH AND STATE GOVERNMENT AGENCIES.

CHAPTER 1

'Did you ever read your history?'

MRS MARY CLARKE

REMEMBERS

MRS MARY CLARKE OF FRAMLINGHAM, WHO PASSED ON IN 1984

Mary Edwards of Cummeragunja Aboriginal Station, on the New South Wales side of the Murray River, married Norman Clarke from the Framlingham Aboriginal community at Echuca on 26 November 1910. She then moved south to live among her husband's people. I interviewed her in her home at the Framlingham Aboriginal Settlement in 1979, five years before she passed on.

In this interview, Mrs Clarke related stories she had heard from her mother-in-law, Alice Clarke, whose parents lived through frontier dispossession. She told of the treatment Aboriginals received when white settlers moved into the Western District from the late 1830s onwards. Alice Clarke, née Dixon, married Frank Clarke in 1879. Their parents were of the generation that was dispossessed, and Frank and Alice would have heard first-hand accounts of what had transpired. The European presence in the Western District of Victoria is so recent that three overlapping lifetimes easily span the period from before European contact to the 1980s.

Mrs Clarke:
Well, what she told me was—she travelled with some tribes from Portland down to Warrnambool there. There was so many that they separated. And they heard, the tribe she was with walking said, 'We'll meet you in the morning.' The other tribe, an overseer popped up and seen all 'em travelling—children and all, and women carrying the babies on the back—and he said to them, spoke to them, but they couldn't understand. When they talked in the language, he couldn't understand that, so he said, 'Are you hungry?' and they shook their heads, and he said, 'Well, you go and sit down over there in that shed.' And they went there. He said, 'I'll make you something to eat,' and he had a great big boiler. He had a boiler there. It was in the shearing shed that he took them to have this meal. The shearing shed. They was finished shearing and they took the Aborigines there to have something to eat. They were weak and hungry, and she said, she said to some of her friends, 'I'm not stopping. I'm gunna go on, I'll go on and I'll come, we'll come back'—she was with her tribe, they split up like, and she was with her tribe—and she said, 'I'll come back next morning.'

So they did come back and—I'm not finished—wait a minute. The overseer made this porridge and he finished them. He put strychnine in it. They didn't know what he was doing, and they're all sitting around looking hungry, all sitting there, little children and all, and he was giving them the porridge, serving the porridge out to them, and they all went—flop. He murdered them with the porridge, the strychnine in the porridge. And when my mother-in-law came back with her tribe, she said she find them all dead. Children on the mothers—the babies on the mother's breast and little tiny fellows and them all laying about all scattered around dead. And, and they went ahead. They came this way to Warrnambool. They came from Portland to Warrnambool, all the rest of them, and there was a place in Tower Hill. There was a lot of people shot there too.

Jan:

Was that squatter's station near Portland?

Mrs Clarke:

Yes, yes, near Portland. I know the man's name, but I really forget it.

He died. He died walking the floor. He died walking about, walking about. He was haunted, he was worried, he died and one old Aboriginal woman was in this place—they had her there for help, the lady of that place—and when she saw him sick and he fell over, and he was dying and she said, she said, 'You—that's what you get,' she said. 'You poison my people, now you dead,' she said. [Pause] 'You are a no good man do that, all my people are dead now.' And so that was the finish of that.

And I was telling you about—oh, I think I told you about the [pause] Condah, Bloody Lake, they called it. Did I tell you?

Jan:

No.

Mrs Clarke:

Well, she [pause] that happened and they finished up all dead, and my mother-in-law and her tribe they come ahead.

What I was gunna tell ya, my mother-in-law—they killed the poor Aboriginal women. No, killed the men and they raped the poor

'Leave us a tiny corner'

NATIVE PLEA

MRS. MARY CLARKE, of Framlingham, descendant of Truganinni, last of the Tasmanian aborigines, made an impassioned plea for the aborigines last night.

She spoke at a meeting in The Australian Church, Russell street, against the eviction of a half-caste woman and her children from a home at the aborigines' settlement at Framlingham, near Warrnambool.

During the discussion it was stated that the Aborigines' Board probably would not give effect to its previous decision to evict the woman and her family from a home which it had considered she wrongfully occupied.

"Police come out to collect our rent," Mrs. Clarke said. "The Aborigines' Protection Board think it is important for the colored people to pay rent.

"But the white people never thought of paying US rent for the whole country that they took from our ancestors.

"Give us a go"

"Leave us this tiny corner where our homes are," said Mrs. Clarke. "Why should we pay rent for it at all? We regard that little bit of land as ours still.

"You have never given us a fair return for this country. . . . Give us a go in our own country."

Resolutions were passed unanimously objecting to the Framlingham eviction. The Government was urged to restrain the Aborigines' Board from selling or removing any cottages from the Framlingham settlement.

The meeting also asked for a more constructive Government policy aimed at the welfare of aboriginal people, and expressed the opinion that the time had arrived for administrative changes for the welfare of the aborigines.

A few weeks ago I went to the Jubilee March. I saw people of many nations. Somebody near me in the street said, "Where are the real Australians?"

I said, "We are a forgotten people, a forgotten race." So we are. Not only in the days of Truganini, but today. Why is it that when functions "for all nations" are held, the aborigines are generally forgotten? Where can my people fit in to the social life of the community. Most of them are shy; someone must step forward to speak, so I will.

The truth is, our people dodge white people because we feel we are not wanted. I know this is not always true. I have met a lot of very sympathetic white people and a few very helpful ones.

Even so, it takes all the courage I have to shake off the old fear of the white community and mix with white people, even when they are kindly.

When I want to help my people I feel I have to nerve myself for a struggle, but now and again, with the help of a few good friends, I have a victory, and it is all worth while.
—MARY CLARK (Queen Victoria Hospital, Melbourne).

THOUGH MARY CLARKE WAS SHY, SHE WAS A FIGHTER FOR THE RIGHTS OF HER PEOPLE, AS THESE NEWSPAPER EXTRACTS SHOW. HER PLEA TO WHITE AUSTRALIANS TO 'LEAVE US A TINY CORNER' APPEARED IN THE MELBOURNE *ARGUS* ON 22 FEBRUARY 1951, AND THE ACCOMPANYING LETTER WAS PUBLISHED IN THE *ARGUS* ON 8 DECEMBER 1951

Aboriginal women, and when the Aboriginal women had their children and they were white, they'd throw 'em away. They'd throw 'em away, get rid of them. They wouldn't have 'em. [Pause] And that happened and it happened in those days. Yes, they didn't like the white child, they'd throw it away—just get it and throw it away, soon as it was born.

And that's what they done. They just done that to the old Aborigines, shot 'em down. And they had a terrible, terrible time. They—they couldn't move. They took over, as a matter of fact. They took over the poor Aboriginal women and killed their husbands. And I always say that some day they gunna answer for that, because some day they gunna be judged for the wrong they've done Aborigines. And that will come very soon, too.

Jan:
Did your mother-in-law tell you that the children that were white were killed? Or did someone else?

Mrs Clarke:
Yes, she told me, she told me that. She said they wouldn't have it. Lots of people today say, 'You're not Aboriginal, you're white.' I was in the hotel having lunch, and two women walked in. They were at the table before me and I came in and sat up at the table, and one of them said to me, 'Where do you come from?' I said, 'I come from the Aboriginal settlement,' I said, 'the Aboriginal settlement at Framlingham.' One of them said, 'Oh, you're not Aboriginal, you're white like us.'

I said, 'Well, did you ever read your history?' I said, 'You may be related to me for all I know,' I said, 'according to history.' I said that to them. [She laughs.] I said that to them. They looked at me and I said, 'I should have been a full-blood Aboriginal woman only for the white man's sin,' I said, 'went amongst the old people, inoffensive Aboriginal women,' I said, 'inoffensive poor things,' I said, 'and killed their men to get at their women,' I said. 'Did you ever read your history?' I said. They said, 'No.' 'Well, you want to read it,' I said, 'because I should have been a full-blood Aboriginal woman.' I said, 'All half-castes is the white man's sin, what they done amongst the Aborigines in the early days, the Aboriginal women.'

I told them straight. I never worried go back in telling them, saying you're not Aborigine, you're white. Well—that happened in the early days, you see. The older women. They disgraced them. But they wouldn't have their white babies. They threw them away.

And I don't know what else I could think of now.

Jan:
You were telling me about the Lake at Condah, the bloody lake.

Mrs Clarke:
There is a lake down at Condah up to this present day. And I went down there for a trip, both myself and my husband, and I had a relation down there and she was telling me everything. She told me everything. And she said, 'You know,' she said, 'that lake over there, they call it "bloody lake", my girl,' she said. I said, 'Why?' She said, 'Because they shoot all the Aboriginal people and children and all—all the convicts, whatever they were. Shot 'em all down and they raced,' she said, 'they raced into the lake and dived in there to get out of the road of the shots. And, shot 'em all, children and all, the mothers with the babies in their arms and some crawled into the burrows, on the side of the bank and—they— that lake was like blood. It was turned into blood and from that day to this, they called it the bloody lake.'

Yes, that was a wicked thing to do, and they had a terrible time with them down there when the convicts were all roaming around and looking for women and that, and so this is what they come across, this settlement, Condah. And ah, the poor Aborigines just walking around, hunting and all that, and they see these fellows all coming and they raced down to this lake, all went into it. And there was one woman, one old Aboriginal woman what told the tale. The rest were all dead. Drowned. She told the tale. She said, she hid in the reeds. She went into the lake with the rest of them, but she hid in the lake from them and they missed her. And that was the one that told the tale to everyone that knew, that's how they know it today.

Oh, some cruel things, some cruel things that were done, they were very cruel people, they were. I said some day they are going to answer for that when they stand before God. And I said that they've gotta answer for all what they've done. I said they were very cruel to our people in the early days. They flogged them and shot them and—and they murdered them.

They were murdered everywhere—all over Australia. They got Australia for nothing and they treated our Aborigines like dirt and murdered them and killed them. It gets on my nerves when I think of it, of what's left . . .

There used to be an old woman in Warrnambool, she was camped about, down near where the guns are, you know [at Cannon Hill]. And she used to come up and sit down in the gutter, sit down in Warrnambool, and smoke her pipe, and a lot of larrikins would come along and laugh at her and tease her and they say she used to get up and chase them—and chase them—she'd be looking about, looking about to see what she had to hit them with, but they'd be gone.

She couldn't find a spear or nothing. They went away. She said, 'I'll kill you, I'll kill you.' They used to tease her—poor old woman.

Oh, yes, there's a lot of stories and I forget a lot and that's only what my mother-in-law told me. But—that's all I can think of.

Jan:
Miss Murray it seems also helped Aborigines . . .*

Mrs Clarke:
They [the Murrays] were lovely people. They used to feed all the Aborigines—everyone from the whole settlement would go in there for the races and go to her place and they would have everything ready for them to eat. They were lovely people, yes. Before they go to the races they would be full. They were very good. They were lovely people.

They [the men] used to travel in the sports—foot-running and hurdling. They used to follow right up to Bendigo and everywhere. That's where I met my husband. He came up there [to Cummeragunja], he came up there while I was there. It was very pleasant there when they used to come, the boys—everyone would make them welcome, like. Oh, it was a beautiful setting!

---

* Sister of John Murray, MLA for Warrnambool 1884–1916 and Premier of Victoria January 1909 to May 1912.

Jan:

Much better than here?

Mrs Clarke:

Oh, there were three hundred children going to school. White children too. There used to be a lot of white people farming on a big hill, big sandhill, a couple of miles off the settlement, and their children used to walk to school on the settlement. Lovely people, they were. There was no prejudice that time.

There was a black man teaching us. He happened to be an Indian, and he married one of our women. He was well educated and he teached us all. Oh, a lovely man, a good Christian man. Mm. I met my husband that way. He come up to New South Wales with all the rest of the boys—they all dead now—they all died. So I've had a very good experience.

Jan:

Did you ever go over and stay at Lake Condah when it was still a mission station?

Mrs Clarke:

No. I came from Cummeragunja down here. It was a big settlement on the Murray River. They had three hundred children going to school, they had a church, they had a chemist, they had a hospital and they had a big store. It was a lovely place—you wouldn't want for anything. Oh, yes, I can picture everything that happened there, yeah, everything. I had lovely friends and all relations. I mixed with people, and young people at that time wasn't like the young people today—wild, abusive language, filthy language. I never heard none of it, any of it. It was clean, clean and everybody was friendly. We used to play games, rounders, and we had a big corroboree there once. We used to have good times. [She laughs with pleasure at the memory.]

Jan:

Who was the mission manager there?

Mrs Clarke:

Mr Harris.

Jan:

Cummeragunja sounds better than any of the mission stations that I've heard about here. None of them here were big enough to have their own shops, chemist shop and that sort of thing.

HUT ON THE FRAMLINGHAM MISSION IN WHICH MARY CLARKE GAVE BIRTH TO HER DAUGHTER AMY. FROM LEFT TO RIGHT: AN UNNAMED VISITOR; BILLY RAWLINGS; MARY'S BROTHERS-IN-LAW, FLEETWOOD CLARKE AND FRANK CLARKE; VISITOR.

Mrs Clarke:

No, when I come down here it was very, very quiet. I was quite a stranger when I come down here. I lived with my mother-in-law down on the river down here, and everybody was sort of shy—some people. They eventually made friends after they got used to me.

And I had a picture here of a poor old Aboriginal man. William Good his name was. [To her grandson:] You heard that name, eh, Raymond? He used to preach the gospel. Have you heard that name?

Jan:

Yes, I've seen pictures of him too.

Mrs Clarke:

I had one ... too, but someone took it from me. He was preaching in the church one day—he was the only minister about, poor old fellow and he wasn't a young man either. The church used to be full, and one Sunday he was preaching and when he was saying prayers—he was praying—and two dogs was fighting outside and all the people walked out of church to look at the dogs! [She laughs.]

THE OLD CHURCH AT FRAMLINGHAM

Jan:

What did he say to that?

Mrs Clarke:

When the poor old fellow, when he opened his eyes he wondered where the people had gone!

Yeah, he opened his eyes and he wondered where all the people were. Then he went outside and he seen them all standing round the dogs. I'll never forget that, it was the funniest thing. He was a good old man, a good old Christian man though. He died of old age.

Yes—that was the funniest thing ever happened. That poor old fellow. He was praying away. And a big mob was in the church too. A big mob in the church, and when he opened his eyes he looked. He couldn't make out where they'd gone to. He walked out and heard the dogs outside fighting and he went out and seen them and they were all there, standing up. Funniest thing that ever happened. I'll never forget that.

He was a good old man, his wife was a good old woman too. There were a few Christian people here at that time when I come, but today there's no church, no anything—no minister comes or nothing. They've all forgot about us. I used to love the church, love the church. It makes me so sad.

That's all I can tell you.

CHAPTER 2

'An old hand'

JIM CAIN

c. 1830–1882

JIM CAIN

Jim (Jem) Cain (Cane or Kane) was an extraordinary character. Born at a time when the only Europeans in the Western District were the whalers and sealers working along the coast, he was later to boast of having shaken hands with the son of the Queen of England. Jim was fond of the races and sporting fixtures, and became well known throughout the district and as far afield as Melbourne, where he attended the Melbourne Cup for several years running. He was sociable and enjoyed a drink or two.

Jim was well liked, and seemingly had no difficulty in gaining help, in cash or kind, from white citizens of the district. He was always 'well supplied with money': 'Western District people were always ready to supply his wants', wrote Richard Osburne, a keen observer of the local scene who was proprietor of the *Warrnambool Examiner* from 1851 to 1880 and author of *The History of Warrnambool*, published in 1887.[1] Michael Heaver, a local policeman, agreed with Osburne's assessment. Jim, he said, 'was a great favourite with all classes. At Races and places of amusement people would treat him to a drink even in spite of the police watching and trying to prevent it.'[2] He was popular with his own people also. William Good, resident on the Framlingham Aboriginal Station, commented that he was 'well liked by all the Blackfellows he was an old hand in this district'.[3]

Though there is not even a hint of this in the Warrnambool sources, Jim Cain claimed that Warrnambool belonged to him, as I learnt from an article published in the *Camperdown Chronicle* in 1882.[4] Jim identified Warrnambool as his 'country', the word Aboriginals use to describe the land to which they are intimately linked and for which they take responsibility. Deborah Bird Rose explains, 'Country is a place that gives and receives life':

Country in Aboriginal English is not only a common noun but also a proper noun. People talk about country in the same way that they would talk about a person: they speak to country, sing to country, visit country, worry about country, feel sorry for country, and long for country. People say that country knows, hears, smells, takes notice, takes care, is sorry or happy . . .

Each [country] has its own people, its own Law, its own way of life ... In Aboriginal Australia each country is surrounded by other countries. The boundaries are rarely absolute; differences are known, respected and culturally elaborated in many ways. As David Turner says, Aboriginal Australia is made up of a series of 'promised lands', each with its own 'chosen people'.[5]

In later years Jim lived mainly in Warrnambool but was often to be seen heading out along Raglan Parade or on the road to Belfast (Port Fairy).[6] He and his wife Nellie—and Kitty, of whom more later—evaded the sedentary life on the 'mission', though in 1876 a government document gave the Framlingham Aboriginal Station as the required place of residence for Jim and Nellie. For this reason their lives provide an interesting contrast to those of Aboriginals residing on the stations.

How Jim gained his name is part of local history. In 1838, so the story is told, Jim Cain 'of whaling renown' was working with another man splitting timber for farm improvements on Yangery Park, a property just a few kilometres to the west of present-day Warrnambool. At lunchtime they took a break, leaving their tools at the work site. When they returned they discovered all their tools had vanished except the cross-cut saw. Aboriginals were blamed. Jim Cain's shirt, which had been thrown over a stump, was also missing. A short time later the shirt was seen 'on a young black boy'. From this time on the lad was called Jim Cain. Although he was threatened and entreated to divulge the whereabouts of the missing tools, he refused to do so.[7]

In seeking more information about Jim Cain, I turned to Mrs Maisie Clarke, a member of the local Koori community, who informed me she had always been told that she was a descendant of the Cains through her mother, Ester Couzens, a daughter of Harriet Blair, who was a daughter of the Cains.

I investigated birth, death and marriage records and local history, hoping to augment what I had learnt. I found that in 1862 there was a Nellie (Aboriginal name, Whitburboin) living with

JIM AND NELLIE CAIN

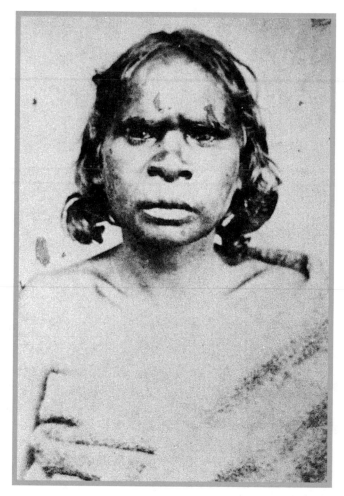

NELLIE CAIN'S APPEARANCE TRIGGERED MUCH SPECULATION
ABOUT HER ANCESTRY

Barney (Aboriginal name, Minimalk). They had five children: Jessie, Harriet, Frank, Willie and Mary Anne. They were living at Terang for part of 1862, but saw themselves as members of the Tooram 'tribe', a group of Aboriginals living at Tooram, the property of John McMahon Allan, just to the east of Warrnambool at Allansford.[8] The word 'tuuram' was the Aboriginal name for the tidal estuary of the Hopkins River.

Marriage and death certificates provide evidence that Nellie Cain was the mother of Jessie and Harriet, but there is conflicting evidence about whether Jim was their father.*

Nellie has a colourful place in Warrnambool's history, as she plays a part in the legend regarding the 'Mahogany Ship', long claimed to be buried in the sandhills west of Warrnambool and seen as proof that the southern coast of Australia was discovered by Portuguese or perhaps Spanish sailors. In 1836 two men, Gibb and Wilson, lost their whaleboat and their mate when they were trying to enter the mouth of the Hopkins River in search of seals. A plaque at the mouth of the Hopkins now commemorates the event. The survivors walked along the coast to Port Fairy. On the way, they came across a wreck on the coast near Tower Hill and reported it to their employers. From then on a number of people reported seeing the wreck, which gradually disappeared from view over the years, probably covered by the shifting sand. Despite energetic searching and offers of government reward, nobody has so far rediscovered the wreck of the ancient ship.

Aldo Massola has claimed that Aboriginal tradition supports the idea that the coast was discovered long before the beginning of the nineteenth century, and that Nellie was descended from these early voyagers. In 1969 Massola wrote:

> *It has been stated that they had a tradition that 'Yellow Men' from the wreck had settled amongst them, intermarrying with the tribe long before the coming of the first 'white men' ... it has been claimed that Nellie ... was quite different from an ordinary Aboriginal. Her colour, her hair, the general contour of her countenance, and particularly her profile were said to suggest some foreign strain.*[9]

---

* Harriet was the younger of the two sisters. After the death of her first husband, James Couzens, she married John Wyselaskie on 31 March 1909. On this marriage certificate her parents are named as Nellie and Barney. On Harriet's death certificate (27 February 1928) her parents are named as James Kane and Nellie Kane. Jessie married Walter Lancaster on 13 February 1909, after the death of her first husband (Brown). On the marriage certificate her parents are named as James Cain and Nellie Allen (many of the Aboriginals living at Tooram took the surname Allan). Jessie, again a widow, married Henry Albert in 1915. This time her mother's name is given as Nellie Cain but the father's name is marked unknown.

Kirrae wurrung Elder Banjo Clarke agrees. He remembers the old people such as Grannie Isabella (Bella) Rawlings talking of people of a different colour being in the area. Banjo also remembers Harriet, daughter of Nellie. She was short and very dark: a quiet, kind old lady. He vividly remembers an incident that occurred when he was only a child. He was on his way down to the Warrumyea Bridge to get a billy of milk from his cousin, who was milking cows. Following a footpath through the mission scrub and trees, he came to Harriet's hut, which was about the centre of the mission, on the Purnim side of Newnham Avenue:

The little footpath went past the hut, and as I went past she called me over. 'Where are you going, my boy?' she said. 'I'm going to get a billy of milk.' 'You want to hurry, big storm coming.' And she said, 'When you come back this way, you come back here.' On the way back the storm clouds were building up in the south-west. It was getting darker. I was hurrying and trying hard not to spill milk out of the billy. I came to the hut. The old lady called me in. She had an old camp oven on the fire. 'Wait a minute, my boy,' she said. 'It won't be long, soon be cooked.' I stood there and watched her as she pulled the oven off the fire, opened it and tipped it over. 'There, my boy, I'll wrap it for you.' I could see it was sweet scone—flour, sugar, dripping, cooked like a damper. I was real happy. She said, 'You take it home and share it with your brothers and sisters.' She gave me an old coat. 'Put this on, my son.' Rain began to fall. I hurried home. They were all happy. 'Where did you get it?' they asked. 'From the old lady down in the hut,' I said.[10]

Born about 1830, Jim Cain grew up in the midst of the inter-racial violence that erupted from west of the Hopkins River to the South Australian border during the early 1840s. As late as 1844 Rolf Boldrewood saw no 'trace of [European] man or habitation' when he camped with cattle at the mouth of the Merri River 'just below where Warrnambool now stands'. As he drove over the sand hummocks bordering the beach, the only movement was that of a number of cattle, an 'outlying group', which galloped off when he disturbed them. 'All else', he wrote, 'was silent and tenantless as before the days of Cook'.[11] But Europeans were near by and had been for some time, and the land was far from untenanted. Had he not heard of the strife that had caused such anguish only two years before his arrival? At that time the residents of the Port Fairy area had appealed to the government for protection against Aboriginal attacks. They complained of the Aboriginals' numbers, ferocity and cunning, 'which render them peculiarly formidable'.[12]

Those who signed the petition included squatters located over a large area to the east, north and west of Port Fairy: from Hunter at Mount Eccles to the west, to Niel Black in the east and others as far north as the Grampians. Boldrewood was himself shortly to face Aboriginal attacks on his property when he took up Squattlesea Mere run, south of Mount Eccles. Like others whose interests were threatened, he soon came to the conclusion that there was no alternative but to fight:

We could not permit our cattle to be harried, our servants to be killed, and ourselves to be hunted out of the good land we had occupied by a few savages . . .

[S]hould we crush the unprovoked émeute [Fr: popular rising], or remove the remnant of our stock, abandon our homesteads, and yield the good land of which we had taken possession?

It would hardly have been English to do the latter. So we had nothing for it but to make the best fight we could.[13]

Even though Jim Cain was a child, he no doubt heard talk around campfires of European violence, of deaths by shooting and poisoning. Or did elders shield the young from such terrifying news?[14] One of the worst cases of poisoning occurred in 1842, inland from Port Fairy at Tarrone, the property of Dr Kilgour and Dr Bernard. A group of Aboriginals crossing the property were invited to stay for a meal and given poisoned food. Three men, three women and three children died from the poisoning. Further inland in the same year, on the station of Smith and Osbrey at Caramut, four Aboriginal women and a child were shot while they lay defenceless, asleep in a tea-tree scrub.

When it appeared that local settlers were shielding those guilty of this unprovoked attack, Sir George Gipps, the Governor of New South Wales, wrote to Charles La Trobe, Superintendent of the Port Phillip District, threatening that in the interest of justice and humanity he might have to close the district to settlement and turn 'the whole into an aboriginal Reserve'.[15]

The 1840s were also the decade of the Port Phillip Protectorate, when the government appointed a Chief Protector, George Augustus Robinson, and four assistants to protect the interests of the Aboriginals as Europeans moved into the district. In the Western District many Aboriginals would have met both Robinson (the same Robinson who 'brought in' the Van Diemen's Land Aboriginals) and the Assistant Protector in charge in the west, Charles Wightman Sievwright. Sievwright established a Protectorate base at Lake Keilambete in early 1841, but moved to Lake Terang shortly afterwards.

In February 1842 Sievwright finally moved to Mount Rouse, where 64 000 acres had been reserved for an Aboriginal Protectorate Station. This was the only Protectorate reserve from Geelong to the South Australian border. Aboriginals were encouraged to move to the Protectorate base, which they were told was an 'asylum ... instituted to provide for their wants'.[16] This station continued for almost eight years but offered little to the Aboriginals. There was no teacher, supplies were few and arrived only intermittently, and the Protectors found they were unable to prevent Aboriginal attacks on European properties or protect Aboriginals from European retaliation.

The Chief Protector journeyed across the district between May and August 1841 with the aim of meeting as many clans as possible, telling them of the government provisions for their protection, taking a census and collecting information on the location of clans and on Aboriginal customs. His official report recorded his meeting with local Aboriginals on the coast eleven miles east of Port Fairy. On arrival he despatched Aboriginal messengers to the various clans with an official invitation—official in terms of both cultures: he adopted the Aboriginal custom of using messengers, and he was the official representative of the Governor of New South Wales and the Superintendent of the Port Phillip District.

> *April 26.—Towards evening, a large body of natives (armed) were seen wending their way among the sandhills. At fifty paces from my tent they halted. I went forward, and, the usual preliminary forms being gone through, I was introduced, and explained through my native inter-preter the object of my visit. One hundred natives at least were present. They were seated on the ground in rows, and continued so with their weapons beside them during the conference. Presents were distributed. Their original names were written down, and ... I gave them new ones ... the evening was spent in song and dance.*

The following day messengers were again despatched, and he met a large group of Aboriginals waiting for him beside the track leading to Port Fairy: 'three hundred at least were collected. The sections were separately formed—the men (armed) in front, the women and children behind. On my approach they stood up'.[17] He estimated that he might have met as many as 400 Aboriginals during his stay in the Port Fairy area.[18]

Robinson returned in 1842 to investigate claims of Aboriginal attacks on properties in the Port Fairy district. On this trip he met at least fifty Tare-rer gunditj men, women and children three miles west of the Merri River. Between the Merri and the Hopkins River he met nine more Aboriginals, and at Allan's property he met the local clan, Pat-tat-gil gunditj.[19]

Jim Cain may have met the Chief Protector. He may have heard of the Protectorate station. But the reality was that he and his people were on their own. The Protectorate offered little, and by the 1850s the entire scheme had been abandoned as an acknowl-edged failure. There was no longer any pretence that anything was being done for the indigenous people of the west.

Aboriginals had become paupers in their own land, forced off their clan territory or allowed on to it only with permission from

Europeans, sometimes excluded from special sites, their numbers greatly reduced, cut off from many of the places where they previously hunted and gathered. Their material circumstances, which Geoffrey Blainey has argued were as good as those of the average western European at the time Captain Phillip and the First Fleet arrived,[20] had deteriorated markedly, both in absolute and relative terms. There were two reasons. First, as Blainey points out, the standard of living of the average person in 'many European nations and outposts' rose significantly in the nineteenth century.[21] Second, European settlement led to the loss of the land and all but destroyed the Aboriginal way of life.

In south-west Victoria Aboriginals began living all year round in simple windbreaks, mia-mias, which before European arrival served mainly as temporary housing in the summer months. In winter the people of the region had used more substantial, durable and warm huts, which they returned to year after year as the cold weather set in. The abundance and variety of foods available were also sharply reduced, partly because Aboriginals were excluded from certain places, but also because some foods became much harder to find. Murnong, a root crop like a parsnip with a yellow buttercup flower, the plant most frequently mentioned in early accounts as a staple Aboriginal food, became increasingly rare as sheep ate off the tops and the Aboriginals were prevented from burning off to encourage its growth. To acquire new products such as tea, flour, sugar, tobacco and alcohol, Aboriginals had to negotiate with Europeans, either through begging or by seeking paid work.

A perceptive local pastoralist, Robert Burke of Mount Shadwell, realised the depth of Aboriginal suffering. He saw the 'loss of a feeling of independence' as Aboriginals grappled with change in every aspect of their lives. He warned:

As a race, I believe the intelligence of the native has been much underrated ... Physically, morally and intellectually the race has undergone and is undergoing an amount of depression which ... tends to the extinction of the race. We should therefore form an unfair estimate of the race if we judged them by their present degraded condition.[22]

Aboriginals were widely employed at least on a casual basis, and were paid in cash, or food and clothing. Their opportunities to find work improved in the 1850s, when many white employees departed for the goldfields in the hope of making a fortune. Many Aboriginal workers did odd jobs, both in the countryside and in the towns. Others took on more demanding tasks such as shearing and fencing, which kept them in work for several months at a time, receiving eight to ten shillings per week and their keep. In the late 1840s and the 1850s, however, it seems few hired themselves out as a European would, agreeing to work full-time for extended periods. One employer explained the situation this way:

> *I only know two or three who hire themselves like white men. They are trustworthy and truthful, seldom neglecting or leaving their charge without notice, but I cannot with any certainty name the time they may stop, as they are generally paid by the week, usually 10s. with rations.*[23]

Jim Cain was one of the local Aboriginals with a reputation as a valued worker. He was well known around the Warrnambool area as a loyal and trusted employee of Richard Rutledge of the Briars, Farnham. Richard's brother, William Rutledge, who moved to Port Fairy in 1843, was to become known as the 'King' of Port Fairy, where he was 'merchant, magistrate, mayor and alderman, all in one'.[24] In 1844 William was granted the Farnham Survey, which gave him ownership of the rich land that stretched west from the Merri River to the Killarney Beach Road. At this time Richard moved to the Survey, and in the following years he made several trips to Sydney to buy and to bring back cattle and horses for his property. He was accompanied on these trips by Jim Cain, who was still a boy at the time. In 1845 Jim would have been about fifteen years of age.

Richard Rutledge left the farm in 1852 and went with a small party of men to try his luck on the goldfields for about twelve months. At the end of this period, before returning to farming, Richard made a trip to Sydney to purchase a number of horses and bring them back overland to Farnham. Richard delighted in telling the story of an incident on this trip in which Jim Cain played a key role. The story is repeated here in the words of one of Richard Rutledge's close friends. The men on their way back approached the crossing place at the Goulburn River to find:

> the government punt in the hands of a mob of diggers who were so exasperated at the exorbitant demands of the puntman that they tied him up to a post, and worked the punt themselves, crossing all who wished free of charge. They were a rowdy lot, and as the hotel was close by, many of them were in high spirits. Mr Rutledge had a considerable sum of money on him, of which Jim Kane was aware; so getting his master away from the crowd he said—'Mr Richard, you had better give me your money. These fellows are a bad lot, they might rob you, but they'll never think of robbing a blackfellow!' Mr Rutledge, acting upon Jim Kane's advice, gave him his money, keeping only a small sum for present expenses. The landlord assisted them to cross their horses at a bend of the river away from the crowd. They crossed themselves by the punt and camped that night some distance from the place.[25]

Richard Rutledge also looked after Jim. Surviving letters demonstrate his concern when his friend and employee, together with George Cain, was charged with the wilful murder of William Baker (Aboriginal) on 24 September 1853. The trial was held in Geelong Circuit Court on 4 February 1854. Witnesses reported seeing the men together on the day of the murder behaving in a very excited manner. There was no evidence that they were drunk. Mr Ireland, for the defence, argued that the prisoners had turned to their own laws to resolve a dispute and dispense justice, and that this was not surprising given 'the little attention paid to the requirements of the native population by their European brethren'. The jury returned a verdict of manslaughter with a strong recommendation for mercy.[26] The two men were sentenced to six months jail to be served in Geelong.

When the time for Jim's release was near, Rutledge contacted Inspector Lydiard at Belfast. He asked that Jim and George be taken to Melbourne and given into the care of Captain Warcus of the schooner *Elizabeth*, who had orders to bring them back to Belfast by sea. Inspector Lydiard wrote to the Chief Commissioner of Police in Melbourne: 'They are belonging to a tribe in this district and would run great risk of being killed should they come overland. All expenses will be paid by Mr Rutledge.'[27]

This correspondence reveals that some Europeans at least were aware of the clans' strong ties to specific territory and of the hostility they felt towards outsiders, 'strangers', Aboriginals whose 'country' was somewhere else. Such hostility could be averted by seeking permission to enter clan territory, but Rutledge was right in thinking that crossing the district was a more hazardous undertaking for Aboriginals than for Europeans. By the time his request arrived, however, the men had already been discharged. Each had been given a couple of pounds and a blanket to help them on their way. All Richard Rutledge could do was wait and hope for their safe return—and express his relief when they were finally spotted coming up the drive.

Charles Flower, nephew of Horace Flower of Port Fairy, worked on Farnham for a time after he arrived in the district in 1854. In his reminiscences he tells of an incident that earned Jim much praise in the local community. An immigrant ship had arrived in Port Fairy and Mrs Rutledge, needing a servant, had gone to Port Fairy, engaged a 'good girl' and arranged for Jim to call for her. Jim was despatched the next day with the bullocks and dray to bring the girl and her luggage to Farnham. On their way home two men accosted them, threw their swags on the dray and told Jim they wanted to go to Koroit. The girl, becoming alarmed at the men's behaviour and their 'boisterous' language, jumped off the dray and sought refuge in a nearby public house. The men continued to insist that they wanted to go to Koroit and even threatened Jim with violence if he did not do as they wanted. Jim appeared to give into their demands, but in fact continued heading for home:

It was now getting late in the evening and while we were at tea, Jim's lubra came in a great state of excitement [to tell us] that something was wrong with Jim. She was quite confident as she had heard him Coo-ee twice and she, frightened, thought wild black fellow after him—then we heard the bullock whip. Rutledge and I then proceeded in the direction the dray was coming. We met it with the two men on it. While Jim was telling the story in very broken English the men got down and one began to contradict Jim, when he hit the men on the head with the butt end of his whip. We then allowed them to go, but after questioning Jim more closely ... it was worse than we thought. It was evidently their intention to have taken the girl, bullock and dray to some place or other. This being so, Rutledge and I decided to follow them. We came up with them at a public house about four miles from Warrnambool on the Merri River; they were there in the bar parlour and had firearms in their swags. The hotelkeeper told us of this ... Rutledge left me as guard ... while he galloped into Warrnambool for the Police, who came out quickly and took them in charge ... They were tried and sentenced to some months imprisonment and Jim was highly commended for his action and a monetary subscription raised for him in the Court.[28]

At this time Aboriginals in the Western District still practised polygamy. John McMahon Allan of Tooram once said that polygamy existed to 'any extent consistent with the supply of opossums and kangaroos'. Asked how widows were treated, he light-heartedly replied, 'Given to husbands as soon as possible'.[29] Jim had two partners, Kitty and Nellie. Of the two, Nellie seems to have been better known, and it is noteworthy that she is the only one of his wives mentioned in the 1876 government document giving Framlingham as the Cains' required place of residence.

The managers of Aboriginal stations, whose task it was to civilise and Christianise the residents in their charge, did not encourage polygamy. This became an issue during an incident on the Buntingdale Methodist Mission at Birregurra in the early 1840s. The missionary expressed his pleasure that one of the residents had built a house for himself and his wife. Others approached and asked if they could also build houses. They had a special request, however. They would need more rooms, because they each had several wives. The missionary was not amused. If it was good enough to adopt one European custom, he said, they could adopt another. They could discard the other wives and keep only one. The Aboriginals went away and showed no further interest in building European-style houses.[30]

In time mention of polygamy became rare. This might have been partly a result of the influence of mission managers in the 1860s and later, but there was another influential factor as well. Fewer women than men appear to have survived the frontier period in the district. An 1853 estimate of the number of Aboriginals in the Portland Bay district listed 325 men but only 209 women.[31] In 1881 there were 325 males over 14 years of age but only 201 females.* There were 130 men whom one might expect to be looking for a partner (unmarried men aged 20 and upwards and widowers of all ages), but only 63 available women (unmarried women aged 15 and upwards and widows of all ages).[32]

For a decade after the end of the Protectorate, there was virtually no government provision for the indigenous peoples of Victoria. Aboriginals in the Western District were largely left free to go their own way, as long as they kept to themselves and didn't infringe against European notions of acceptable behaviour. In the frontier period it was made clear that taking even one sheep was stealing: it was an attack on property and as such must be punished. Killing too would not be tolerated. The lessons were well learnt. There was little stealing of any kind by 1850, and little if any violence against European individuals.[33]

Where once settlers carried guns whenever they ventured outside their hut or home, now Aboriginals carried guns without comment. They were widely regarded as quiet, honest and

---

* It is wise to be cautious of census and Board figures, especially after 1877, for two reasons: first, the continuous migration between Victoria and New South Wales; and secondly, changes in the official definition of 'Aborigines'. The change of Board policy towards 'half-castes' in 1886, for example, meant that those who were recorded as 'legally white' were no longer counted as Aboriginal. Neither of these reservations applies to the 1881 census figures. The 1877 Aboriginal census also supports my general point about the excess of men in the population. For more detail, see Diane Barwick, 'Changes in the Aboriginal Population of Victoria, 1863–1966'.

trustworthy. Sergeant Archibald of Warrnambool, for example, wrote in the late 1850s: 'The Aborigines of this district . . . are very quiet, and have not, to the knowledge of the police, committed depredations against the life or property of the inhabitants'.[34] Similarly, Robert Burke of Mount Shadwell pastoral run commented in 1858: 'In my district the natives are perfectly quiet. In former times depredations of a serious character were committed, and many lives were sacrificed.'[35]

The situation changed in 1860 with the appointment of the Central Board to Watch over the Interests of the Aborigines. The Board established Aboriginal stations in various parts of the colony, in line with its policy of moving Aboriginals on to land temporarily reserved for their use with the aim of civilising and Christianising them for eventual merging with the general population. The Board was slow to establish stations in the south-west, but it appointed Honorary Correspondents, who were able to claim and distribute provisions for the Aboriginals.

It was 1865 before the Framlingham Aboriginal Station opened, and even then it had a chequered start. The Central Board decided that Lake Condah was a better place for a station and in 1867 closed Framlingham and opened Lake Condah. Local Aboriginals, however, preferred Framlingham, and the Board was forced to reopen the station in 1869. For the next twenty years there were two stations in the south-west.

Once stations were established, Aboriginals were required to move to them and came under the control and supervision of the manager. Official pressure would have been exerted to persuade Jim and Nellie to move to the Framlingham Aboriginal Station, but they continued living in the general community for the rest of their lives. In this way they avoided the loss of freedom of movement and the supervision of all aspects of life that was part and parcel of being resident on an Aboriginal station.

In December 1867 there was great excitement when His Royal Highness Prince Alfred, Duke of Edinburgh and son of Queen Victoria, visited the Western District. Emotions ran high as communities vied to outdo each other in demonstrations of gratitude and loyalty. The public turned out 'almost *en masse*' for a glimpse of the Duke. At various stopping places he paused to receive addresses from the communities and make short speeches in return. Amid all the fervour one of the few members of the Western District public to be introduced to the Duke, and one of only two to shake his hand, was Jim Cain.

Warrnambool was not on the Duke's route. People eager to show their loyalty had to ride to Camperdown or Mortlake (where the largest crowd ever assembled in the region waited for four hours to catch sight of the Duke) or gather at the Moffat property, Hopkins Hill, at Chatsworth, where Warrnambool community leaders were to deliver their Address. This document assured the Prince that they felt the 'liveliest feelings of attachment' to him as an 'Officer of the Navy which has ever been the glory and might of Great Britain, and the boast of Englishmen'. In 'no part of the Queen's dominions' were her subjects 'more loyal and devoted'.[36]

The Duke had evidently heard of Jim, for he asked to meet him. The introduction took place at Hopkins Hill. The *Warrnambool Examiner* reported the event and the delight of Jim, who:

> *will probably never cease boasting of the fact that he shook hands with 'big one Queen's piccaninny'. The circumstance has made him proud as Lucifer, and from the time of the hand shaking, Jim has evinced a great disinclination to lower his dignity by performing any kind of work. Having heard that it was not the custom of His Royal Highness to shake hands with anyone, and that only one of Mr Moffat's guests (Mr Richmond Henty) had been so honoured, Jim's conceit knew no bounds. 'Mine big fellow now', said Jim; 'Duke shake hands along o' me ... Duke no shake hands with Billy Rutledge even ... mine fust-rate chap now.'*[37]

He was 'so deeply impressed with the honour that for some time after he kept his right hand sacred from contact with "common people"'.[38]

Though Aboriginals and settlers were in contact, and sometimes very close contact over several decades, on pastoral properties, on farms and in homes where Aboriginal women worked as servants, there was an official attempt to keep a distance between the races. Mixing to the extent of actually living together was strongly discouraged; it was illegal for a non-Aboriginal to live with Aboriginals. Henry Attwood, for example, was fined in the Warrnambool Court of Petty Sessions for doing so.[39]

People employing Aboriginals without permission were also fined. In October 1876 Daniel Twomey was fined 20s. and £5 5s. costs in the Penshurst Court of Petty Sessions for 'giving food and employment' to two Aboriginals from one of the Aboriginal stations. Twomey explained that 'One of them had been in a very weak state: he had taken compassion on both and taken care to see that they had not been given alcohol'. In passing sentence the magistrate 'cautioned persons too kindly disposed' towards members of the Aboriginal race that the law would be enforced.[40] The Aborigines Protection Act, the *Warrnambool Standard* warned its readers in early 1877, 'forbids any person'—an Aboriginal obviously not being a person!—from harbouring

> *any aboriginal unless such aboriginal shall have a certificate, or unless a contract of service shall have been made on his behalf and be then in force, or unless such aboriginal shall from illness or from the result of any accident or other cause be in urgent need of succour, and such cause be reported to the Board or a local committee or local guardian or to a magistrate within one week.*[41]

All these certificates and contracts of service had to be signed by the Board.

It was also illegal to supply Aboriginals with alcohol, but it was almost impossible to prevent their obtaining it. Aboriginals favoured 'ardent spirits', which had serious effects, leading to fights and sometimes murder. To prevent these problems, the Guardian of the Aborigines, William Thomas, argued in 1858 that it would be beneficial to prevent Aboriginals 'from coming within the precincts of a town'.[42] This did not become law, but after the establishment of the Central Board to Watch over the Interests of the Aborigines the police were encouraged to be more active in seeking out and punishing publicans who broke the law. They could be fined up to £5 for supplying Aboriginals with alcohol.[43]

Court records indicate that pacification had its price for dispossessed Aboriginals. Over the years Jim Cain went to court many times. From 1864 to 1876, the period for which I have been able to get full details of 'Aborigines confined in Her Majesty's Gaols and Lock-ups', Jim had at least one stay in prison every year except 1871; in all, he was incarcerated on thirteen occasions.[44] On five occasions he was only held briefly and discharged without sentencing, a clear indication that the offence was a mild one. The remaining offences, committed over eleven years, consisted of five charges of being drunk or drunk and disorderly, and three of assault. Two of the assaults were on one or other of his wives, and it is likely that the other was on a fellow Aboriginal. It is probable that alcohol was involved in all cases. The usual sentence for being drunk or drunk and disorderly was twenty-four, forty-eight or seventy-two hours imprisonment. Often imprisonment could be avoided if one had the money to pay a fine, but Aboriginals usually went to jail. On 26 January 1872, for example, Jim was ordered to pay ten shillings or go to jail for forty-eight hours. Not having the money, he 'was marched off to the lock-up looking ill-used', reported the *Warrnambool Examiner*.[45] The sentence for assault was more severe, ranging from imprisonment for a month to three months imprisonment with hard labour.

Nellie and Kitty also spent time in the lock-up over the same period. Their only offence was being 'drunk and disorderly'. They were often discharged without sentencing, though Nellie on one occasion was sentenced to fourteen days imprisonment.

One can see the difficulty of their situation. Drinking alcohol was widespread in the community. It was regarded as a sociable thing to do, and Aboriginals found alcohol reasonably easy to obtain. Yet they were forced to drink away from the hotels and public places and try to avoid being noticed when drunk—rather hard when one lived in a town such as Warrnambool, where one's behaviour was easily seen. It is surprising in the circumstances that Jim and his partners were not in trouble more often.

'Drunk' and 'drunk and disorderly' were the most common offences with which Aboriginals were charged in the second half of the nineteenth century. Between mid-1861 and the end of 1870 there were 617 occasions on which Aboriginals in Victoria were confined in 'Her Majesty's Gaols and Lock-ups'. Of these 288 (47 per cent) were in the Western District, which accounted for one-third of the Aboriginal population of Victoria in 1864. Analysis of the offences for which Aboriginals were confined reveals that 194 out of the 288 (67 per cent) were for being 'drunk', 'drunk and disorderly' or 'drunk using obscene language'. If one combines these with charges arising out of police action against them (resisting arrest, assaulting police, using obscene language, using threatening language) the total becomes 220 out of 288—76 per cent.[46] A pattern well documented in the modern period, that 'the Aboriginal offence *par excellence* is drunkenness', was established early in the post-frontier years.[47]

Drinking, or at least being drunk, led to problems. Jim Cain saw this. Even in grappling with the effects of alcohol, he showed an inimitable style. He could easily have felt sorry for himself when he reflected on what he had watched happen to his people. He could have felt bitter that the whites had come uninvited, taken the land, killed and stolen, and left his people with nothing. And now they were punishing him for drinking when all around him he saw plenty of people having a drink and a good time without being put in the lock-up. He didn't. Instead, he thought of how he could appeal to the community to help deal with the effects of having too much to drink. Like anyone else, he could put an advertisement in the local newspaper, and this was what he did. He lodged the following advertisements:

Caution. — I, Jim Cane, aboriginal, hereby caution any publican against giving my lubra NELLY any intoxicating liquors.[48]

Caution.—I, JIM CANE, aboriginal, hereby caution any publican against giving my lubra NELLY any intoxicating liquors.

And:

Jem Cain in company with his two lubras, got tipsy lately, and on suffering a recovery found that some one had stolen three rings from his fingers, and two from his cravat. Jem will be obliged for information which will lead to their recovery.[49]

These were not Jim's only dealings with the local press. At the end of November 1879 he and Wilmot Abraham (see chapter 3) called into the *Standard* office to lodge a complaint. They and their partners were being molested by larrikins who were throwing stones at them and using bad language. The *Standard* reported what they had said and reprimanded the lads—'any ... who have been guilty of such behaviour should be ashamed of themselves'— but finished by blaming Jim and his friends for enticing the larrikins to attack them. It described 'these blackfellows' as 'a perpetual nuisance ... when half drunk ... they become trouble-some, and tempt the abuse of thoughtless boys'.[50]

Jim took his concerns about 'larrikins' further. To his mind, the judicial system that dealt with him when he offended against the code of acceptable behaviour should operate just as effec-tively against those whose behaviour offended him and his fellow Aboriginals. He therefore took a complaint to the Warrnambool Court. He waited discreetly in the background until the court had dealt with its business of the day, then raised the matter of the larrikins' swearing and cursing. 'Blackfellow no like.' He told the magistrates that he and Kitty had been subjected to the grossest language, and he left his listeners in no doubt about the horror of the experience. He suggested a remedy: the placing of 'Bills' near the Commercial and Western hotels and other places where drinkers congregated. He suggested they should carry the message: 'Larrikins no swear. Plice put um long a lock-up if they do.' The *Standard* reported that he had received a sympathetic hearing, but expressed the view that nothing would come of it.[51]

Nellie died on 3 December 1880, aged forty-five, at Farnham, Dennington. The cause of death was given as phthisis and pneumonia. She was buried in the Warrnambool Cemetery.[52]

By this time the population of the Warrnambool district was 14 435 (4837 Europeans in the town and 9495 in the country, plus 75 Aboriginals and 28 Chinese).[53] Warrnambool was a thriving centre, and was proclaimed a town in 1883. Most of the Aboriginals lived on the Framlingham Aboriginal Station. Whenever Jim was asked why he didn't move to Framlingham, he always said he preferred knocking about the town, and this he did until his death in 1882.

The last time anyone saw Jim alive was at a football match between the Warrnambool team and the Framlingham Aboriginal footballers, played on the Jetty Flat near the swamp known as Lake Pertobe in mid-1882. On the following Tuesday Jim Cain's dog walked into the Framlingham settlement without his master. Worried friends reported Jim missing and made several searches, as did the police, but to no avail.

On 11 November 1882 a local man, John Kenny, decided to investigate an object in Lake Pertobe. He had first noticed something about three weeks earlier and thought it was a swan. He swam out about a hundred yards into the water and discovered the object to be a man's body. Taking hold of the man's shoulder, he brought the body ashore. The police were then contacted.

A magisterial inquiry held the following day established what appeared to have happened.[54] Both William Good and John Brown from the Framlingham Aboriginal community remembered seeing Jim at the football match. William Good commented, 'he was pretty well on from drinking on that day'. Countering any suggestion of foul play, he added 'no one was meddling with him'.

Constable Heaver remembered that the water in the swamp was unusually high at the time and right up 'to the metalled road'. The post-mortem revealed that Jim was 'well-nourished' and healthy at the time of death. There were no signs of violence on his body. There were signs that Jim had died from asphyxia subsequent to drowning. It was agreed that he had accidentally drowned after the football match while under the influence of alcohol. He had been carrying few possessions; his pockets contained just one sixpence and two pipes.

In March 1886 a second man, Patrick Kelly, was found drowned at almost the same spot where Jim was found. The verdict of the magisterial inquiry was that Kelly too had accidentally drowned, but the Deputy Coroner added a rider to his finding: 'either a portion of the lake should be fenced, or lights provided, to prevent people accidentally walking into it', indicating a realisation of how dangerous it was to walk at night in that particular area.[55]

Jim was buried on 12 November 1882 in the Warrnambool Cemetery.[56] He would have wanted it that way. Warrnambool was his country. But there was a strong bond between Jim and the Framlingham Aboriginal community. While written records give the impression that Jim rarely visited the Aboriginal station, there is no doubt that there was a well-beaten track out to the reserve. When Jim disappeared, his dog walked the fifteen kilometres to the mission. There were the people who mattered, the ones who understood.

CHAPTER 3

'I'm your half-brother, and I'm here to stay'

WILMOT ABRAHAM

DIED 7 JULY 1916

ABORIGINAL NAME: CORWHORONG

A POSTCARD OF WILMOT ABRAHAM POPULAR EARLY THIS CENTURY, FROM THE JORDAN SERIES

No Aboriginal has been more strongly identified with Warrnambool than Wilmot Abraham. He lives on in the sketches, photos and postcards that in his day made him the best-known Aboriginal of the Warrnambool area, and a strong visual reminder of Warrnambool to many visitors. In the late nineteenth and early twentieth centuries, images of Wilmot formally seated in a studio or sitting outside his mia-mia featured on numerous postcards, both black-and-white and colour, sold to tourists in the coastal resort.

Wilmot was a favourite subject for artists and photographers. It was a sketch of Wilmot sitting by the fire in front of his mia-mia in Selby's paddock near the Hopkins River that gave Warrnambool's Arthur Jordan the career break that would make him one of the first press photographers in Melbourne. A friend showed the sketch to David Syme, proprietor of the *Age* and other papers, who invited Jordan to Melbourne to meet him. As a result he was appointed as a photographer on the *Leader* newspaper, where he worked until his return to Warrnambool to take over his father's Liebig Street photography studio. Jordan's pen-and-ink sketch of Wilmot was sold to a Warrnambool woman for £5. She was later to turn down £25 for it, but she lent it to Jordan so he could make copies of it.[1]

Local Kooris have a different memory of Wilmot, as I found out when interviewing the late Mrs Mary Clarke in 1979. Her story went back to Wilmot's youth in the early years of European occupation of the Western District, a time of terror and sadness for many local Aboriginals. Mrs Clarke was reluctant to tell me what she knew in case it upset me. She asked her son Banjo, who had entered the room, 'Will I tell her about poor old Wilmot?'

'Tell her all about it,' Banjo replied. 'You're not embarrassing anyone by telling the truth.'

I too insisted, and this is what she said:

Yes, dear old man. I saw a picture the other day and I never seen him since I seen him alive and he's dead a long, long time.

Old Wilmot, he was from a tribe—I forget the name of the tribe—but they used to go out for a day's outing, shooting, going out hunting, and this poor old Wilmot had his brother on his back, carrying him. They were all the children there looking around there for witchetty grubs and all that, and this poor old Wilmot was carrying his brother and up came a lot of men on horsebacks. Up came a lot of men on horsebacks and they were shooting and shooting them down like animals and shooting and shooting them, and this poor old Wilmot had his brother on his back, a little boy on his back, and they shot the poor little boy, and they took Wilmot. Wilmot, you know, he was terrible, poor old fellow. He was young then, wasn't old like when I saw him. They got him. They took the little boy away. To Mr Murray . . .

And that's where he was there with his mia-mia and they were very good to him and looked after him till he died. Poor little fellow. I think the tribe took him and, you know, buried him, the little boy, and that's what happened.

I could find no mention of this death in official records. The event survives in the oral tradition only.

Wilmot was one of the Tooram Aboriginals who camped on John M. Allan's property at Allansford, just to the east of Warrnambool. His native name was Corwhorong and he was born at Panmure.[2] There were twenty-six Aboriginals living at Tooram in 1862, when a public meeting was held in Warrnambool to establish 'the best means of ameliorating the present wretched conditions of the Aborigines' of the district. The meeting passed resolutions recommending that land be reserved for the Aboriginals' use, that they be brought together there under a superintendent, that J. M. Allan be the superintendent, and that a memorial be presented to the Governor embodying the resolutions. The memorial to the Governor was signed by many people from Belfast, Tower Hill, Woodford, Elephant Bridge, Terang, Camperdown and Mortlake, as well as Warrnambool.

Land had already been reserved for Aboriginal use beside the Hopkins River in 1861, but the Central Board to Watch over the

Interests of the Aborigines was suspicious of the activity on behalf of the Aboriginals around Warrnambool and refused to agree to the formation of an Aboriginal station on the land until its meeting of 8 September 1865. Then it responded positively to a request from the Church of England Mission to the Aborigines of Victoria, which proposed to occupy the Framlingham reserve and open a station with Daniel Clarke as missionary manager.

The Framlingham Aboriginal Station was established in 1865 and most local Aboriginals moved there, for it was government policy that Aboriginals be required to do so. Wilmot, however, refused. Like Jim Cain, he preferred his freedom. Instead he moved around his 'country', camping in favourite spots. For a time I thought he lived in Warrnambool or on its outskirts, but I later learnt he was a familiar figure much further afield. At Nullawarre, for example, he is regarded as a local Aboriginal. In 1870 James Burleigh bought the first land there and discovered that it was a favourite camping place for Wilmot and his fellow Aboriginals:

> *The last of the full-blooded Aboriginals camped in mia-mias on this property until 1880. A south-east paddock is still called 'The Blacks Camp Paddock'. The four blacks were Wilmot and Peter, who caught and ate possums, and Lily and Diana, who made rush baskets. Wilmot (the last living) moved to Warrnambool ... One small picture 'The last of his tribe' is in the Nirranda Hall.[3]*

There is a story of how Wilmot remonstrated with a descendant of that first James Burleigh for shooting possums in the moonlight. 'You shoot too many possums, this blackfellow die,' Wilmot said.[4]

Wilmot and his partner, Diana, were also well known at Peterborough and further east. Diana's name became a household word, as Alice Goldstraw recalls in *The Border of the Heytesbury*: '"You are as black as Diana", was a reproof I heard frequently, when, as a child, I objected to having my face and hands washed'.[5] Goldstraw also recalled that when local white children began to study the classics, 'they found it difficult at first to reconcile the name Diana with a goddess chaste and fair garbed

WILMOT IN FRONT OF HIS MIA-MIA

in green and silver, so long had they associated it with the coal brown skin, red blouse and purple skirt of Wilmot's lubra'.[6]

In 1862 Wilmot and another Aboriginal man, Paddy, both of whom were familiar with the coastal area east of Warrnambool, were selected to accompany a public expedition organised to prospect for gold in the inhospitable Otway Ranges. The party, led by J. M. Allan, left Warrnambool in November. It returned with tales of some success, and a further party set out on 12 January 1863, again accompanied by Wilmot and Paddy. The venture was abandoned in February, though others were to continue searching in what was believed to be a very promising area for prospecting.

Wilmot had the unenviable distinction of having appeared before the court for drunkenness 'more frequently than any other person in the district'.[7] He always had an excuse. Some were delightfully appropriate. When the familiar charge was read out in the court on 26 May 1891, Wilmot informed the bench with an indignant air that it had been the Queen's birthday, and as a loyal person he had been drinking toasts to her health. 'The presiding magistrate could not withstand his confession of loyalty . . . Wilmot escaped with a caution.'[8]

When Wilmot appeared before the court for being 'drunk' or 'drunk and disorderly', he was usually either cautioned and discharged, or sentenced to twenty-four or forty-eight hours imprisonment. On only one occasion did he face a more serious charge, that of assault, for which he was sentenced to three months imprisonment with hard labour. He had thrown a jug at Miss Tieman, who had refused to serve him in the bar of the Victoria Market Hotel.[9]

One night a friend said to Wilmot, 'You'll never get to heaven when you die, Wilmot, if you get drunk all the time like this'. Wilmot grinned and replied that Lily, who had replaced Diana as his partner, would look after that. 'She will tell St Peter at the gate, "He's only a poor old blackfellow", and St Peter will let me in.'[10]

The white community saw Wilmot as someone to whom they could appeal on matters Aboriginal. A case in point occurred during the 1870s when there was much public discussion about Queen Fanny, who was 'the heroine of an episode that, had it occurred to a white woman would have rendered her famous over the wide world':

> It was years ago, when Fanny was a young lubra ... the country stretching from Lakes Gnotuk and Bullen-merri to Mount Noorat and the Sisters was held under squatting license from the Crown by a person called Taylor who was the immediate predecessor of Messrs Neil Black and Co. At that period of the settlement of the country the blacks were, of course, very numerous, and by no means satisfied with the manner in which their country was being settled, and themselves improved off the face of the earth. They sometimes stole a lot of sheep ... and some-times ... would try to spear a shepherd or two ... After their sheep-stealing exploits they were hunted and shot down ... it so happened that Fanny's tribe was camped somewhere on the west side of Lake

Bullen-merri, and the warriors had indulged themselves in a raid on
Taylor's sheep or shepherds. The result was of course, a hunt in retalia-
tion ... There being no other means of escape many of them, not killed
or wounded in the first onslaught, made for the lake and amongst the
number was Fanny. Carrying her picaninny, she took to the water ...
and with the little one on her back swam across the lake ... a distance of
about a mile. Out of the whole campful at that time she was the only
lubra and her's was the only picaninny that escaped death.[11]

There was much local discussion of the accuracy of this story and
of Queen Fanny's parentage. James Dawson, who was a great
friend to Western District Aboriginals and would have spoken to
them about this, believed the account.[12] Others claimed that
Queen Fanny was a half-caste and a daughter of Buckley, the
escaped convict who lived with Aboriginals until he surrendered to
John Helder Wedge in the Geelong district on 7 August 1835.
Wilmot's advice was sought. Peterborough pioneer Jessie Scott
MacGillivray remembered what he said and recorded it. The claim
that Fanny was a half-caste, she said, 'is not true. She was a full-
blooded black, on the authority of Wilmot—the well known old
black chieftan ... the last of his tribe, who stated, "She was as
black as blacker than me".'[13]

Because Wilmot used the surname Abraham, those who
thought about this may have assumed, as the photographer Arthur
Jordan did, that Wilmot had been adopted by the Abraham family,
who were among the district's earliest white settlers. The truth is
far more interesting. Wilmot was the son of a white man, William
(Billy) Abraham, who came to the area with the pioneering Allan
family, after whom Allansford is named.

I learnt of this from Reg Grauer of Allansford, a great-grandson
of William Abraham. Wilmot's white parentage was not widely
known in the Warrnambool community during his lifetime. Even
among the Abrahams Wilmot's membership of the family, obviously once accepted, became something best not talked about
from about the 1920s to the 1960s. All mention of it was avoided.

Children grew up knowing nothing about Wilmot's connection with their family. Imagine Reg Grauer's surprise, then, when he learnt the truth from an elderly aunt who realised that unless she told what she knew she would take the family secret to the grave. This is what Reg told me in December 1996:

The Abraham family came with the Allans to Allansford in 1839 . . . from the Riverina. They heard of the good lands down south, so they moved a mob of cattle and their family belongings to take up land in the south. My great-grandfather, Billy Abraham, was then approximately fourteen years of age and a drover and a freeman for them. He wanted to come with them, but on the first night on the drive they decided that he was too young. They sent him back and told him that he was too young to come.

But, being a determined kind of boy, he made a pact with the cook to leave him provisions at the camp and he kept half a day's travel behind them. For some couple of months he kept a safe distance in the rear, but within travelling distance of the stock movement. After they got over the Great Dividing Range he thought he was that far down the track they wouldn't send him back, and they didn't. He rode into camp and continued on with them to Allansford, where the Allans settled in late 1839.

To make sure of him as a drover the Allans appointed him as a boundary rider to the east of Allansford, where they made him a slab hut and stocked it with provisions on a fortnightly basis, and his duties were to stop the cattle from roaming further eastward than the Childers Cove area. This he apparently did for a number of years.

Jan:
Where did they build this hut for him, Reg?

Reg:
They built him a hut down Allan's Flat Road, a road which runs down due south from the Great Ocean Road at round about Allan's Forest, where the Allan's Forest School previously was—it would be about two to three miles east of the Warrnambool Butter Factory.

A RARE SIGHT—WILMOT WITHOUT HIS HAT

He had a slab hut there and his duties were to stop the cattle roaming eastwards. Being a virile young boy he was quite active in doing this job.

The story so relates that some period after this time my maiden aunt called me to her bedside, round about the 1950s,* insisting that I take my family responsibilities of having the secrets of the Abraham family bestowed upon me. She wanted to tell me about the skeletons in the cupboard. Included in those skeletons was the fact that I was to become the proud wearer of Grandfather's Orange Sash. He'd been an Orangeman who came out . . . The world hasn't changed much since that time but fortunately—or unfortunately for her—I refused her kind offer. As I had good Catholic neighbours, I didn't want to continue the war.

Included in those family skeletons in the cupboard she told me about the misdeeds of her grandfather Billy, my great-grandfather. Billy, she said, being a young active buck in those days, took himself a gin, and after some time she begat him a child. After the child was born, both the gin and the child disappeared from the area for a number of years. After this Billy married a white by the name of Mary White, and they had a family. Then their children married and had children themselves. My aunt was about the fourth or fifth child in a family of thirteen.

She as a child remembers this black man coming up the path to the house one night and dumping his bundle on the veranda. She rushed inside and said, 'Father, there's a black man outside.' Father Billy, the son of Billy, said, 'What do you think you're doing, my good man?' He answered, 'Well I'm Wilmot, I'm your half-brother, and I'm here to stay. This is my home.' He deposited his belongings and made himself at home.

---

* We checked later and Reg's Aunt Ruby died in 1978 aged eighty-two. He was called to her bedside when she was in her seventies, so it was likely that this was in the 1960s rather than the 1950s.

I've no reason to doubt this statement as Ruby, my aunt, was a very astute lady, very honest and trustworthy. I have no doubt that what she was telling me was the truth. Wilmot said, 'I'm Wilmot Abraham.' He used the family name, and my aunt told me from that date onward Wilmot was accepted as a member of the Abraham family. He was fed, housed and clothed by them and even that, when he passed on, his burial was paid for by the Abraham family. It is only hearsay from her, but I believe it to be true.

Jan:

But he didn't live with the family all the time, did he?

Reg:

No. Wilmot was a roamer. He moved around in a circuit from the [Abrahams'] Durnsley Park property at Mepunga—a mile south of the Mepunga East School—towards Warrnambool, where he had a mia-mia at Huntingfield,* which is just behind Ethel Mitchell House. He camped there under some cypress trees. He also moved round towards Lake Gillear and fished there, and round the coast to Nirranda and some of the bays there. He fished along the rock shelves and generally hunted back to Durnsley Park. He had quite a circuit he used to travel on a periodic basis. That was typical of the Aboriginal families of those days, they were just roamers.

He had a partner called Diana and there are photos of Wilmot and Diana in residence in their mia-mia in the family albums, which more or less confirms that there was some connection. I was surprised when I went through the albums on the death of my parents that these photos turned up. It led me to believe that what I was told was factual. So we do have some inkling that Wilmot, instead of being one of the last of the 'full-bloods', was actually first of the 'half-castes'.

Jan:

Wilmot's birthplace is given as Panmure in a list collected by Collin Hood's daughter. I'm not sure that Wilmot provided the information. Does it seem likely that he was born at Panmure?

---

* A property on the Princes Highway, just west of the Deakin University campus, recently owned by a Mayor of Warrnambool, Pat O'Sullivan.

Reg:

Panmure is a possibility, because it is only about four miles from Durnsley Park.

Jan:

Mrs Mary Clarke remembered Wilmot telling her that he was shot at as a young child, and that his brother, who he had on his back, was shot and killed. They brought the dead child to the Murrays' before the tribe took away the dead child and buried it. I wonder where these hostile actions took place.

Reg:

I have no recollection of hearing that story, but the Murrays lived at what later became known as Murray's Hill, a mile west of Allansford. Summer Hill was the name of the property. If that was the property he was taken to, it was within the ambit of his travels.[14]

It appears that Wilmot moved closer to Warrnambool in old age and also found the Framlingham Aboriginal Reserve more acceptable, perhaps because there was no longer a manager or control over people's comings and goings. The Murray family were lifetime friends to the local Aboriginal community, and Wilmot's second partner Lily lived the last part of her life at John Murray's property, Summer Hill, on what was then called the Allansford Road. She died there on 21 September 1884.[15]

Wilmot lived for a considerable time longer. He died on 7 July 1916 at Waikato, the Warrnambool home of Miss Murray, John Murray's sister. According to the *Warrnambool Standard*, in old age he lived for several years in a hut at Waikato, Miss Murray having undertaken to provide him with food and accommodation at the request of the Board for the Protection of the Aborigines. In the last weeks of his life his strength failed him and arrangements were being made to move him to Framlingham, 'where he would receive attention from his own people', but he died before he could be moved.[16] He was buried in the Warrnambool Cemetery.

On the death certificate his age was given as eighty: it was more likely to have been seventy-two or three. It might seem a surprisingly long life for one who was described as being of 'wandering and dissipated habits',[17] but the old ways and the food that was traditionally eaten guaranteed a much healthier life than one could achieve in what was supposed to be the superior circumstances of the Aboriginal stations. Even the Board for the Protection of the Aborigines came to acknowledge this. In 1879 the Vice-Chairman of the BPA reported to the Chief Secretary that:

> *Whilst individuals of thirty or thirty-five years of age who take up their residence on our stations as a rule preserve their health, are able to work hard, and bid fair in many cases to live to sixty or seventy years of age, those who are born on or enter our establishments in childhood on attaining a suitable age are unable to work for any time without inducing spitting of blood, and for the most part die between their twelfth and twenty-fifth years, and seem in few cases likely to reach thirty. From this it happens that instances are daily becoming more frequent of parents who have buried two, four, or six children, and occasionally have been left childless.*[18]

Wilmot's biography points to the problematic nature of Aboriginality for the people of Warrnambool and district. It was comparatively easy to embrace the Aboriginal who was 'the last of his tribe'—a phrase originating among members of the white community, reassuring words that were taken as read, their truth left untested. But the evidence is that in the early twentieth century, after what the community perceived as the last of the 'tribal' people died, it was regarded as best to distance oneself from Aboriginal links. This was the case even for the Abraham family, who—contrary to the usual practice of European pioneers—had accepted into their bosom an Aboriginal member, the result of a cross-cultural liaison on the Western District frontier.

CHAPTER 4

The Three Pompeys

I: THE FIRST TWO POMPEYS: THE WRITTEN RECORD

ALBERT AUSTIN, CHRIS AUSTIN

c. 1846–1889   1874–1939

ABORIGINALS AT THE FRAMLINGHAM ABORIGINAL RESERVE IN 1867. BACK ROW
LEFT TO RIGHT: JOSEPH LIVINGSTONE, POMPEY AUSTIN, TOM LIVINGSTONE. MIDDLE
ROW LEFT TO RIGHT: WILLIAM GOOD, DICK PATTERSON, HENRY DAWSON, JOSEPH,
ROBERT CLARK, JOHN DAWSON, KING DAVID, LUTMAN, CAMPERDOWN GEORGE,
JIM CROW, KING GEORGE. FRONT ROW LEFT TO RIGHT: ANDY MCKINNON, NORMAN
ROBERTSON, WILL CLARK, WILLIAM RAWLINGS, FRANK BLAIR, HENRY ALBERTS

Little is known of the life of Albert Austin, the first of three members of his family to be known as 'Pompey'. His date of birth is unknown, but his death is recorded in 1889. He is in the group photograph of the Aboriginal men on the Framlingham Aboriginal Station reproduced on the facing page. Apparently he died in the East Melbourne Hospital and was buried in Melbourne.[1] In 1867, when he married Rosanna Francis, his age was given as about twenty-one; his father was named as Charlie and his mother as Alice.[2] According to the late Diane Barwick, who had a detailed knowledge of the records of the Board for the Protection of the Aborigines (BPA), Alice was from Lake Bolac.

The Pompey of European history, 'Pompey the Great', was a Roman general and statesman of the time of Julius Caesar. How then did Albert Austin gain such an illustrious name? Perhaps he was given it by George Augustus Robinson, the Chief Protector of Aborigines, during his journeys across the district during the 1840s. Meeting large groups of Aboriginals and eager to give them European names, Robinson tended to draw on the great names of history as well as the planets and more pedestrian names such as Kitty, Maria and Mary. For this to be true, though, the first Pompey would have had to be older than the records indicate. Maybe Robinson gave the name to someone else, and it was then passed on to Albert by someone in his own community. Another possibility is that local Europeans gave Albert the name Pompey in recognition of his military prowess. This is unlikely, but there is no doubt that Pompey, his peers and their parents' generation fought against those who came on to their land and decided to stay.

Among the first Europeans to arrive in Pompey's country were the Manifold brothers. Pleased with the freshwater lake they found just to the east of present-day Camperdown, in late 1838 the Manifolds took out a lease on 100 000 acres [40 500 hectares] of fine grazing land. The local Aboriginals resented their presence. In the historical records there is a reference to an incident in which Arthur Lloyd and Peter Manifold joined forces to deal with

ALBERT, THE FIRST POMPEY AUSTIN

Aboriginals who were taking their sheep. Lloyd told the Geelong Police Court, 'They presented their spears and showed signs of resistance, upon which we fired on them. I have no doubt some of them were wounded.' According to historian Michael Cannon, 'No further inquiry was made or charges laid'.[3] 'The blacks in those early days gave a lot of trouble', wrote Henry Matson, who went to work at Purrumbete in 1855.[4] W. G. Manifold, in his history of the Manifold family, mentions three incidents in which Aboriginals attacked the pioneering Manifolds, and notes that two of these attacks 'could have led to the death of one of the brothers'.[5]

The land about Camperdown is commonly thought of as Manifold country, but earlier it belonged to Pompey's clan. The evidence for this comes largely from the reminiscences and writing of John S. Manifold, one of Australia's most famous folk poets and a member of the pioneering family. John Manifold knew and admired the original Pompey's son, Chris Austin. Manifold was also well aware that the Aboriginals had made life difficult for his ancestors. He told Rodney Hall:

The first homestead was built there [by Lake Purrumbete] ... the blackfellows burnt it down. So my ancestors put up another and the blackfellows burnt that down too, while the men were away sinking a well ... Then they put up a third and, by God, this time it was stone. The nursery where I spent my early youth was part of this third homestead; and we reckoned as kids that if you chipped away at the plaster with your thumbnails you'd come on the old loopholes [shooting apertures] sooner or later. The nursery got a bit of a bashing one way and another from the inside, because we were intent on finding those loopholes. Anyhow, the blackfellows failed to take a third homestead—it wouldn't burn so readily. And it got expanded and extended.[6]

At the age of nine John Manifold was sent away from home to become a boarder at Geelong Grammar School. By that stage Chris Austin, the second Pompey, was fifty. Many years later, in a poem simply called 'The Land', Manifold wrote of how during his school years he had ached for the land he left behind, and envied Pompey Austin his oneness with the country:

The hurt I hated most at nine years old
Was separation, not from kith and kin
But from the land, the factual tawny-gold
Acres whose barley brushed a rider's shin.

Fragrant in summer, kind to peregrine
And painted quail, yet cruel to withhold
Itself from me and not to let me in.
I was a moody little boy, I'm told.

Angry at being made to feel a fool—
I couldn't eat it, kiss it, hold its hand
Or suck its breast—I tried to turn my back

But used to dream of it at boarding-school
And envy Pompey Austin whom the land
Seemed to enfold and bless, since he was black.

As a child John Manifold sought Pompey's company, listening to the old man's stories and learning about Aboriginal ways of thinking and doing. Manifold would later turn one of Pompey's stories into a story of his own, which is published here for the first time. At one level Pompey's story is simply a legend about how the flatfish comes to be in the Milky Way, but it is perhaps much more than this. Am I reading too much into it when I see it as an allegory of the effect of European invasion on the Aboriginals—a means of expressing the powerlessness of their position?

THE FLATFISH

BY J. S. MANIFOLD, 1915–1985

Pompey Austin told me this story when I was seven. Pompey was an old man; he claimed to be the son of the chief who fought against my great-grandfather back in the 1830s, and probably he was right. He had a white beard, unusually thick for an aborigine, and a very black face, and I thought him the noblest and kindest and wisest of men.

It was after sundown, and we were sitting out by the woodpile watching the stars come out.

'Your people say the stars are other worlds,' said Pompey, 'and that Heaven lies beyond them. My people say that Heaven is an island in the river overhead, and that the stars are waterlilies in it.'

'It says in the Bible,' said I, 'that there is water above the firmament. Would the firmament be the sky?'

'It could be,' he said. 'Do you see that long mob of little stars?'

'Yes,' I said, 'it's the Milky Way.'

'Do you see the dark patch in the middle of it? What does that look like to you? We say it is a flatfish in the water.'

'It ought to move about more,' said I. We had been after flatfish with the spear, and I knew how they could move.

'It doesn't move much,' said he; 'It can't get away. I'll tell you why, and then you must run inside and get ready for bed, or I shall be blamed for keeping you.'

'In the beginning there were no men. There was the earth, there were trees, grass, water, and some of the trees had fruit. It wasn't ordinary fruit; when it ripened, it became wallabies and goannas and all sorts of animals. There were devils on earth, and they lived on this fruit. There were gods too, but they lived in heaven, and came to earth only for short visits.

'The gods were not satisfied with earth as it was. They kept on making improvements. One god took the magic fruit, and made it grow into a man. This pleased him, and by and by he made more men. The men grew and multiplied, and he was delighted.

'But the devils were not at all pleased. The new-made men were taking all the food. Besides, the devils found the men very tough and wary and hard to catch; and they got angrier and angrier with the interfering gods, as they had to work harder and harder to get their tucker.

'Then the head devil decided to go and make his complaint to the head god.'

'Was the head devil called Satan,' I asked, 'or was it Lucifer?'

'He may have had those names,' said Pompey, 'but he has other names too. He turned into a crow, and went flying up and up and up. Devils can do that. Any time you see a crow, it does no harm to take a shot at him.'

'But not at eagles,' I said, 'I know. An eagle might be a god, any day.'

'Quite right,' said Pompey. 'Gods travel as eagles, devils travel as crows. Then he turned himself into a flatfish.'

'Gosh!' said I. 'Are you sure it's all right to eat flatfish?'

'I've never known it to do any harm,' Pompey admitted, 'but you shouldn't eat them raw. This flatfish swam and swam in the sky until he came to the beach of the island of heaven. He walked up the beach in his own shape, and there he found the gods sitting at tucker. So he dropped on his heels, and sat where they could see him, like a well-mannered person.

'By and by the head god called to him, saying "Have some tucker?" And the devil replied, "I should be glad to: tucker is scarce."

'The gods were puzzled at this, and asked, "Why, what has gone wrong with the good food on earth?" "Everything has gone wrong," said the devil, "since some meddlesome fool began improving things," and with that he felt so angry that he came walking right up to the fire. "Why couldn't you leave things alone?" said the devil. "Why couldn't you have left things as they were? Here are these new-fangled human beings eating us out of existence. If you think that's an improvement, you're a lot of old fools."

'The head god was angry. "You have no manners," he said. "You came uninvited, yet we offered you food. Instead of thanking us, you start abusing us. You have no manners, and no sense. If I think things need changing, here or on earth, I shall change them. You can take that for an answer. Now clear out!"

'When he saw the head god jump up, the devil turned and ran. Clear to the water's edge he ran, shouting, "No more changes if I can stop them!" Then he turned back into a flatfish, and dived.

'The chief god laughed. "No more changes?" he said. "Then stay as you are, flatfish!" And he pointed the magic stick after him.'

The night was darker now, and Pompey pointed to the Milky Way. 'Don't you see him?' he asked. I saw him, and said so. That dark patch *is* like a flatfish, once it has been pointed out to you.

'Well, that's the head devil,' said Pompey. 'He doesn't move very much, and it's quite easy to keep an eye on him. What you want to look out for is the day when you can see *no* flatfish in the Milky Way; because that will mean that he's got loose.'

'Might he?' I asked. It seemed quite possible.

'He's been there a long time,' said Pompey doubtfully.

'We'll be able to recognise him if he gets loose,' I said, 'because he will be going round saying "Why can't you leave things as they are?"'

'I think that's quite likely,' said Pompey, 'But just now it's your bed-time.'

According to John Manifold, Chris Austin claimed that his father fought the pioneering Manifolds, but it is more likely that it was Chris's grandfather who did so. If the first Pompey was twenty-one when he married in 1867, this would mean he was born about 1846, when the worst of the frontier conflict was over. No doubt the events of the contact period were so dramatic and so significant, and Chris's grandfather talked of them with such feeling, that his son, as he told the stories of the invasion, took on the persona of the person directly involved, as sometimes seems to happen when the oral tradition is kept alive.

Later it was the turn of the squatters to have their right to the land attacked by selectors—small farmers who purchased land with government assistance. In this situation Manifold's sympathies were with the squatters: 'They had done the hard work, they pioneered the district, fought the blacks and made treaties with the blacks'. The mention of 'treaties' is perhaps a reference to an informal understanding reached with the Aboriginals. How and exactly when this was achieved is not clear, but in 1857 James Bonwick, who was travelling through the district, noticed that the Manifolds employed Aboriginals as stockmen: 'The Messrs Manifold prefer Blacks to Whites as being far better acquainted with stock, more active in duty, more ready and willing, and not more expensive'.[7] But at heart John Manifold believed that the Aboriginals had the greatest claim: 'If anybody actually owned the land it was the blacks. If there was anybody next in line, it was us.'[8]

Sixty years after his death, Chris Austin lives on in the memories of his people. I found him alive in the stories told by Banjo Clarke, Kirrae wurrung Elder, who agreed to share his memories both of Chris Austin (to him, 'Old Pompey') and Chris's son Cyril, also known as Pompey. In these stories Chris Austin is not the revered family retainer of childhood, as Manifold nostalgically remembered him, but one who shared the everyday life of his community, living by his Aboriginal principles, even when this might mean an occasional trip to jail.

Banjo's stories, like others in the oral tradition, reveal Aboriginal attitudes to the white man's world and how it does its business—its violence at the time of dispossession, its paternalism and sense of superiority, its use of police as agents of control, its punitive courts, jails and fines, and the continuing discrimination to which it subjects Aboriginal people. When Banjo speaks, he also gives us insight into the nature and strength of Aboriginal culture and the means by which Indigenous people survived all kinds of difficulties imposed on them in circumstances that were beyond their power to change.

But first, a few words about Banjo, the teller of stories.

INTRODUCING BANJO CLARKE

BANJO CLARKE IN A REFLECTIVE MOOD: PHOTO TAKEN IN LATE 1994

Henry (Banjo) Clarke was born in a bark hut at the Framlingham Aboriginal mission in 1921 or 1922. He has lived most of his life at Framlingham, but in the dark days of the 1930s depression the family moved to Melbourne in search of work.

Making ends meet was difficult for most people then, but more so for the Framlingham Aboriginals. As John Sutton Egan pointed out in early 1934, before the depression the people at Framlingham 'battled their way by cutting wood and splitting posts. Now, however, they find it difficult to exist, as even the most wealthy dairymen cut their own wood and split their own posts in the forests.'[9] Banjo's mother went to the city and found work, then his father and the children joined her.

Banjo had little formal education. He didn't have much time for schools. He attended school at Purnim: 'Two days, my record was,' he says. He attended a church school in Melbourne for a time: 'they were feeding the children then that went to school, that's why I went'. He gained his education from the old people in the bush, in the camps, helping them and hearing lots of stories of the old days from them—and from the old people in the city also. He grew up in Melbourne and then began carrying his swag out of town looking for work in the country and visiting Framlingham, 'my homeland'. 'I still had feelings for it,' Banjo says.

Among the places Banjo worked at was Weatherhead's sawmill at Tynong North. He first went there with an Aboriginal mate, and returned many times, because he knew he could always rely on finding work there. Arthur Weatherhead, the proprietor, had a young daughter by the name of Muriel. When she discovered that Banjo couldn't read or write, she set out to teach him. Years later he met up with Muriel again and discovered she had become a schoolteacher:

I laughed and said, 'You a schoolteacher!' I said, 'Bush girl!' She said, 'Don't forget, Clarkie, you was my first pupil!' I said, 'You're right there, too.'

When he was about fifteen years old, Banjo joined the boxing troupes that travelled around rural Australia. At different times he was with both Harry Johns' and Jimmy Sharman's troupes:

They did a lot of [agricultural] shows, wherever shows were on. They'd do two or three shows sometimes. Other times when there wasn't any shows they'd go to some big town and they'd put their own show on in this town on a vacant allotment. They'd drive around the streets in the big truck and broadcast that the fight's on and to get your local champs to come and fight. They'd get a big crowd there too, without any show.

Banjo's love of boxing started when he was young. He used to 'hang around gymnasiums' in Melbourne. His brother and many of his Aboriginal mates used to fight in the Fitzroy Stadium:

I used to go with them and watch them. Then when they all left and went their different ways I used to still go. Old Jack Murray was a trainer in Russell Street and I used to go there. 'Could you fight, son?'

'No,' I said, 'I spar with my mates.' 'Come down in the morning,' he said, 'and put on a pair of sandshoes and start skipping.' I done that and I was right. I was a good skipper. Then he put me on a speedball and taught me all about the speedball. Sometimes he'd put me in the ring to spar with some good fighters. They all looked after me, as I was the only Aboriginal kid going to the gym then.

Although he won a lot of fights, Banjo says he wasn't ambitious to be a champion: 'We went in for the money or just the fun of it.' Money was limited. 'Only time we saw gloves was when we got in the ring.' Even shoes were shared. Henry Alberts, who was also from Framlingham, boxed alongside Banjo, and they had a pair of boots between them. When one had finished fighting, the boots went to the other. Racist comments from the crowd strengthened Banjo's resolve to win. When people said things like 'Kill the nigger', it just made him determined to do his best, and he knew he could deal with the racists in the ring without being up on a charge of assault.

Banjo boxed for twenty-five years or more. He was with a boxing troupe in Mount Gambier when World War II broke out. He remembers the old cook, who had gone up the street to buy some meat and vegetables, coming back and saying, 'Righto, all you bloody fighters, you'll get bloody fight now.'

War brought a change of lifestyle for Banjo. He thought of joining the army, but was steered into civil construction work instead. He and an Aboriginal mate were walking around Fitzroy when they saw 'a bit of an army depot' and decided to sign up. When they said they would like to join the army, the recruiting officer replied:

'Why should *you* want to join the army?' I said, 'Oh well, everyone else join it.' This young officer said, 'Well,' he said, 'I don't know. You can join the army if you want to, but you fellows have got nothing to fight for. You've got nothing, mate,' he said. 'But there's other jobs you can get to help the war effort,' and he told us about this civil construction. And that's what we done.

Banjo worked in large construction camps all through northern Queensland and the Northern Territory, building roads and bridges to enable the troops to move quickly from one part of Australia to another. He saw a lot of Australia at the same time. He was in a group that reached Darwin just after the town was bombed and took part in the cleaning up. After the war ended he returned to Fitzroy by way of Adelaide.

He stayed for a while in Fitzroy, where he went back to boxing and found work wherever he could: 'mostly getting jobs in the country, woodcutting. We liked woodcutting because we done that most of our lives. And we used to roll our swags in Melbourne and head off for the country in search of work.' Yet he kept returning to Framlingham. Eventually the lure of his 'homeland' proved irresistible, and he returned there. He married Audrey Couzens and obtained work in Coleman's stone quarry at Panmure as a crusher operator. It was a job that he enjoyed, and he held it for many years. He only left because he was advised to do so for health reasons: exposure to dust had given him recurrent bouts of pneumonia every summer.

In his spare time, he taught many people to box, including Lawrence Austin, 'Baby Cassius', a descendant of old Pompey Austin. 'Baby Cassius', born at Framlingham in 1954, was to hold national titles in three weight divisions. He was Australian junior welterweight champion, welterweight champion and lightweight champion. He twice held the Commonwealth lightweight championship, in 1977 and 1978. Of 48 fights, he won 34, drew 2, lost 12.[10]

He used to be a little kid waiting for me, sitting in the grass with gloves when I was walking home from the quarry. Aw, here's this little fellow here again. And I'd be tired and wanting to get home, and he'd say, 'Unc, you've got to learn me,' and I'd put the gloves on with him and learn him. And sometimes I'd hit him hard and I thought he would stop. He'd say, 'Now, Unc, you have to stay a bit longer to learn me how to stop that punch and how to rock it in.' Then I'd be there for another hour! He wouldn't give in, and he ended up a champion.

After giving up work at the quarry Banjo worked for the Shire Council, and also did woodcutting and whatever else came up. Finally he spent three years as caretaker for the Warrnambool Surf Club, a position in which he made lots of friends.

When the bicentenary of European settlement approached in 1988, Banjo decided it was time to make a stand:

When that come on some of my Aboriginal mates was saying, 'Don't celebrate in '88 because this's when hardly any white people was here. This has to be an Aboriginal year—things have to be focused on Aboriginals and all the troubles they went through since the white man come here.' I was lying down in bed listening and thinking to myself, are they fair dinkum or what? I had some beer, and I thought to myself it must have been beautiful when old Aboriginals never drank and no one ever seen them going to jail, and lying in the gutters, in the parks, all drunk and nowhere to go. I thought to myself, right, in respect for my Aboriginal people and my Elders who've suffered all them years, I'm going to knock off drink for all this year.

Then I went out to the kitchen [where the conversation was taking place]. The men were saying 'Don't celebrate Unc in '88, because this is an Aboriginal year.' 'I'm not,' I said, 'because I'm going to have respect for all the Aborigines what were introduced to grog and died in jail and in the gutters and parks. Here,' I said, 'you can have my grog.' They were drinking and talking. 'Here, want a drink?' I said, 'No! I'm not drinking for twelve months in respect for my Aboriginal people. A one-man protest for all the ill-treatment they had!'

I went to the pub and bought the lemon squash. They all laughed at me and had a bet to say how long it'd last. I went for twelve months, no trouble at all. I liked it that much, going off the grog, I stayed off it ever since.

In retirement Banjo still lives beside the Hopkins River on the mission, and often visits the forest and the cemetery where many of those he remembers lie. A well-known figure both locally and interstate, he has many visitors and a very large number of friends. Over the years he has shared many stories with me. I have been particularly interested in those he tells about men and women I have encountered in the written records. Here he tells his stories of Chris Austin, who to him was 'Old Pompey', and Chris's son Cyril, also known as Pompey.[11]

FRAMLINGHAM ABORIGINAL SETTLEMENT SCHOOL HOUSE CHURCH SERVICE, ABOUT 1918. BACK ROW LEFT TO RIGHT: ELEN BLAIR, ALICE CLARKE, ELLSIE CLARKE, FRANK CLARKE, DAVID TAYLOR, JACK WYSELASKIE. MIDDLE ROW LEFT TO RIGHT: MRS. WYSELASKIE, BESSIE RAWLINGS, AMILLA ROSE, JESSE TAYLOR, ISABELLA COUZANS, FRANK CLARKE, JIM ROSE, GEORGE ROSE, CHRIS AUSTIN, JOHNNY ROSE, BILLY RAWLINGS, VISITOR, JOHN ROSE, VISITOR. FRONT ROW (CHILDREN) LEFT TO RIGHT: GRACIE ROSE, DOLLY EDWARDS, EMILY ROSE, EADY CLARKE, ALICE CLARKE, MARY ROSE, NELLIE AUSTIN, VERA AUSTIN, PERCY CLARKE, DORIS RAWLINGS, ARTHUR AUSTIN, STEVIE AUSTIN, CYRIL AUSTIN (POMPEY), GIRL STANDING BEHIND: LOUY RAWLINGS. ALL NAMES AND SPELLINGS AS ON THE ORIGINAL PHOTO, WHICH WAS IN THE POSSESSION OF THE LATE JIM ROSE

II: BANJO CLARKE'S STORIES

CHRIS AUSTIN

'OLD POMPEY'

1874–15 JULY 1939 [12]

CHRIS AUSTIN WITH HIS DAUGHTERS PHOTOGRAPHED FOR AN ARTICLE ON THE
PLIGHT OF THE FRAMLINGHAM ABORIGINES DURING THE DEPRESSION OF THE
1930S. ADELAIDE (RIGHT) IS THE GRANDMOTHER OF LIONEL ROSE

He was a real old Aboriginal hunter round the place, putting in fish
traps for the people and all the little children helping him. All the little
children used to love to see him coming. He'd have his trousers rolled
up and barefoot and his spear and all the little children would follow
him down the hill here,* where he made his fish traps, and he'd be
helping them, showing them where to put the stone and making the
nets. He knew the right time to put the nets in.

When the fresh water comes he would go down early in the
morning and see the nets full of eels. All the little kids would put them
in bags and climb them up the steep hill and wait. He'd come up here

---

* To the Hopkins River near Banjo's present house.

with his knife and he would skin the eels and clean them. He'd have a nice clean piece of rag—white rag—and he'd roll them up in it. He was real clean and everything, like a butcher, real fussy with his work. Pillow slips or whatever he had were snow-white, and he'd put the eels in them. He'd get a sugarbag and keep some alive. He'd go to Warrnambool—hitchhike right along Purnim Road with all the nice, fresh eels—and he'd sell them on a Thursday to the Catholic people. They'd eat the fish, eels or whatever they had on a Friday, an old Catholic custom.

He'd have some eels in his wet bag, and he'd go to Warrnambool, they'd be the live ones. He'd cut across. There was a dam about three miles out of Warrnambool—I'll show you one of these days. He used to put the live eels in that dam. He'd stay for two or three days and if the people wanted eels, instead of him coming way back here, he'd go to the dam and spear a couple and take them back to Warrnambool.

There were eels in that dam for years after he passed away. One of his great-grandsons had a look in that dam one day and he seen this big eel. He caught it and brought it to the mission. When I told him the story about his grandfather he was real happy. I said, 'That must have been one of the eels he left there years ago, breeding in that dam.'

The old tucker man wouldn't let nobody starve. If he could help out, he'd help out. He'd go steal a squatter's sheep or a stray young bullock, a cleanskin—no brand, no earmarks, nobody's—what was wandering around the bush. Well, he'd butcher that too, and everyone would have a feed. He'd go in the paddocks in the night. He'd have his little dog with him to catch the sheep and hang on to him, and the old fellow would run up and grab the sheep, cut his throat and skin him.

We kids used to be playing in the bush there—the mission used to be all scrub and trees when we were little. We'd be playing in the moonlight, playing, then some kid would stop and say, 'What's that?' We'd smell meat cooking on the coals, nice fresh meat cooking in the bush, and we'd all head for that direction. Then we'd see the big fire and the old fellow would be there, chops cut up and on the coals. All the kids would sit around and never ask any questions where he'd got the meat, never said nothing. He'd give them all a feed. Then he'd take the best part, a leg of mutton or something, and give the rest to other people that had none, then he'd go.

He went to jail a lot of times for that—three months, six months—and one time he was asked, 'When are you going to stop from doing this, old fellow?' 'Ah,' he said, 'For as long as my little children are hungry I'll steal the sheep off the white man.' He said, 'They've got all their good tucker on our land and we've got no more native food now and the white man took over all the land. Why should my little Aboriginal children go hungry when the white man next door got plenty, plenty tucker? That's why I go and get it—little children come first. I'm not frightened about jail as long as my little children are full and happy.' And he done that over and over again.

The police used to wait for him in the night, and then he realised the police was waiting 'cause he seen strange signs, and then he went late in the evening when it's daylight. He caught the sheep in the day-light, see! He did the same thing, and then at night cooked for everyone. He used to go on real stormy nights too, as no one else would be out in that weather. That's how he got away with a lot. Well, he got away with a lot but they also caught up with him a few times and sent him to jail.

I remember when I was walking with my dad through the scrub and heard this truck going—the motor. 'There, your old mate is going there.' 'Who's that?' 'Grandfather Austin,' he said. I said, 'Where are they taking him?' 'They're taking him to jail.' My dad lifted me up on his shoulder and said, 'Wave a hand to him.' We were about five hundred yards back near the scrub, in the clearing. He was looking across to our camp and I waved a hand. I said, 'He's not waving a hand.' Poor old Dad said, 'No, but he can see ya.' He said, 'He can't wave a hand because he's got his hand tied behind his back, sitting on the truck—handcuffs.' I think they had tied him with rope too, to the truck, so he wouldn't get off. But he wouldn't have got off.

When he used to go in the daylight he'd do everything nice and clean like a top butcher, as he was. He used to take a dish with him. When he cut the sheep's neck he held it over the dish so that the blood ran into the dish. His little dog what helped him would drink the blood up. So he got rid of the evidence. When he was about to go sheep-stealing he had a big butcher's knife and he'd be standing there sharpening it with a sharpening stone, and nobody would say anything to him because they all knew what he was going to do. The little dog knew too. The dog would be sitting down there on his haunches watching his master. He'd be wagging his tail. He knew what it was all about. Then away they would go.

He'd go to jail. Sometimes he done it in Geelong, sometimes he done it in Pentridge. He'd do whatever sentence he got, and everybody was happy when he came home.

He was there [in Pentridge] when Angus Murray got hung.* He used to clean the cells out and he was up on the top tier, they call it, where the gallows are, and he cleaned along the cells there and came to the condemned cell, where they kept the prisoners before they take them out to the gallows. He was reading the names on the wall what prisoners carved on the wall, and he seen this old hymn carved in on the wall:

All my petitions I shall bear,
And I'll shout while passing through the air
Farewell, farewell, sweet hour of prayer.

They were the words Angus Murray wrote on the cell wall before he was hung. All the people said he was innocent and protested about his death sentence, and thousands of petitions went to the government. They never took no notice of the petitions because he was found guilty, but everyone knew he wasn't guilty. He wasn't the fellow who bought the gun.

---

* Angus Murray was arrested for his part in a bank hold-up on 8 October 1923, in the course of which the manager of the bank was shot. On 21 October 1923 the manager died as a result of his wounds, but not before he had seen Murray and said that he was not the man who shot him. Murray's accomplice was never apprehended. At the trial, evidence was given that Murray was not carrying a gun and that his accomplice shot the bank manager. Murray was nevertheless found guilty on the grounds that, if two men conspire to commit an offence that subsequently becomes murder, both are equally guilty of the crime.

Murray petitioned the Executive Council protesting his innocence, and he gained widespread support. A public meeting held on 8 April 1924 was attended by 10 000 people. On 10 April the Premier received a deputation from various groups protesting on Murray's behalf. A petition signed by more than 60 000 people was handed to the Governor on 12 April. But it was all to no avail. Murray was hanged in the Old Melbourne Gaol on 14 April. About 2000 people gathered outside the jail on the morning of his hanging, twice the number who turned out when Ronald Ryan was hanged in 1967.

The story was that he wasn't carrying a gun because he was frightened of somebody tackling him and the gun would go off accidentally. He said, 'No way in the world.' He said, 'I'm not going to get hung for shooting someone or carrying a gun. I'll never get hung for shooting anyone,' he said, and that's what he got hung for. And he never carried a gun. His mate carried the gun. He promised him that he wouldn't take the gun with him. The old fellow came home and told us all the story.

There used to be a lot of church. Different times, different religions come here, and all Aboriginals would go to church and pick their favourite hymn. They were all good singers, good musicians. One of the old fellow's sons was an organist, and he used to play all the hymns in the church. They used to ask, 'What's your favourite hymn?' And he'd say—thinking of Angus Murray and what he had seen on the wall in the condemned man's cell—'Sweet hour of prayer'. He'd say the number and they'd all sing that in remembrance of that poor fellow who got hung.

Young Pompey, the old fellow's son, had a shield over one eye. He got his eye knocked out once. I don't know what the story is but there was a dispute, some kind of dispute— domestic dispute I think it was, something like that. Kids wasn't allowed to listen to anything like that, them days.

I remember that old fellow. I was only a little fellow then. We were living in a hut. That was all forest over there, and there used to be a fence running across the boundary there. When we was playing in the bush near our hut I heard my eldest brother talking to my dad. He said, 'There he goes now. The old fellow must be taking him to the hospital.' I remember looking across toward this fence-line and seeing the old dad walking in front and the young fellow was walking behind. He was following his dad 'cause his eye was knocked out. I think it was speared. I think his father speared him: in some dispute, against the old fellow's laws and wishes, or something. But I never heard no more about that, and the old fellow took him to the hospital. They probably walked all the way in to the hospital and they cleaned the rest of his eye out and took it out.

He used to wear a glass eye then. But he didn't like the glass eye. Sometimes he'd lose it if he was riding the horse or something. He'd tell us kids and we'd go and find it for him. I think he must have carried it in his pocket, and he had the shield over his eye then. Most of the time he just had the shield and everyone knew him, see, from that shield too— oh, yeah, that's Pompey. But the old dad, I think he regretted doing that spearing, that was his tribal way of punishing people, must have been something bad—but the old fellow took him to the hospital. And there was no more said about it. Not a thing!

Jan:
How did the old fellow die?

Banjo:
The old fellow was on one of his trips to Warrnambool with things to sell and to buy a bit of meat, and probably a bottle of wine, a quart of wine, and was on his way home. He never made it home that night. No one took much notice of that. The next thing we knew about him, word came that he was found dead on the side of the road, on the Wangoom road, near the culvert. My eldest brother and the old fellow's son, Pompey, walked to Warrnambool to see if they could see anything. Down Russell Creek on the Mortlake Road they found some blood and his shoe. That was a mile and a half to two miles from where he was found. It was in the paper that he was found dead on the road. Everybody believed that: that he was found dead.

Years and years after—it must have been forty to fifty years after— when I was in the hospital, this old gentleman over in the next bed asked me could I remember Pompey Austin. I thought he was talking about the young fellow. 'Yeah,' I said, 'yeah, he died in Warrnambool jail.' He said, 'Oh, yeah, I know that, but not him, the old fellow, his dad.' I said, 'Yes, he was found dead on the road years ago.' 'No,' he said, 'he was found alive.' 'No,' I said, 'it was said over and over again that he was found dead.' He said, 'I know that,' he said, 'but he was alive when they brought him to the hospital.'

That stopped me.

'That means he died in the hospital.' 'Yes,' he said, 'not on the road' and he said he had a real strong voice. He said he thought to himself, there's nothing wrong with this old fellow. He was growling that he needed his bag and to find the things along the road because he had to get home—his people would be wondering where he was, and he had some things for the little children who helped him at his fish traps.

I didn't know the fellow worked at the hospital. I just thought he was another old bloke in the hospital at that time. I said, 'How do you know all this?' He said, 'I was the person who looked at him.'*

'Well, there you are,' I said. 'After all these years we are finding out the real truth now.' 'I gave him a cup of tea,' he said. '"Never mind, old timer, you drink that tea, settle down and I'll get you right back along the road to get your things",' and the old fellow was still growling that he shouldn't be in there.' He heard the cup drop and it broke: he looked around and the old fellow fell off the chair. When he went up and examined him he was dead, he'd passed away.

When he did a post-mortem on him to see what his injuries was, he said he'd never seen anything like it. His liver was cut right in two, clean cut, right in two! The fellow said, 'I never, never know from that day to this how he didn't die straight away. By rights he should have been dead right away. The only explanation I got is that the old man willed himself to live to find the things for the children and say goodbye to his people.'

He'd been buried a long time when I heard this story, and I went and looked for his grave [in the Framlingham Aboriginal Cemetery]. I knew where it was. You wouldn't have known there was a grave there. I knew where it was, because it was near the fence post, and I knew where the fence post was. I was telling Camilla [a friend] and this other young lady, 'We'll walk down the river and mark the grave, build it up so we don't forget him.'

His grave is still there now. People who didn't remember said, 'What's that grave doing there? There's no grave there.' 'There's a grave there all right,' I said. 'That's the old fellow what was supposed to be found dead on the road, who died in the hospital—that's why I am doing his grave up, so people won't forget him and pay respect to him.'

---

* My research suggests that Banjo's informant was Frank Goodreid, who was employed at the hospital as a porter. He was very gentlemanly, dressed like a doctor and had the manner of a doctor. He took patients to theatre, helped administer the ether or chloroform, gave injections, helped with the post-mortems and was the 'Keeper of the Morgue'. In his later years he was also an in-patient a number of times, as he had diabetes.

I remember that for years and years there used to be a boomerang on the head of his grave. And when the dirt levelled off and the grass grew over, only the boomerang was left, and that's why I knew the grave was there. He was a great boomerang thrower, boomerang maker, and he went round the Warrnambool Show throwing the boomerang and taking his hat around to collect a few bob.

Yes. Them old people, them's the sort of people I remember. I have a real vivid memory of them old folk. There was something special about them. I think it was their kindness and understanding about people, their knowledge about life and the way they coped with it and all the hardships.

THE PASSING OF CHRIS.

Leaving the old weather-worn home, a small procession of cars and trucks wound its way through the bush, to the little Framlingham Reserve cemetery. There they laid Chris., of boomerang fame, a one-time skilled rider, a colored man of happy temperament. Chris. was loved by all the children on the Reserve. He was often spoiled by the white man's drink. Chris. was a strange mixture. He loved hymns even as he loved alcohol. Just before his remains were committed to mother earth, his request that his two favorite hymns be sung at his graveside, was complied with—"Sweet Hour of Prayer" and "Pass Me Not, Oh Gentle Saviour"—and just as his life was a strange mixture, so, was the choir that sang these two hymns. In this assembly round the little grave, was practically everyone on the Reserve, together with representatives from the Shire of Warrnambool, the police force, church committee, Rotary Club, O.S.T., Salvation Army, School Committee, Framlingham Reserve Board of Management, and several farmers and business men. Together with the coloured people, they said goodbye to Chris., and left him among the gum trees—an Australian native at rest—in a very small part of the land previously occupied by his race.

OLD POMPEY'S OBITUARY, *WARRNAMBOOL STANDARD*, 19 JULY 1939

When I followed up the records of Old Pompey's death, I discovered that Banjo's recollections are different from the account of events given in the newspaper and in the Proceedings of Inquest (no. 970/1939) which say that Pompey was hit by a car at Russell's Creek and was still alive when taken to the hospital. The driver, John Kelly, was unlicensed and had been drinking, though evidence was given that he did not appear to be affected by alcohol shortly after the accident. The car did not stop when the accident occurred, despite the fact that Kelly knew Pompey well. Kelly claimed at the inquest that he did not recognise Pompey and that, though he knew he had hit somebody, he thought he was not hurt.

He drove on, turned on to the Wangoom Road and ran into a culvert. The inquest verdict was that Pompey died as a result of 'shock and internal haemorrhage received ... by misadventure'.

Banjo says that there was much confusion among the Aboriginal community about what happened. People suspected that the facts of the situation were being covered up. Why, for example, did the car turn on to the Wangoom Road? The Kellys lived at Purnim and didn't normally travel on the Wangoom Road. Although the Kellys were friendly with the Aboriginal community (as their descendants still are today), they did not talk to Pompey's family about what happened. Probably, Banjo says, young John Kelly would have liked to talk to the Aboriginal community about it, but he didn't. It was an unfortunate accident, and one about which there is still quite a degree of confusion.

CYRIL AUSTIN

'YOUNG POMPEY'

5 MAY 1905–27 APRIL 1946

People would see Pompey—the young one—in town when he had a job, perhaps cutting wood. He'd camp at Mr George Jinkins', who had a wood yard in Koroit Street [Warrnambool]. He gave Aborigines work. Pompey would walk around the streets. He didn't get served much in the hotels those days, so he'd get a mate to go and get him a bottle of wine—this was the cheapest drink, cheaper than beer. He'd go up a lane and drink the wine. People would see him and his friends and say, 'There's the Aborigines again drinking.' Sometimes they'd get under the weather and would get locked up. Why they got drunk was they had to drink it all in one go. They didn't have the right to go in the pub and have a social drink.*

---

* In Victoria the section of the Licensing Act that prohibited supplying alcohol to Aborigines was not repealed until 1957.

Those who saw him and didn't understand the Aboriginal way of life, they'd say, 'He doesn't work. All he does is bite people for a few bob.' But he did a lot of odd jobs around town. What did they expect him to do? He could only do the work he was offered and live his culture, his Aboriginal culture. Perhaps some white people could see what he had, his culture, and envy him for it, like that poet fellow [J. S. Manifold]. What was the point of trying to save for the future like white people do? There was no future. That went with the taking of the land and the government being busy reducing our rights.

Lots of times he ended up in jail drunk. The attitude of white people was, don't trust Aborigines. Don't let them in your house. You can talk to them in the street, but don't let them in your house. Aborigines hanging around town was seen as something evil, cadging here and there. Many people thought of him as a lazy man, hanging around the white man's town, someone always in and out of jail. Not all people thought this way, but most—enough to make it awkward for Aboriginal people. But he wasn't like that. Sometimes mates gave him a few bob, but he would work when he could get work.

He could only get a job when it was offered to him, and he took them when offered. He also helped his brother, Uncle Billy Austin, who was a share dairy farmer for various farmers around the Camperdown, Cudgee and Allansford areas.

When things got tough he'd cut wood in Warrnambool, and he'd walk around in his leisure hours. He wasn't a slave to anyone. He liked to go walkabout every so often, to visit the old places. He also worked for a mate of his called Tom Clark, and Pompey used to go there a lot and help him out with milking the cows and harvesting and things like that. When he got an order for wood he'd go into the Framlingham Forest from Tom Clark's—Tom Clark used to work for Wormalds at Panmure—and cut the wood.

He was the kindest man out, helping his mates, and would do anything for little children. He was a great man for the races, Warrnambool May Races especially, and liked a bet. He'd walk across the paddocks on the day picking mushrooms to sell so he could have a bet. In all the years I knew him I never knew him to be in a fight with anyone.

He used to live a similar lifestyle to the old people. Every year he would get the fish traps ready at 'fishery bend' in the Hopkins* before the floods come. When the river starts to rise the clear water comes first, and that's when the eels start to travel. Before the river rose he would have the fish traps in place. He'd have all the children helping. He used to make nets out of fencing wire what farmers discarded and use reeds to guide the eels into the nets. The nets would last for a season. In the morning he would go with the children to clear the nets. He was the main person to provide food in this way when there was no government assistance, and to teach other Aborigines to do it also. Most people left this work to the old fellow. He was the hunter and the fisherman. A lot of people knew him as he was, a man who lived an Aboriginal lifestyle.

He died in Warrnambool jail—heart attack, I think. He and his nephews were locked up, maybe about taking rabbit skins or some other small thing—certainly not gold! Maybe he wasn't even guilty. Pompey would never tell on anyone: his lips were sealed.

When I was a young fellow I used to help him, camp in town and walk up the street with him. One day when I was around fourteen years old, when we were up the street we met two of his white mates who used to help him out now and then. One asked, 'Been up the lane where you usually go for a drink? I've left a bottle of wine and a glass there for you.' Pompey said, 'Thanks, mate, I'll go up there.'

The mate looked at me and said, 'You've got a little mate there. What's his name?' 'This is my nephew, Banjo Clarke,' Pompey said. The mate said, 'How are you going, son?' and he reached out and shook my hand. He said, 'You're with a good old mate: Pompey will look after you.' Then I thanked the white man, because I knew Pompey would look after me. He already did. They said a few words. Pompey thanked his mate and we walked away.

We went around to the lane where the man put the wine. Pompey got the wine and the glass and took it back to the wood yard, where he

---

* The bend in the Hopkins River near where Banjo now lives.

worked splitting wood for Mr George Jinkins. He used to have a nip now
and then while he was splitting the wood.

I never heard that name [Banjo] in my life before, and it stuck all
my life. Lots of people don't know my real name. They only know me as
Banjo. And it was Pompey that gave me that name.

I don't know why. I think I used to recite bits of Banjo Paterson's
poems when I was young. Maybe it was because of this. I used to like
being with the old people telling stories around the campfire.

Much, much later Pompey and his two nephews were taken to jail
on suspicion of stealing rabbit skins—maybe in the '40s. He was happy-
go-lucky and a good singer. He liked singing religious songs. All the
Austins had good singing voices. I think they went to church to enjoy
the singing.

They were dragged in for questioning about the stealing of some
rabbit skins. They must have had some money on them, so the police
were suspicious about where it had come from. Rabbit skins had been
stolen the night before. Pompey would probably have said that he had
earned the money.

They were kept in for questioning—I'm not sure whether they went
to court. Pompey walked up and down in the corridor in the jail singing
away, his voice loud and clear. He said, 'I feel so happy singing these old
gospel songs. I don't know why I am so happy in a situation like this.'

Throw out the lifeline
Someone is sinking today
Throw out the lifeline
With an arm quick and strong
There is a brother whom someone should save . . .

His nephews walked up and down, wondering whether they
would get off, but Pompey sang on, one gospel song after the other.
Then he grabbed his heart and fell down. When the police came he
was dead.

The police brought his nephews out to the funeral. It was a real sad
day for the Framlingham people when their favourite uncle was being
buried.

CHAPTER 5

'Why did they take them away?'

ELIZABETH (LIZZIE) AND HENRY McCRAE

1889–1936   1890–1938

HEADSTONE ERECTED OVER THE McCRAES' GRAVE BY THE CITIZENS OF
WARRNAMBOOL, WARRNAMBOOL CEMETERY

'Why would they do it?' Banjo asked. 'Why would they bury them away from their people—the ones who lived with them, shared their lives and loved them? I can't understand it,' he said.

'When Lizzie died we dug the burial place up in the [Framlingham] cemetery ready for the funeral. When one of us died everyone took part in digging the hole for the grave. It was the last thing we could do for the person. Then the word came that she wasn't going to be buried in the cemetery. She was being buried in Warrnambool. Everyone was very upset. Everyone went to funerals—even the little children—to say their last farewells. Why would they do it? Why would the white people bury her apart from her people? For a long time nobody filled in her burial place. It was next to where Jim Rose is buried.'

Banjo suspected the motives of the Europeans who decided to bury Lizzie in the white cemetery. 'Is she buried there?' he asked. 'And the others buried in the Warrnambool cemetery? Are their bodies there? Or were their bodies taken to be studied by the white professors and doctors, as examples of primitive people? That's what they did with many of our people. Grannie Truganini* was frightened that they would take her body when she died. They hung it in the museum and kept her bones in a box in the museum. Then they cremated her. But were they her bones that were cremated, or someone else's? You can't be sure.'[1]

I had no answer to Banjo's questions.

From previous research I already knew a little about the McCraes.† I had discovered that Mrs Elizabeth (Lizzie) McCrae was born at Ramahyuck Aboriginal Station, and was the daughter of Sam Hamilton of Ramahyuck and Ellen Foster. Her grandmother, Norah Foster, was brought from Western Australia to Victoria to live on the Ramahyuck station. Her father, a Queenslander from Rockhampton, was found as a child on his dead mother during a 'raid' and was eventually placed on Ramahyuck as well.[2]

---

* Truganini, the famous Van Diemen's Land Aboriginal woman, who died in 1876.

† The spelling of the McCraes' name varied; on their headstone it was 'McCrae', which is also the form used by their descendants, but in other sources it was spelt 'McRae' or 'McRea'.

HENRY AND LIZZIE MCCRAE WHEN LIZZIE WAS WORKING AS A NURSE. THE
PHOTOGRAPH IS THOUGHT TO HAVE BEEN TAKEN AT LAKE TYERS OR HEALESVILLE

Lizzie married Henry McCrae on 25 August 1909 at Coranderrk
Aboriginal Station. I could not find out when they moved to
Purnim. They were not survived by any children.

Lizzie had a beautiful voice. Banjo says white people would
pack the mission church to hear her sing.

By the 1930s many Europeans believed that the Aboriginal
people of Australia were on the verge of extinction. This thinking
was reflected in a number of events. The artist Percy Leason, for
example, held an exhibition of Aboriginal portraits in Melbourne

in September 1934. He called it 'The Last of the Victorian Aborigines'. In a pamphlet issued in connection with the exhibition he pointed out that there remained in Victoria 'only forty-six listed full-bloods'. 'Only this small group, the last of six thousand—only these survive our occupation of Victoria for one hundred years.' These forty-six, he wrote, were 'the best representatives of Victoria's vanishing aborigines'. Two of the forty-six were the McCraes. Whether he painted them or not is not clear.[3]

Why did the white people bury the McCraes in the Warrnambool Cemetery? I had looked for an answer in the old files of the *Warrnambool Standard*. The extracts from the *Standard* echoed the words of Percy Leason. The Aboriginals were 'a vanishing race', and the McCraes were 'the last of a great tribe'. They were well known and liked. Mrs McCrae had 'a particularly fine voice'. '[O]n the occasion of her appearance in several vocal numbers at the Framlingham benefit concert in the Town Hall last year, she was given a rousing reception.' Mr McCrae was 'a Christian gentleman' who, 'although having very little ... constantly gave kindly help to those about him'. Erecting the headstone 'was the least the people of Warrnambool and district could do to mark the last of the first inhabitants of our country'.[4]

Banjo and I had discussed the McCraes several times before. Each time he'd asked, 'Why did they do it?', I'd told him what I had learnt from reading the *Warrnambool Standard*. This time I just sat. I'd told him all I knew and I had nothing more to say.

'But why did they do it?' Banjo insisted, the pain as real as it was sixty years ago.

I sat there, a representative of my culture, stunned, hardly conscious of Banjo as I at last comprehended what he had been trying to make me understand. We not only took the land, institutionalised the people, separated them from their children, allowed skeletal and other remains to be taken overseas, put their skeletons on show in museums and kept personal collections of the tools we found scattered across the paddocks, we had also

HENRY McCRAE (LEFT) WITH MARY AUSTIN (CHRIS AUSTIN'S WIFE) AND
WILLIAM (BILL) AUSTIN, SON OF MARY AND CHRIS

claimed the right to bury their dead with us if it suited us. No! I wanted to say. We're not like that! But the evidence was overwhelming.

I thought more deeply about my culture, about how—often with the best of intentions—we have done things to Aboriginal people without any idea of the hurt we have inflicted. Why didn't the citizens of Warrnambool think of the McCraes' own people, the ones with whom they shared their lives? Now, like Banjo, I ask, 'Why did they do it? Why did they take them away?'

CHAPTER 6

In defence of
Framlingham

COLLIN HOOD

c. 1836–1914

ABORIGINAL NAME: MERANG

TRIBE: TJAPWURONG (THE LANGUAGE IS USUALLY REFERRED TO AS
DJAB WURRUNG OR CHAAP WURRUNG)

TOTEM: JALLAN (BOA SNAKE; WHIPSNAKE)

COLLIN HOOD, HENRY ALBERTS, JIMMY HAMMOND AND MRS BROWN, ABOUT 1910.
NOTE THE ABORIGINAL BASKETS IN THE CENTRE OF THE PHOTOGRAPH

Collin Hood was born about 1836[1] and died in 1914. He was the son of King Blackwood and Mary, also known as Charles and Mary Hood.[2] A member of the Tjapwurong tribe, he was born on Muston's Creek, a western tributary of the Hopkins River, on the south-eastern edge of the tribal territory, which stretched west to Hamilton and north up to Stawell in the Grampians. At various times he gave his birthplace as Muston's Creek, Hexham, Ballangeich and Barwidgee (a station on the north-west boundary of Merrang run, later the home of the Hood family, after whom Collin took his name): all are within walking distance of each other. Hexham is on the Hopkins River, just a little to the north-west of Mortlake.

Of all the Western District Aboriginals who appear in this book, Collin is the only one whose totem is recorded. His totem was jallan: 'challan' is the Djab wurrung word for boa snake.[3] There were elaborate rules in Aboriginal society governing whom one could marry. The aim was to prevent marriages between those who were too closely related—'of one flesh', as James Dawson put it in his book *Australian Aborigines*, which documented the customs of Western District Aboriginals. The phrase they used for this relationship was 'Tow'wil yerr'.[4]

Aboriginals married outside the clan, but Western District Aboriginals were also divided into five classes, and there were rules about which classes could intermarry. The classes took their names from certain animals—the long-billed cockatoo, the pelican, the banksian cockatoo, the boa snake and the quail. Each person was thus forbidden to marry certain people and encouraged to marry others. Collin, for example, told the Reverend John Bulmer, manager of the Lake Tyers Aboriginal Station, that as a jallan he must marry a white cockatoo. His daughter, a white cockatoo, could marry a black cockatoo.[5]

Collin Hood's story illustrates how links to place altered in post-European Aboriginal culture. The dispossession brought about by European occupation of the tribal lands forced a reduction and sometimes a brutal breaking of the strong ties that had previously bound Aboriginals to a specific area of land, the clan

territory. In Collin's case, Europeans were on the border of his
'country' by 1838, when David Fisher and others established a
pastoral run at Mount Shadwell (Mortlake). A year later dispossession had occurred: the land west and south of the Hopkins had
been taken up by Europeans. In 1841, when Chief Protector
Robinson passed through Collin's clan territory, there were already
so many European land-holders in the area between Mount
Noorat and the coast at Warrnambool that Robinson was able to
move from one white property to the next in easy stages, as the
notes in his journal show:

> *from Kilambete [John Thomson at Lake Keilambete] to Black's [Niel
> Black's] and return to Kilambete, 12 [miles] . . .*

> *from Kilambete to Thomson's outstation, 7;*

> *from Thomson's to Webster's [Mount Shadwell station], 7;*

> *from Webster's to Hopkins [River], 10;*

> *from Woolshed [later Hexham] to Fairie's [Merrang], 7;*

> *from Fairie's to Bolden's [on the west bank of the Hopkins, south of
> Merrang], 3;*

> *from Bolden's upper station to Bolden's lower station [close to the present
> site of Warrnambool], 20;*

> *from the farm to Campbell's [on the Merri River near Tower Hill], 12*[6]

In the area west of the Hopkins River, interracial violence reached
a peak in 1842, but Aboriginal people living in the vicinity of the
river itself, as Collin Hood did, were being dispossessed from 1839
onwards. As a child Collin would have heard talk of his people
being whipped off the runs, or chased and shot at by the
newcomers. He may even have had to run to save his own life.
Local Aboriginal oral tradition tells of such brutality and the
written records confirm that such things occurred at the Mount
Shadwell run, at Merrang and on the Boldens' property.

Dispossession effectively made Aboriginals intruders on their own land. To what extent it meant total exclusion depended on the individual squatters' wishes. Some Aboriginals negotiated the right to remain and camp on what had been their own land, but all of them lost the right to care for and use the land in the old ways.

Ties to specific places were further eroded after the establishment of the Central Board in 1860. The forced removal of Aboriginal people to the stations weakened their links to 'country', and in some cases bonds were completely severed when officials insisted that Aboriginals reside on distant stations. At the same time, Board policy led to the growth of new ties and attachments. People ordered to reside on one Aboriginal station might be forced to go to another by Order in Council as punishment for misconduct, or because the Board had decided to close the station. Alternatively, an individual or family might visit a distant Aboriginal station and gain permission to stay. As people forged new relationships, kinship ties stretched to embrace all Victoria and beyond. The Board also brought Aboriginals from outside Victoria on to the stations. The result was that relationships expanded across the European-created state borders to South Australia, Western Australia and Queensland until there were networks of kin stretching throughout Australia.[7] Of the 780 Victorian people recorded as Aboriginal in 1881, 44 were born in New South Wales, 17 in Queensland, 10 in South Australia and one in Western Australia.[8]

Aboriginals initially found the enforced close contact with 'strangers' on the stations difficult to cope with. Kirrae wurrung Elder Banjo Clarke says:

At first those brought together on the missions from distant places were suspicious of each other, were different mobs. But as traditions declined on the Aboriginal stations the suspicions lessened, though even now there is still awareness of a difference, a slight barrier with those from a different group. But more important is the shared

Aboriginality, a different interpretation from that of Europeans, a difference that comes from the heart.[9]

By the late 1850s many of the Aboriginal survivors of the frontier conflict were working on pastoral runs. The earliest record I have found of Collin is at Robert Hood's run, Merrang. Hood bought the property in 1856, when dispossession was well and truly complete. Collin was not the only Aboriginal working on the property, but his use of the surname 'Hood' indicates he had a strong link to the Hood family. Aboriginal men were employed at Merrang to do gardening, hay-making, shepherding, shearing, digging potatoes and cutting thistles. 'Black Jeni' (Jeanie Farie) worked in the house.

The fact that Merrang is both the name of the pastoral run and Collin's Aboriginal name[10] suggests that he was in his own 'country'. Collin was already referred to by his Anglicised name in the Merrang pastoral records in December 1858. He alone of the Aboriginals was paid for horse-breaking early in 1863. Collin is named as receiving payment during 1858, 1859, 1862 and 1863. His pay in 1858 was £38 17s 8d, indicating that he was then working full-time. In that year he bought a horse from Merrang for £20.[11] In the early 1860s William Hood described Collin as his 'best man', meaning his best worker.[12] He had a reputation for being a very flashy dresser, turning out on Sundays and holidays 'in white breeches and shirt'.

Collin's first wife was Nora, who according to Robert Hood was the 'virtual head' of what Europeans called the Hopkins River or Hexham blacks.[13] Her uncle, King John, was the 'sacred man' or 'doctor'. She was exceptional in that she could read and write before there was any government provision for teaching Aboriginals. As early as 1863 Robert Hood described Nora as 'a highly-civilised woman ... who can read and write'.[14]

According to the Reverend William Hamilton, Presbyterian minister of Mortlake, Nora was 'educated, baptised and regularly married. A domestic servant till married.'[15] I found the record of her baptism, which was performed by the Reverend P. Teulon Beamish on 24 June 1853. Beamish was the first local Anglican priest, and his vast parish stretched from Port Fairy to Cape Otway and inland as far as, but not including, Hamilton. The record of baptism gave Nora's date of birth as 14 January 1836, and her parents' names as Ningi Burning and Nango burn. Her surname was given as Villiers, which is the name of the county in which she was living. This is interesting, because Aboriginals were usually named after their parents or friends, or from something in the neighbourhood such as a swamp, waterhole or rivulet.[16] After dispossession Aboriginals at first continued this practice but used European place names. There are examples in the very early records of Aboriginals' adopting place names as their surnames, as apparently in this case, rather than the name of a European family such as Clarke, Hood or Austin.

The Reverend Hamilton named Nora as one of two Aboriginal women he had met during his twenty-six years residence in New South Wales and Victoria 'possessing a greater amount of religious knowledge than many of our white population'.[17] She 'owed her instruction and conversion to Mrs. MacKenzie', probably the wife of Anthony MacKenzie of Woolongoon, a property not far from Merrang. 'I conversed with her according to the usage of the Presbyterian Church', Reverend Hamilton wrote, 'and I believe her to be a sincere and intelligent Christian. I baptised her children without hesitation.'[18]

The missionary John G. Paton called on Nora unannounced while on a fund-raising tour of Victoria in 1863. He found her in a hut in the Aboriginal camp near Hexham. She and her children were 'clean and tidily dressed'. To his surprise, she had been reading the *Presbyterian Messenger*, and a copy of the Bible was at hand. When he asked if she read the *Messenger*, she replied, 'Yes I like to know what is going on in the Church'.[19]

Collin Hood and Nora appear to have had six children. They had previously owned a comfortable home, but had lost it through Collin's drinking. Nora told friends that there was some consolation. Their circumstances, she said, had brought her 'poor husband to his senses', and he was trying not to drink.

Nora's fame spread to Melbourne, where Paton made his meeting with Nora central to his appeal for greater efforts to Christianise the Aboriginals. At the meeting to farewell him in Melbourne, Paton used letters Nora had written to him to illustrate his contention that Aboriginals were 'above the brutes of the field' and capable 'of taking in the Gospel'. In one of these letters Nora spoke of her efforts to spread the gospel among her people:

I am telling the blacks always about God our Saviour and the salvation of their souls. They are so very wicked. They go from place to place, and they don't stop long with me. I am always teaching my children to pray, and would like to send them to School if I could ... I hope you will go home to England safely, get more Missionaries, and then go back to your poor blacks on the Islands. I will be glad to hear from you. May the Lord God bless you, wherever you go! Your affectionate, Nora Hood.

He also showed objects that he had collected from her used by 'the sacred man' to influence events for good or ill:

At my farewell meeting in Melbourne, Sir Henry Barkley presiding, I pleaded that the Colony should put forth greater efforts to give the Gospel to the Aborigines; I showed the idols which I had discovered amongst them; I read Nora's letters; and, I may, without presumption, say, the 'brute-in-human-shape' theory has been pretty effectually buried ever since.[20]

In 1860, when the Central Board took on the task of implementing the government's Aboriginal policy, it was decreed that land was to be reserved for Aboriginal use and Aboriginal stations established in places where there were considerable numbers of Aboriginals. The stations were to be run preferably by a minister of religion with some experience of agriculture. Once the Board was operating, communities sought to have land reserved for local Aboriginals. In May 1861 Dr John Singleton, on behalf of an Aboriginal mission formed by the Church of England in

CAPTIONED 'ABORIGINES, WARRNAMBOOL, VICTORIA', THIS APPEARS TO BE A PHOTO
TAKEN IN THE BUSH ON THE FRAMLINGHAM MISSION IN THE VERY EARLY DAYS

Warrnambool, applied for land for an Aboriginal reserve. In response, a reserve of 3500 acres by the Hopkins River was gazetted on 17 September 1861. It was on this land that the Framlingham Aboriginal Station began in 1865.

Collin and Nora were well aware of these developments. They were perhaps the first Aboriginals to ask for an individual grant of land when the government introduced its new policy. On 11 June 1860 the Board received their application for a grant of land near Hexham.[21] This was followed in November by a letter from Mr Scott, a local surveyor who was also an Honorary Correspondent for the Central Board, recommending a plan for a reserve for Aboriginals in the parish of Connewarra, including a suitable piece of land for Nora and Collin.[22] It appears that the Board approved this grant, and the District Surveyor is on record as stating that it might be given.[23] It is not absolutely clear whether the Hoods

received title to the land, but circumstantial evidence suggests that they did.[24]

In 1865 the Central Board agreed to a proposal from the Church of England Mission to open a station on the reserved land, with Daniel Clarke as missionary manager. The station had barely begun when the mission surrendered the station to the Board. A shortage of funds and a disagreement with Daniel Clarke over the terms of his engagement were given as reasons for the change of heart. The Clarkes continued at the station as Board employees, but it was not long before Clarke was in trouble with the Board, which accepted his resignation in May 1867.

What had Daniel Clarke done? Board Minutes give little idea, but it is clear that Collin was involved. In May 1867 a number of Aboriginals faced the Police Court in Warrnambool, charged with assaulting and threatening the life of Daniel Clarke and assaulting Mrs Clarke. Those charged were Collin Hood, Jemmy Brooks, Sam Robinson, Jemmy Delford, Old Joe, King John, Dicky, King Jack and Jemmy McLean. The brief notes of the case published in the

Warrnambool Standard indicate that the issue had been some action of Daniel Clarke's with regard to Aboriginal children, which led to the men threatening the Clarkes both verbally and physically. The large number of people involved and the presence of several Elders indicate the seriousness of the Aboriginal concern. Only three of the nine were convicted. Collin was obviously seen as a leader of the protest; he and Jemmy Brooks were sentenced to fourteen days imprisonment. Old Joe was sentenced to forty-eight hours with hard labour. The journalist recording the details of the case reported that those sentenced appeared to be enjoying their time in prison: 'Yesterday we notice the three evidently pleased at working in the police garden, and we have no doubt their sentence will ... prove an agreeable change'.[25] At the time it was widely believed that prison was an improvement on normal Aboriginal living conditions.[26]

What was the reason for the Aboriginal protest? It seems likely that the Clarkes tried to separate the children from their families, a policy that was fashionable at the time among those who saw themselves as helping the Aboriginals. This was the practice at the Ramahyuck Aboriginal Station, for example, where the children slept in a boarding house.[27]

CERTIFICATE OF MARRIAGE OF COLLIN HOOD AND LOUISA LUTTON

On 4 October 1867 the Board decided to close the station and move the Aboriginals from Framlingham to Lake Condah, where a new station was being established. Some of the Framlingham Aboriginals refused to go; others went, but quarrelled with the people at Lake Condah and returned home. In September 1868 the Framlingham Aboriginals contacted the Central Board asking for the re-establishment of the Framlingham station. In April 1869 they sent a deputation to see the Chief Secretary, and before the end of the month the Board had decided to employ a master and matron at Framlingham. The station was again in operation.

I am not sure whether Collin and Nora were on the station at this time, but Nora died on 20 March 1871, shortly after it was reopened. She had been a patient at the Melbourne Hospital, and was buried in the New Cemetery, Melbourne.[28]

It was not long before Collin remarried. On 6 August 1872 he and Louisa Lutton, who had been widowed the previous year, were married at the Framlingham Aboriginal Station according to the rites of the Congregational Church, the Reverend Uriah Coombs taking the service. Both gave their age as thirty at the time. Louisa, who came from near Mount Rouse, was the daughter of King George and Mary. They had four children:

SCHEDULE D.

in the Colony of Victoria.

Rank or Profession.	Ages.	Residence.		Parents.	
		Present.	Usual.	Names. (Mother's Maiden Name.)	Father's Rank or Profession.
Stockrider	30	Framlingham	Framlingham	Blackwood Mary	King
Domestic Servant	30	Framlingham	Framlingham	George Mary	King

Marriage, *after declaration duly made*, was solemnized between us according to the rites of the Congregational Church. { *Collin Hood* *Louisa × Lutton* (her mark) }

Witnesses { *William Goodall* *Ellen good* }

> A MARRIAGE ceremony was performed on Tuesday last at the Aboriginal Station at Framlingham, by the Rev. U. Coombs. The husband is Collin, son of " King Blackwood," who was united in wedlock to Louisa, daughter of " King George." After the marriage, a festival on temperance principles was given by Mr. W. Goodall, in celebration of the event. The happy couple, and witnesses, appended their native names to the register, also to the Government document.

NEWSPAPER REPORT OF THE WEDDING OF COLLIN HOOD AND LOUISA LUTTON IN THE *WARRNAMBOOL EXAMINER*, 9 AUGUST 1872

Leah (1873–1894), an un-named male who died the day he was born, Wallace, who died in 1881 at the age of two-and-a-half of a hepatic abscess, and Minna Martha (1883–1915).

The Hoods were named among those required to reside on the Framlingham Aboriginal Station in 1876. Board records in the 1880s include references to Leah's ill-health, Collin's appointment as stock-keeper on the Aboriginal station and to his taking the pledge to abstain from drinking alcohol.

In October 1882 Leah was reported to be 'very ill'. Her ill-health continued after Martha was born in April 1883. In the manager's report for July 1884, Leah Hood was mentioned as needing an operation for hydatids. The manager commented that the number of cases of hydatids was on the increase, and added that the doctors he had spoken to had blamed the problem on the fact that dogs were polluting the drinking water. He expressed a wish to reduce the number of dogs on the station, but was reluctant to do so without an order from the Board: 'the people put such a value on them and regard with such horror the idea of destroying them that I do not care to move in the matter except under the express direction of the Board', he wrote. On 1 September he recorded that Leah was the most seriously ill person on the station and needed an operation. At the end of the month he commented that she had improved but was now ill again.

Collin had few appearances in court, but one occasion is worth commenting on. On 21 July 1874 he was charged with being 'drunk and disorderly'. The penalty was to pay a fine of five shillings or be imprisoned for twenty-four hours. Collin, unusually for an Aboriginal, paid the fine.[29]

Drunkenness was a problem on the Aboriginal stations. At Framlingham the managers tried to prevent the residents from gaining access to alcohol by ensuring that publicans who supplied it to them were prosecuted. They also tried to persuade Aboriginals to take the pledge to abstain from drinking. It appears that Collin provided some moral support for those who were determined to overcome their problem. In April 1885 the Framlingham manager at the time, Reverend Robert Thwaites, had two men who had been violent towards their wives while drunk brought before the Warrnambool Bench, but he agreed that they be discharged with a caution provided they promised to sign the pledge.* Thwaites reported to the Board that Collin Hood had joined the men and their wives in signing the pledge.[30]

AN ACCOUNT OF A CRICKET MATCH FROM THE *WARRNAMBOOL EXAMINER* , 20 FEBRUARY 1875. THE REPORT IS OF GREAT INTEREST, BECAUSE IT PROVIDES A RARE MENTION OF THE ABORIGINAL NAMES OF SEVERAL FRAMLINGHAM MEN

Cricket was a favourite pastime of those on 'the mission' in the 1870s and early 1880s. The Aboriginal team played regularly against the Warrnambool team and sometimes against the Koroit team. The cricketers bought themselves a

* One of these men was King David; for a further discussion of this incident, see chapter 7.

CRICKET.

ABORIGINALS V. FRIENDLY SOCIETIES.

A match between the above clubs was played in the Friendly Societies' Park, on Wednesday last. The weather was all that could be desired; but the ground was rough and bumpy. Mr. Goodall captained the Aboriginals, and Mr. D. R. Evans, the Friendlies. The darkies appeared to be in splendid form, and played with great spirit, defeating their opponents in one innings, with 15 runs to spare. The Friendlies went in first, to the bowling of Blair and Cousins, who soon disposed of the lot for 27 runs, the highest scorer being F. Manning, who made 11. The Aboriginals then went to the wickets, and made 92, to which Cousins contributed 30, obtained in his usual careful style; J. Brown 21, and J. Fairie 11. The Friendlies, in their second innings, made 50, Ivor Williams making 15, J. Waters 11, and F. Manning 7. The batting and fielding of the darkies in this match was especially noticeable as being greatly improved. The bowling of Cousins and Blair was very destructive, and the wicket keeping of Wyselaskie greatly admired. The Friendlies did not seem to be in their usual form, either in the field or at the wicket, and there was nothing in their play worthy of special remark. The game was over by four o'clock, and a scratch match between sides chosen by Messrs. R. G. Begley and J. Collyer concluded the afternoon's sport. The following is the score :—

ABORIGINAL PLAYERS.—F. Blair (Mirnmulk), b Molan, 5 ; J. Cousins (Koongerong). b Manning, 30 ; J. Wyeslaskie (Woorookie Larnock) b Molan, 6 ; P. Austin (Poorne Yarriworri), c Watson b Molan, 5 ; W. Good (Porrom-meit Coorong), c Crisp, b Manning, 0 ; W. Goodall (captain), b Manning, 0 ; J. Dawson (Koroitch Tiyer), c Williams b Manning, 4 ; J. Brown (Poorae Yallon - cork). b Waters, 2I ; J. Fairie (Llahweit Tarnim). b Wilson, 11 ; H. Sanders,

ABORIGINAL PLAYERS.—F. Blair (Mirnmulk), b Molan, 5 ; J. Cousins (Koongerong). b Manning, 30 ; J. Wyeslaskie (Woorookie Larnock) b Molan, 6 ; P. Austin (Poorne Yarriworri), c Watson b Molan, 5 ; W. Good (Porrom-meit Coorong), c Crisp, b Manning, 0 ; W. Goodall (captain), b Manning, 0 ; J. Dawson (Koroitch Tiyer), c Williams b Manning, 4 ; J. Brown (Poorae Yallon - cork). b Waters, 2I ; J. Fairie (Llahweit Tarnim), b Wilson, 11 ; H. Sanders, (Nunnewarne), c and b Waters, 0 ; D. Dickey (Tullum Tullum), not out, 0 ; Byes, 10 ; Total, 92.

34 balls, 15 runs, 2 maiden overs, 5 wickets. *Second Innings.*—H. Saunders, bowled 66 runs, 27 runs, 2 maiden overs, 4 wickets. F. Blair, bowled 48 balls, 18 runs, 2 maiden overs, 3 wickets. J. Cousins, bowled 18 balls, 5 runs, 3 wickets.

ABORIGINALS.—F. Manning, bowled 60 balls, 31 runs, 4 wickets. D. Molan, bowled 66 balls, 47 runs, 2 maiden overs, 3 wickets. J. Walters, bowled 19 balls, 10 runs, 2 wickets. E. Wilson, bowled 6 balls, 4 runs, 1 wicket.

wagonette in early 1878 so that they could get to the matches in style. Readers of the *Warrnambool Standard* were reminded of the fact that James Cousins* (Mosquito), who took an active part in organising the Aboriginal cricketers, had been a member of the Aboriginal team that toured England in 1868. This team of Aboriginal players from western Victoria was the first Australian team to play at Lord's.[31] Collin often played as a member of the Framlingham team,[32] though he did not receive any special mention. The *Warrnambool Standard* reported that the bowling of Cousins and Blair was 'very destructive'.[33] Frank Blair on one occasion 'played a very pretty innings, putting together 20 in artistic style and without giving a chance till he was neatly caught at point'. John Wyselaskie was described as 'the W. G. Grace of the Framlingham team, resembling the great cricketer not a little in size and frame, though a better looking fellow',[34] while William Rawlings was expected to develop into 'a first class bowler'.[35]

Like Robert Hood at Merrang, Thwaites found Collin a useful employee. He worked 'willingly and more constantly than most men', and Thwaites appointed him stockman in the early 1880s. Thwaites also had other motives. As he told his superiors, Collin 'has a hot temper and is a bit of a bounce [bragger], that is partly why he was made stockman. It isolates him to a great extent and prevents collisions.' It made life difficult for Collin, however. In June 1884 he wrote to Captain Page at the Board for the Protection of the Aborigines (BPA) to explain a little 'upsetment' and ask the Board not to listen to complaints they might receive about him from people on the station. They were behaving in an odd way, and he wasn't sure why. Yet in his own description of his job one can see how he was being cut off from his fellows:

> *I have got a bilit [billet: a job] of stock-keeping from Mr Thwaites. Sir I am very strict from letting the people taking the cattle. Sir he's doing well and getting paid for all the graziers. I am taking the butchering and giving out the meat only one piece all round and salting them to [too] for*

---

* The family name was elsewhere spelt as Couzens.

A PHOTOGRAPH OF ABORIGINAL WOMEN AND CHILDREN, BELIEVED TO BE HAVE BEEN TAKEN IN THE GARDEN OF GRANNY ALICE CLARKE'S HOUSE NEAR THE WARRUMYEA BRIDGE, ON THE FRAMLINGHAM ABORIGINAL MISSION IN THE LATE 1880S. THE WOMAN STANDING AT THE BACK, SECOND FROM THE LEFT, MAY BE GRANNY CLARKE

the mens that works regular and those thats doing no work shall get no more without they work like the rest.[36]

Thwaites called the people together and spoke to them of their duty as Christians 'to bear one another's burdens'. Then he asked them individually what complaint they had to make about Collin. No one made a complaint and the situation became settled again.

The Aboriginals were expected to work for their keep on the station, but those interested in work off the station could sign on for seasonal work such as shearing when it was available. To do so they had to have a permit from the BPA. This had been the practice in the Western District from the time the Aboriginal stations had been established, and the Aboriginals prized the opportunity to earn money, but the competition Aboriginal shearers posed to

ABORIGINAL WOMAN (POSSIBLY EMILY EDWARDS) AND CHILDREN PHOTOGRAPHED
IN THE BUSH ON THE FRAMLINGHAM ABORIGINAL MISSION, PROBABLY IN THE
LATE 1880s

white labour became a sore point in late 1887, when a militant new Amalgamated Shearers' Union was moving to establish uniform rates of pay throughout the district.

The issue was raised in Parliament by Mr Toohey, the Member of the Legislative Assembly for Villiers and Heytesbury, who claimed that Framlingham Aboriginals were shearing for less than the Shearers' Union rate. He asked the Chief Secretary to take steps to stop this clash with the interests of white shearers. The Chief Secretary promised to take up the matter with the BPA, which also received a letter from the Secretary of the Trades Hall Council asking if the Aboriginals were hired out and whether they were members of the union. The BPA asked the Framlingham manager, William Goodall, to provide details. Goodall reported that all but two of the Aboriginals who were away shearing belonged to the Shearers' Union, and the two non-unionists were shearing at the same rate as whites in the district. James Dawson, ever alert to any move against Aboriginal interests, used the letters column of the *Camperdown Chronicle* to voice his disbelief at the parliamentarians' actions:

> *Do these two members of our Legislature [Mr Toohey and Alfred Deakin, the Chief Secretary] really require to be told that the Aborigines of this colony are as much the subjects of the Queen as they are, and cannot be debarred from the rights of citizens, and of labour[?]*[37]

On 7 August 1889 the Board decided to close the Framlingham station, and it reaffirmed the decision on 4 September. It envisaged this as the first of a series of closures. The move was supported by local farmers, who wished to see the site turned over to an agricultural college and experimental farm. The decision came as a great shock to the Aboriginals, and they and their supporters fought hard to save the station. Collin played a leading role in this campaign.

In fighting for their cause the Aboriginals had a loyal friend in Robert Hood, on whose property many of them had worked over the years. He contested the claim that the Aboriginals came from other parts of Victoria and therefore had no particular attachment to the locality, an argument that was often used by those trying to close the station. He wrote to the *Standard*:

> *I think I know almost, if not every one, of the full-blooded blacks at Framlingham, and knew them all before they were located there as belonging to the Western District, and they all knew each other. [T]hough belonging to different tribes originally, they latterly were all on visiting terms, constantly meeting on the different stations about ... Some people who don't know the native character, may fancy they have no love of country or locality. This I am sure is not a fact ... I am convinced that it would be a great wrench to move them from what they naturally considered their home for life.*[38]

James Dawson immediately wrote to the *Standard* expressing 'satisfaction' with his friend's letter:

For among all the wealthy occupants and owners of this magnificent district, from which the rightful owners were hunted, expelled, and very many of them massacred in cold blood, and poisoned, it is almost the only one evincing a kindly feeling for the remnant and courage to express it publicly.[39]

On 1 November 1889 the Chief Secretary, Alfred Deakin, arrived in Warrnambool on his way to visit Framlingham. Two of the Aboriginals addressed Mr Deakin on behalf of the Framlingham residents. They were Collin Hood and William Good.

A *Warrnambool Standard* reporter was on hand to record the Chief Secretary's visit and he provided the following account of what Collin had to say:

The first speaker—Collin Hood by name—said he hoped the board would not remove them from Framlingham. It had been their hunting grounds, and they hoped to be allowed to live there for the few remaining years of their lives. They had nice homes there and were happy, and if removed to other places would not agree. They only wanted enough land to be allowed to live quietly and comfortably as at present.[40]

Mr Deakin assured the Aboriginals that he wanted to see them happy and comfortable, and said he believed that their wishes should be taken into account. He promised to see the Board again and endeavour to get the members to change their decision. He couldn't see why both proposals couldn't be accommodated: that about 500 or 600 acres be set aside for the Aboriginals and the remainder reclaimed by the Crown for use as an experimental farm. The newspaper reported that the Aboriginals received this response with satisfaction.

Deakin's support, however, did not sway the Board. On 1 November 1889 the Reverend Friedrich Hagenauer, Acting General Inspector of Aborigines, reported to Dr Morrison, Vice-Chairman of the BPA, on his visit to Framlingham just after its official closure. He stated that William Goodall and his wife had left the station only a few hours before his visit, and he 'found some of the Blacks in a rather excited state of mind their leader using expressions of a very unpleasant kind'. He claimed that only six or seven of the eighty people present were born in the locality. Nine had already left the station, and a further thirty had agreed to go elsewhere. Once they left, he assured the Board, the remaining few would soon follow. He pointed, however, to some determined resistance led by Collin:

> A few of the blacks from the locality have been crammed in the idea of getting a few hundred acres of land from the reserve either as a hunting ground or for small farms, and their leader Collin Hood, seems very earnest in his request. He seems to have had land of his own at Hexham Park in former years, but does not know how he lost it, which might be the same in the future as it has been in the past.[41]

At the end of the month Hagenauer's claim that the Framlingham residents were not locals was again challenged by Robert Hood, who had followed up his letter to the *Standard* by asking Collin Hood, whom he described as 'a very intelligent blackfellow', to make 'a list of the pure blacks at present at Framlingham, their names and birth places'. The list, which was published with the letter on 29 November 1889, showed that of the Aboriginals Collin listed ('39 pure blacks and 4 half-castes') there was only 'one pure black man at Framlingham who was born outside the district'. Hood concluded that it would therefore be a 'great hardship to remove them from what they look on as their home, and place them amongst strangers'. It is interesting to note that while the white community, and even the Board, dealt with 'half-castes' and 'pure bloods' as two completely different groups, Collin felt it necessary to include four 'half-castes' among those he believed belonged. Robert Hood commented that the list had been prepared by Collin's daughter, who had been educated at the Aboriginal station.

A small group of Aboriginals, including the Hoods, refused to leave the station even after it was closed, the manager had been removed, and all the stock and farming implements had been taken away. On 8 September 1890, amid all the uncertainty and reduced circumstances, Collin's second wife, Louisa, died and was buried in the Aboriginal cemetery. Elder Banjo Clarke remembers being told by the old people that a Hood is buried under the very tall pine tree in the cemetery. It is likely that this is the site of her grave.

In their attempts to close Framlingham, the Board and Hagenauer, its Inspector and Secretary, had not reckoned on the stubbornness of the Aboriginals and the effectiveness of their friend John Murray, MLA for Warrnambool. Back in September 1889 Murray had drawn Parliament's attention to what was happening at Framlingham, describing it as 'the first big case of eviction' in the colony. The Chief Secretary assured him that matters would not be finalised without Parliament's having a chance to express its opinion.[42]

One year later, on 23 September 1890, hearing that the BPA was on the verge of handing the reserve land over to the Council of Agricultural Education without consulting Parliament, Murray again stood up in Parliament and spoke on the Framlingham issue. He asked for a definite promise from the Chief Secretary that 500 or 600 acres would be reserved for the use of the Aboriginals. When Deakin was unable to make such a promise, John Murray moved an adjournment of the House to speak on the subject 'That the proposal to hand over to the Council of Agricultural Education the Framlingham Aboriginal Station is harsh and unjust to the aboriginals there'.

Having gained the adjournment, John Murray read a letter from a friend who had visited the station the previous week:

> I went out to the camp and found the poor blacks very much upset. Altogether there were 42 at the camp. William Good said they were giving up all hope, as they expected Mr. Hagenauer down to wind up the camp and send them all about their business.

When Mr Hagenauer came down, John Murray claimed, he did so 'like a wolf on the fold'. The Aboriginals had come to regard him as 'their evil spirit'. The letter continued, 'Three of the houses have already been disposed of, and the people about Purnim are looking at some of the others, and are to put in tenders for them'. There were other grievances. One man's ration had been stopped because he had been incorrectly considered a 'half-caste', and two half-castes over the age of forty had been denied rations, although by law they should have been receiving them. Then, with a dry humour that captured the interest, if not the sympathy, of his listeners, Murray explained why he was not satisfied with leaving the Council of Agricultural Education to make arrangements for the Aboriginals:

> *He had no doubt that were it necessary for the advancement of the agricultural interests of the colony, they would have no scruple in converting the aborigines into manure and fertilising the land with them. Then there would be a Bulletin from the Agricultural department giving an analysis of the constituent parts of the manure.*[43]

His intervention was timely. Deakin in reply promised that the Parliament, the Government and Board would be 'generous' to the Aboriginals. One member said that John Murray had handed him a letter from James Dawson conveying the concerns of a 'Colin', no doubt Collin Hood:

> *From what Colin said, they never knew the day their comfortable huts might not be pulled down, should they leave them for a day or two and he tells me that several of them have been treated in this way … I do not know who is at the bottom of this cool and unfeeling way of treating a subjected race, but it ill accords with a professedly Christian Government, and ought to be denounced.*[44]

Two MLAs who were members of the Board spoke. C. M. Officer, Chairman of the Board, stated that he had no problems with the Chief Secretary's promise but he wished that those who sided with the Aboriginals would cease their interference. '[H]ad it not been for the undue influence brought to bear on the aborigines, who were simply so many children, they would all by this time have been removed from Framlingham with their own consent'. He had no sympathy for the Aboriginal claim to be locals of the area: 'In no special sense or way could they be said to specially belong to Framlingham'. He defended Mr Hagenauer: 'a more vigilant, kind-hearted, and deeply-interested friend than the Rev. Mr. Hagenauer the blacks never had'. He found it hard to understand what motivated Murray:

> He thoroughly sympathised with the remarks of the honourable member for Warrnambool about railways for the western district, but he could not understand him standing for a moment in the way of the people there obtaining what they had almost more at heart, namely, the establishment of a local agricultural college.

He agreed with Murray that the Aborigines should not be evicted, but believed that the BPA was not even contemplating such a move.

William Anderson, MLA for Villiers and Heytesbury, had divided loyalties. He commented: 'While he would not like to see all the aboriginals removed from Framlingham, he would caution the House against reserving too much land for them'. Mr Woods, MLA for Stawell, retorted, 'They have not got any yet'.

Murray's intervention achieved its aim. In October came the news that the Chief Secretary had decided to reserve about 500 acres of the land for the exclusive use of the Aboriginals. The small group of twenty-five who were allowed to remain included the Hood family. No doubt they were pleased with the decision, but all that was part of a functioning station had gone. Now they received supplies only.

By March 1891 Collin was living at Hexham, having gained Board permission to do so and to receive his supplies there.[45] His daughter Martha attended the Hexham School during the first half of 1891.[46] Collin, however, was concerned about his now motherless girls, Martha and Leah, and asked the Board whether they could return to Framlingham to live with the Gibbs, a young married couple. The Board was strongly opposed, and wrote back that he had to either keep his daughters with him or go with them to the reserve. He was warned that if the girls returned on their own to Framlingham, the Board would obtain an Order in Council to send them to the Coranderrk station or a similar place where they could be under the care of a manager and matron.

Those who had been given the right to stay on the reserve applied for land for their individual use. In time land was approved for Frank Clarke, William Good, John Brown and John Wyselaskie. The land remained Crown land, though as far as most people were concerned it belonged to these individuals. The men applied for items needed to make something of their farms: a draught horse, a cart, a milking cow and seed potatoes. Collin, who was now living at Worndoo, not far from Hexham, applied for a ton and a half of potatoes. His request was refused. Living off the reserve, he was in a different category as far as the Board was concerned. They replied that as he was receiving full rations he was not entitled to anything more.[47] Yet those on the reserve were receiving rations as well as farming assistance. The Board hoped that with a little help those granted land would become self-supporting and no longer need rations. Why the same thinking did not apply to Collin, who had a long record of working, is difficult to see.

Throughout the 1890s the Board was troubled by the fact that people not legally entitled to be at Framlingham were moving back to the reserve. It worried Collin as well, even though he was not on the reserve. In mid-1892 he wrote to the Board asking that such people be removed. William Good was another who complained of the noise, the quarrelling and unrest caused by people who had no right to be on the reserve. He eventually received permission to move his house to a quieter part of the mission. The Board welcomed such requests and complaints, for they strengthened its hand in carrying out its plans. Framlingham station had been closed and the Board was determined not to back down. During a heated exchange with John Murray in the House of Assembly, Mr Cameron, one of the members of the Board, said that 'If he . . . had his way, he would remove the whole lot, and the honourable member would not be bothered with them any further'.[48]

OLD COTTAGES AT LAKE TYERS, 1895: COLLIN HOOD'S HOUSE IS THE THIRD FROM
THE TOP OF THE HILL

At this stage of my research into Collin Hood's life, all the leads from the Western District petered out. But then new information came from Gippsland, thanks to Hood descendants at Drouin and Lake Tyers. With the aid of a genealogy they shared with me, I was able to establish the details of Collin's third family.

I can only speculate about what attracted Collin Hood to the other end of Victoria, but by April 1897 he was living at Ramahyuck.[49] It may have been the closure of the Framlingham station and the Board's reluctance to help him gain his independence that caused him to look elsewhere. Certainly the Reverend Hagenauer, who was manager at Ramahyuck as well as General Inspector for the BPA, was at this time eagerly pointing out to Aboriginals the advantages of moving from a place where there was not an operating station to a flourishing station where the government was making proper provision for them. Collin may also have been influenced by the fact that his friends the Gibbs applied in 1896 to transfer to Ramahyuck,[50] although in fact they didn't follow this up by moving. Collin's stepdaughter Susan Murray (née Lutton, his second wife's daughter), her husband Fred and their five children applied to go to Lake Tyers in 1889 when Framlingham was being closed.[51] He may have felt that he should move near to them for the sake of his two girls. This appears probable, because Collin and the Murrays were together at Ramahyuck in 1902.[52] A shortage of eligible marriage partners in the Framlingham area may also have influenced his decision to join the large Aboriginal communities in eastern Victoria.

On 17 March 1898 Collin married Helen Rivers, a Kurnai woman, the daughter of Larry Johnson and Kitty Perry and widow of Charlie Rivers, who died on 3 December 1893. At this time he was living at Ramahyuck, but the couple were married at the Lake Tyers church. Collin must have been at least sixty at the time, but he gave his age as fifty. He had good reason to do so, as Helen was only twenty-three. A relatively old man, he was marrying a young bride and starting a third family.

HELEN HOOD (RIGHT) WITH SARAH MOFFAT AND CHILDREN

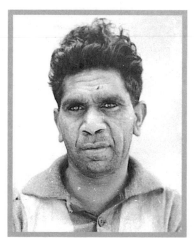

TOP 4: COLLIN AND HELEN HOOD'S
SONS, PHOTOGRAPHED AT LAKE TYERS
BY NORMAN TINDALE IN JANUARY
1939. CLOCKWISE FROM TOP LEFT:
STEWART HOOD AGED 32,
JACK HOOD AGED 38, CLIVE HOOD
AGED 30, JULIAN HOOD AGED 37.

LEFT: NOEL HOOD, SON OF
JACK HOOD AND ETHEL HOOD
(NEÉ MOBOURNE): GRANDSON OF
COLLIN AND HELEN HOOD AND
FATHER OF TERRY HOOD,
PHOTOGRAPHED AGED 21 AT
LAKE TYERS BY NORMAN TINDALE
IN JANUARY 1939

According to the marriage registration details, by this time Collin had fathered ten children, only two of whom were still alive.[53] He and Helen, however, were to have a large family of seven children: Jack, born in 1897; Minna, 1899; Lara Johnson, 1900; Alexander Stewart, 1902; Julian, 1905; Daisy Leah, 1906; and Clive Colin, 1908. Lara and Alexander were born at Stratford, and all the other children at Lake Tyers.

When Collin died in 1914, he was survived by six children. On his death certificate the surviving children are listed with their ages at the time. They were Martha, 28; Jack, 17; Minna, 15; Alexander Stewart, 12; Julian, 10; and Clive, 6. Helen died shortly after Collin in September 1915 as a result of drowning, leaving a number of young children to be cared for by others.[54]

If white commentators believed the Aboriginals were dying out, it seems nobody told Collin Hood or his family! Today the Hoods are 'a big mob'. There are more than 300 descendants living in Victoria, mainly in Gippsland. There is not enough space here to mention all those who have distinguished themselves in one way or another. The best-known of Collin's descendants, however, is his great-grandson, Lionel Rose, who was Australian amateur flyweight boxing champion in 1963, Australian bantamweight champion 1966–69 and won the world bantamweight title in Tokyo in 1968 against Fighting Harada. Over his boxing career, he won forty-two out of fifty-three fights.[55]

Lionel's cousins the Mulletts—Cheryl, Sandra, Pauline, Phillip and Russell—have also been outstanding in sport at the national and State level. Their chosen sport was badminton. Cheryl (married name Drayton) won three Australian junior singles, the Australian women's doubles and mixed doubles titles. In 1969 she won five titles at the same championships, and was awarded the Maxfield Trophy for the best individual performance of the year. In 1988 she was awarded a special medal for achievement at the National Aboriginal Sports Awards. Cheryl also won five major doubles titles with her sister, Sandra. Sandra won four Victorian under-17 singles, three Australian under-17 singles, and eleven major doubles titles. Four of her mixed doubles titles were with Russell, and one with Phillip. Pauline was Victorian under-15 champion in 1972. Phillip was twice Victorian under-17, and three times under-19 singles champion. In 1967 he won the Australian junior singles. Russell won the State under-17 singles and six doubles titles.[56]

It is symbolic of the new circumstances in which Aboriginals formed relationships in places far distant from their own country that the descendants of two men from the Western District were to marry at Lake Tyers: Jack Hood, son of Collin Hood, a fighter for the rights of his people during the closure of the Framlingham Aboriginal Station, married Ethel, the daughter of Ernest Mobourne, who fought against the closure of the Lake Condah Aboriginal station twenty years later, as we shall see in chapter 9. Collin Hood had moved to Lake Tyers by choice; the Mobournes were moved against their will; but both families ultimately remained in Gippsland, far from their homelands.

Collin Hood, Tjapwurong, lies buried at Lake Tyers, which he had made a second home.

CHAPTER 7

Double Dispossession

KING DAVID

C. 1820–1889

CHIEF OF THE KIRRAE WURRUNG—THE BLOOD LIP TRIBE

ABORIGINAL NAME: KAAWIRN KUUNAWARN—'HISSING SWAN'

TRIBE: KIRRAE WURRUNG (SOMETIMES NOW SPELT GIRAI WURRUNG)

CLAN: KON.NE.WURT (OR CONERWURT GUNDITJ, KONEEWURRER; NOW SOMETIMES SPELT GUNAWARD GUNDITJ)

KING DAVID

Old Davie (Hissing Swan) dead. Idea of leaving home killed him. Buried on Thursday.[1]

This was the wording of a telegram sent by William Goodall, manager of the Framlingham Aboriginal Station, to James Dawson, Local Guardian of the Aborigines in Camperdown, on 24 or 25 September 1889. It was a private communication, but one that was rapidly made public. It appeared in the *Camperdown Chronicle* on 26 September 1889 and the *Terang Express* on the following day. In different circumstances one might have expected an obituary or a brief note in the district news column in the *Warrnambool Standard*, but these were far from ordinary times. The death of King David, chief of the Mount Shadwell tribe, polarised feelings in the district. Few would have been unaware of his death, as it came at a critical time in a campaign that had pitted white farmers against the interests of the Framlingham Aboriginal community.

The decision to close the Framlingham Aboriginal Station was the result of two developments: a change in policy by the Board for the Protection of the Aborigines (BPA), and a local campaign to obtain an agricultural college and experimental farm for the Western District.

In 1886 an Act was passed under which all 'able-bodied half-castes'—to use the BPA's terminology—under the age of thirty-five were to be regarded as 'white'. Under the new Act, colloquially known as the 'Half-Caste Act', they would no longer be cared for by the BPA, and would have to leave the Aboriginal stations and support themselves by working for their keep. While the new policy was being implemented, the BPA proceeded to the next stage in its plans: the amalgamation of the remaining Aboriginals on a smaller number of stations. The BPA intended to close the stations one by one until all the remaining Aboriginals were concentrated at the Lake Tyers station in Gippsland.

The new policy implemented from 1 January 1887 arose out of a growing belief that the Aboriginal race was dying out.[2] This can be seen in the report of the 1877 Royal Commission established to advise the government on the best means of caring for the Aboriginal people in the future. The main question facing the Royal Commissioners was whether the Aboriginals had made such progress since 1860 that the system of Aboriginal stations could be abandoned and the Aboriginals merged into the general community. They recommended the continuance of the system on the grounds that, 'even if the race is fated to disappear', the stations would be valuable as public property and the government would have done its duty.

A census of the Aboriginal population taken in 1877 showed that numbers had almost halved since 1863 (from 1920 to 1067). While there were 636 'full-blood' adult Aboriginals as opposed to only 134 'half-castes', 'half-caste' children outnumbered those described as 'full-blood' by 159 to 138. It was commonly believed as a law of nature that the 'full-blood' Aboriginals would die out, but not so the 'half-castes', for they had 'white' blood. It was such thinking that led the BPA to introduce its new policy, the intent of which is made clear in its report for 1887, which stated that the number of people the Board had to care for was substantially reduced:

> Already the Board has made a fair beginning of a policy which is the beginning of the end, and which, in the course of a few years, will leave only a few pure blacks under the care of Government.[3]

The total population of the stations in August 1886 was 556. Of these, 233 'half-castes' came under the operation of the new Act. Numbers on the stations immediately began to decline. Having reduced the number for whom it was responsible, the Board was determined to make sure that the population would not again increase. From the time the 1886 Act came into operation, 'full-blood' Aboriginals were prohibited from marrying 'half-castes', other than those who were over-age. As Hagenauer, the Board Secretary and General Inspector, wrote to the Chief Secretary, an Aboriginal marrying a 'half-caste' would in effect be marrying a person 'considered in the eyes of the Law as . . . white . . . and an Aboriginal marrying such a one cannot claim rations nor reside with the Aborigines'.[4]

The BPA discussions about reducing the number of stations coincided with a campaign by the *Warrnambool Standard*, backed by the Villiers and Heytesbury Agricultural Association (VHAA), to gain an agricultural college for the Western District. The campaign concentrated at first on winning people over to the idea of an experimental farm. It was only after this was achieved and the *Standard* began to look for a suitable site that the project began to affect the Framlingham community. In a fateful editorial in April 1887, the *Standard* listed the possible sites: among them was the Framlingham Aboriginal Station. As cleared Crown land, it was 'an admirable site'. From this time on, the Framlingham reserve and the rights of Aboriginals to be there were often in the local news.

From a local viewpoint the *Standard* and the VHAA seemed a formidable combination. Apart from the municipal councils, the VHAA was 'far and away the most important body in the Western district'.[5] On the other hand, it is unlikely that their plans for the Aboriginal reserve would have been successful if it had not been for the change in BPA policy. It was the combination of local and Board interests that brought about the closing of the station.

In August 1889 the BPA, eager to begin the amalgamation of the Aboriginal population, was considering the future of the Ebenezer station in the Wimmera when it received a letter from the Secretary of Lands asking that land be granted from the Framlingham reserve for an agricultural college. The Board considered the question on 4 August 1889 and unanimously decided to give up Framlingham. The 'half-castes' at the station were organising a petition to the government about their plight when the news arrived that the station was to be closed. Suddenly the whole community was fearful for its future.

In late August three of the Framlingham Aboriginals and the station manager, William Goodall, accompanied by Mr Officer MLA and Dr Morrison, vice-chairman of the BPA, met with the Chief Secretary in Melbourne to protest against the plans to close the station. They then waited on the Board, hoping that they could sway its members. The *Standard* saw this as a 'counter-deputation' and reminded readers not to feel sentimental about the Aboriginals, though it expressed its belief that there was plenty of room for them to keep part of the land while some was used for the college. The *Standard* accused Goodall of schooling the Aboriginals in their mission and of being motivated by a desire to protect his 'snug billet'.

Goodall responded angrily in a letter to the editor, taking exception to a number of the comments. The Aboriginals had made no reference to the experimental farm. They had 'merely protested against the proposal ... to remove them entirely ... from ... their own home. Surely there is nothing wrong in that', he wrote, 'and I don't see why they should be castigated for it'. They had not been prompted by him or, as far as he knew, anyone else:

> [They] required no schooling to enter a protest against what they considered a great wrong as well as a hardship and an injustice seeing that many of them were induced to come here in the first instance under representations that it was their own property and they were not to be disturbed as long as they chose to occupy it.

As for his own position, he added, 'The snugness of our positions is only a matter of opinion, and to those who hold such opinions, I would simply say "come and try your hand for a month".'[6]

The Board reaffirmed its decision on 4 September, and Goodall was notified that he had been appointed to the Industrial Schools Department. He ceased to work for the Board on 30 September.

King David died on 24 September 1889, shortly before Goodall left, his life ending with the closing of the Aboriginal station. It was a second dispossession. Though the BPA argued that the Aboriginals would be cared for on the remaining Aboriginal stations, for them this meant another upheaval and a forced removal from their country. The *Standard* and the VHAA were pleased that things had gone their way, but were wary that the decision might yet be overturned.

James Dawson's response to the news of Hissing Swan's death was published in the *Camperdown Chronicle*:

> *Poor Davie, my good faithful friend of forty years, as honest a man as ever breathed, sacrificed to the greed of a race of men, who, not satisfied with having deprived him and his friends of their hunting grounds, now seek to turn them, in their old age, out of their established homes and associations.[7]*

A sympathiser dramatised the circumstances:

> *Now to Framlingham—Time last Sunday week. Old 'Davie' (who like the whole of the station, is in sore distress about the breaking up of their home) to Mr. Goodall, who has just returned from Melbourne, 'Well, Mr. Goodall, what is it going to be.' Mr. Goodall—'Well, Davie, we will have to go.' The blackfellow retired, went to bed, and forty-eight hours afterwards was dead. Mr. Goodall and the other blacks asserting that the idea of leaving home killed him.[8]*

Goodall's telegram aroused much sympathy for the Aboriginals. Seeing its potential to sway people towards the Aboriginal cause, Robert Vickers, a Western District resident who supported the decision to close the station, wrote immediately to the Hon. J. L. Dow, MLA, enclosing a copy of the telegram. Vickers underlined the words, 'Idea of leaving home killed him'. The telegram was 'a strained effort to produce a sensational effect', Vickers stated, warning Dow that it might be raised in Parliament by those friendly to the Aboriginals.[9]

Dawson's comment on the death of King David elicited a reply from the *Hamilton Spectator*'s 'Warrnambool Correspondent':

> *What a whole-souled euphemism that was, appearing in a contemporary, to the effect that 'Hissing Swan' ... had pegged out because they threatened to remove him to Condah. The 'Hissing Swan' is the gentleman who some years ago tried to get at the dura mater of his*

lubra's cranium with a waddy, and frequently performed other such delicate attentions towards his black-skinned brotherhood. He was a very violent old rascal, devoid of all romance, and a few broken heads were saved, to his womenkind especially, when the gin-soddened, possum-gorging old warrior was laid hors de combat. But this occurred some years ago, and his death at this juncture has as much to do with the proposed removal of the pure blacks to Condah, as with the translation of these people to the planet Mercury, if such were contemplated. He was eighty years of age or over, and seems to have had a pretty good innings at the expense of the white man, for he never did a harder day's work in his life, than groping for his neighbours' kidney fat or smashing up his lubras.[10]

Horrified and disgusted, Dawson penned a counter-blast to the editor of the *Camperdown Chronicle*:

Sir,—In a contemporary of the eleventh inst., a 'Warrnambool correspondent' refers to my letter on the death of 'Hissing Swan' . . . evidently with the intense satisfaction of having an ill word to say of the dead, and although I make it a rule to take no notice of the writings of persons who have not the courage to put their names to their effusions, I cannot allow this correspondent's comments on the character of the deceased chief to pass unnoticed, and I must confess I do so with extreme reluctance and disgust. He says, 'Davie was a very violent old rascal, a gin sodden, possum gorging old warrior, devoid of all romance, was 80 years of age and over, and had a pretty good innings at the expense of the white man, for he never did a harder day's work in his life than groping for his neighbour's kidney fat, or smashing up his lubras.' A very nice obituary certificate of character to be sure, worthy of the writer and his final 'kick at the dying lion'. My personal knowledge of Davie is, that he came into the employment of Dawson and Mitchell, squatters, Kangatong, in the year 1845 or 1846, at the age of 23 or 24, and, with other aborigines, male and female, was employed as shepherd and general worker, under a written agreement and wages. This continued for about twenty years, with such short intervals of absence as are demanded by the laws of the tribes, and the services were performed with the strictest fidelity, and at times when white men could not be depended upon. The Warrnambool Correspondent then says, 'Davie seems to have had a pretty good innings at the expense of the white man', which means that the poor fellow and his friends must be unspeakably grateful to a race of 'aliens' who shot, poisoned wholesale, committed on them the grossest crimes, drove them off their hunting grounds, and in very recent instances deprived them of a chance to earn a living when brought into fair competition with their white oppressors. And now, as a fitting conclusion, it is attempted to fix a stigma on the memory of a man, whose character can bear favourable comparison with the actions of his enemies and slanderers, who are straining every nerve to rob the remnant of the aborigines of their homes and property. I shall now leave the field to these oppressors, as they are too contemptible to be further noticed by me.[11]

The man about whom there was so much fuss was born well before there were any Europeans in the district. He was one of the chief informants for James Dawson's detailed study of 'the languages and customs of several tribes of Aborigines in the Western District of Victoria'. This was a task the Aboriginals took seriously. Dawson described it as tedious, taking several years to complete, but 'if any levity was shown by any person present who could not always resist a pun on the word in question', Kaawirn Kuunawarn would 'at once reprove the wag, and restore order and attention to the business on hand'.[12] Dawson included only two photos of Aboriginals in his book, which was published in 1881. One was of Kaawirn Kuunawarn. It was Kaawirn Kuunawarn again whom nineteenth-century readers saw posed in front of the obelisk raised by Dawson in the Camperdown cemetery to honour the passing of the last of the Camperdown Aboriginals, Wombeetch Puuyun.

Kaawirn Kuunawarn was also the inspiration behind Muutchaka, the main Aboriginal character in Louis Bayer's opera about colonial life, *Muutchaka or The Last of his Tribe*. Bayer said he had been impressed by the chief's nobility of bearing, which was apparent in the photo in Dawson's book. He was looking for an individual who showed all the superior qualities of human nature Bayer believed widespread among Aboriginals before the destructive effects of European invasion. Listening to the praise of Kaawirn Kuunawarn by both Dawson and Goodall, he decided that here was someone with the qualities he was looking for. Dedicated to James Dawson, the opera was first staged at Camperdown on 24 May 1887 and has been produced at least twenty-nine times since.[13]

Kaawirn Kuunawarn was born about 1822 at Lake Connewarren, near Ellerslie, about five miles south-west of Mortlake. He belonged to the Kon.ne.wurt clan. Early in 1841 members of the clan gathered with many others at Lake Keilambete to meet Charles Wightman Sievwright, Assistant Protector of the Aborigines, who claimed that he had come to help and protect them in the new circumstances, in which their land was being rapidly taken up by Europeans.

They were joined on 6 April by George Augustus Robinson, the Chief Protector. Robinson brought with him a message of government goodwill and gifts to give as evidence of this. He distributed gifts to the Kon.ne.wurt and others at Lake Keilambete—headbands, Victoria and Albert medals on a tape to be worn as a pendant and, believe it or not, handkerchiefs. The Aboriginals made short work of the handkerchiefs, tearing them into strips to make headbands. Not all of them were impressed by his generosity. Robinson took a fancy to a small root being carried by a Kon.ne.wurt clansman, but his request for it was refused: 'a proof of greediness scarcely to be surpassed', he noted in his journal.[14]

Each of the clans used distinguishing marks on both the face and body for ceremonial purposes. In this way they used their bodies to indicate to others who they were. Robinson sketched the markings used by local clans. Among the sketches is one of the facial markings used by the Kon.ne.wurt.[15]

King David's father was Carrowan, who died not long after the arrival of Europeans in this part of the district. Sievwright reported

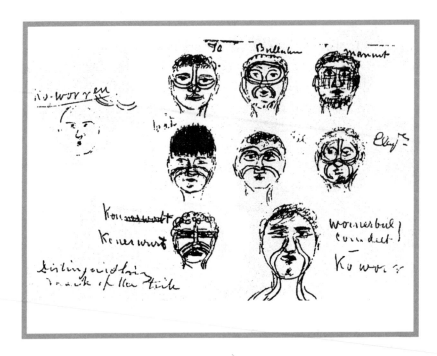

G. A. ROBINSON'S SKETCH SHOWING THE DISTINGUISHING MARKS OF WESTERN
DISTRICT CLANS: THE TC (JARCOURT), BULLERBURER (BOLOKEBURER), MANMOT
(MANMATE), WDR (WADDWRO), COL. (COLIJON), ELENG. (ELLENGERMOT),
KONERWURT (KON.NE.WURT) AND WORNERBUL (WARNABUL)

from the temporary Protectorate base at Lake Terang that on
19 May 1841 'Conawaree, the chief of the Conawane tribe' died at
Lake Connewarren from inflammation of the bowel.[16]

Eels were to be found in abundance at Lake Connewarren. It
was a popular Aboriginal camping place, as one could see from the
number of large mounds beside the lake, evidence of Aboriginal
occupation over many generations. R. Brough Smyth, for example,
provided the accompanying sketch in a book published in 1878,
and described the mounds as follows:

> No. 1 is 102 by 90 feet in diameter, 310 feet in circumference, and 8 feet
> high from the east side, and 6 feet from the west side.
>
> No. 2 is 104 by 99 feet in diameter, 318 feet in circumference, and
> 5 feet high.

No. 3 is 96 by 84 feet in diameter, and 3 feet high.

No. 4 is 87 by 75 feet in diameter, 3 and a half feet high on east, and 2 feet high on the west side . . .

They must be of great antiquity, for there is but little firewood in the vicinity, and only small fires would suffice to cook the eels taken from the adjacent lagoon.

Smyth also mentioned that a few years earlier, when floodwaters caused the lake to overflow, 'eels escaped from their overcrowded breeding basin in scores of tons'. Some Aboriginals were observed standing beside the outlet 'bewailing the sad fact' that there were so few of them left to eat the eels.[17]

Each mound was the site of an Aboriginal dwelling place. The Chief Protector saw similar mounds just before he reached the Hopkins on his journey westward. Curious about the short pieces of wood sticking out of the mounds and the signs of fire having destroyed whatever had been there, he enquired what these were.

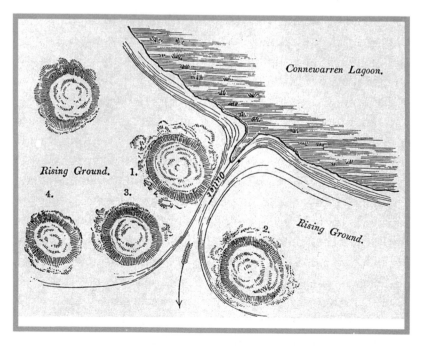

R. BROUGH SMYTH'S SKETCH OF THE MOUNDS AT LAKE CONNEWARREN

His Aboriginal companion replied that each mound was '[the site of] a black man's house, a large one like a white man's house'.[18] These were the strongly constructed winter houses that Western District Aboriginals returned to year after year. The mounds built up over time through the accumulation of debris—from domestic fires, from decomposing building materials and the destructive effects of frequent bushfires.[19]

While mounds were not primarily burial places,[20] all the mounds excavated on Connewarren were found to contain skulls, bones and skeletons as well as stones and artefacts.

Lake Connewarren and its mounds no longer exist. The lake was drained between 1890 and 1900.[21] A few years earlier, in April 1884, twelve mounds on Connewarren were removed, the soil being scattered 'by means of plough and scoop'. Rabbits attracted by the loose soil in the mounds had turned them into warrens, and they were dispersed in the hope of reducing the number of rabbits in the area.[22]

Exactly when King David was born is harder to establish than where he was born. James Dawson knew him from 1845 or 1846.[23] Looking back he estimated Kaawirn Kuunawarn to be twenty-three or twenty-four years old at that time. A note from 1886 found in Dawson's scrapbook stated that 'King Davie', as he was more often known, must be sixty-four.[24] These comments suggest a birth date of 1822. Other evidence supports this. In 1889 King David's age was given as seventy on his death certificate, where the witness to the burial was William Goodall, manager of the Framlingham Aboriginal Station from 1869, and therefore someone who knew him well. There is some conflicting evidence, however. On the certificate of his marriage to Queen Mary, which took place at Coranderrk in 1879, his age is given as forty. This appears to be a mistake; if correct, he would have been a mere boy of six or seven when Dawson first knew him. It is inconceivable that Dawson could have mistaken a boy of six for a man in his early twenties.

King David's name meant 'Hissing Swan', after the hissing of the swans at Lake Connewarren. He was recognised as a tribal leader at the time of European arrival, as Dawson found out when he asked his informants about the customs they observed when holding their great meetings. Kaawirn Kuunawarn described how he had called one such meeting of about 1000 people, which Dawson estimated took place just before the arrival of Europeans. Europeans may have already been in the area, but there were so few that a large meeting could still be held without danger. Kaawirn Kuunawarn made James Dawson a facsimile of the spear-thrower he had used as a message stick to summon three tribes to this meeting with him and his tribe at Lake Connewarren.

If Kaawirn Kuunawarn's date of birth was between 1819 and 1822, as seems reasonable, he would have been a young adult when Europeans moved into his country. The intruders had no conception of any prior Aboriginal rights to land. Europeans seeking land for running sheep and cattle moved steadily closer in the late 1830s. Frederick Taylor took up land at nearby Mount Noorat in March 1839 for G. Mackillop and J. Smith. A little earlier an agent for the Derwent Company took up the Mount Shadwell run, which at this time extended right across to the Hopkins River. The Lake Connewarren area, Kaawirn Kuunawarn's country, was now occupied by others, and the Aboriginals were increasingly made to feel unwanted on their land.

By the last quarter of 1839 all the Aboriginals in the area across to the Hopkins and beyond must have been experiencing shock as news spread of a massacre on Taylor's run in which about thirty-five people—men, women and children, virtually a whole clan—were killed. On the western side of the Hopkins, Merrang had been taken up by the Watson brothers in early 1839, and by August 1840 the Bolden brothers had taken up a vast tract of land to the west of Merrang, stretching south down to the coast at Warrnambool. For the Kon.ne.wurt there was no longer any escape from the reality of European presence and the power wielded by those on horseback carrying guns.

In early 1841, when the Assistant Protector arrived at Lake Keilambete, there had already been conflict between the

Kon.ne.wurt and Europeans. John Thomson of Keilambete had abandoned his outstation nine miles from the Hopkins after a shepherd had been killed by Aboriginals. Robinson was told that three Kon.ne.wurt were responsible.[25]

A month later there was further trouble, this time on the Boldens' run. Sievwright reported to the Chief Protector that on 28 October some of the 'Conawarn Tribe' came to him with a boy who reported that:

> *On the previous day he and a native named 'Tatkier' with his wife named 'Terang-gerang coe' were on their way to join me when four white men 'two gentlemen, and two poor men' came upon them ... and after beating them severely a considerable time, with their whips, one of the gentlemen ... shot Tatkier through the body—and that the female had been so much beaten by the poor man 'Bill' that she died— that he fled up a tree and witnessed what happened—and that when the white people went away he went to where the bodies were left and saw them both dead—he described the man, as having been shot through the body and head and the woman, as much wounded about the head.*
>
> *The grief and rage which this intelligence occasioned amongst the Natives who were with me cannot well be described—the men of two of the tribes immediately armed themselves declaring 'they would go and kill the white people['] and called upon me in a manner the most peremptory and energetic to accompany them.*[26]

It is possible to reconstruct the events of that day from evidence given in statements to Assistant Protector Sievwright.[27] On 27 October George and Samuel Bolden and two stockmen, out riding on the property, came across three Aboriginals—a man (Tatkier), a woman and a boy. The stockmen accosted the Aboriginals, asking what they were doing on the run. When they replied that they were on their way to Sievwright's camp, the whites refused to believe them, and claimed they were looking for cattle. George Bolden and the stockmen then proceeded to drive the Aboriginals off the run. The fleeing Aboriginals were urged on with whips.

When they reached a flat area, Tatkier turned and swung an implement at George Bolden, who was riding just behind him. George fired, shooting him in the stomach. Tatkier then fled to a waterhole. While the stockmen stayed behind with orders not to let Tatkier escape, Bolden returned to the home station for more firearms. Tatkier tried to escape, and attacked one of the stockmen. Bolden, returning at this time, fired and again shot Tatkier, whose body fell into a waterhole and sank, not to be seen again.

Meanwhile the Aboriginal woman had been run over by Peter Carney on his horse. William Kiernan, one of the two stockmen, wrote in his signed statement:

> The horse of Peter Carney while galloping after the native ran foul of the Woman and knocked her down. I afterwards saw her lying against a tree ... she was not dead but might have been hurt from the running over her.

The boy watched these events from the tree where he had fled.

After hearing the story Sievwright and some Aboriginals went to the site. Sievwright left the Aboriginals to recover the bodies, while he went to see the Boldens. George Bolden at first appeared to have no knowledge of any 'collision' but then, since Sievwright seemed to know the details, he asked whether the bodies had been found. To this Sievwright replied, 'I believe so'. Bolden then stated, 'It was I who shot the Native'. Since he appeared 'agitated', Sievwright told him he would return the next day to take his statement.

In the murder trial that followed, Sandford George Bolden, one of the few white men ever tried in the Port Phillip District for the killing of an Aboriginal, was acquitted of the charge despite his admission of guilt. Judge Willis emphasised that the body of the dead man had not been found, and without it there was no evidence that a crime had been committed. The case could not rest on the evidence taken from a 'a savage boy's statement'. Nor could Bolden's admission that he had shot Tatkier be used as evidence, because Sievwright had led him to believe that a body had been found before he made the confession. In fact, Judge Willis stated that 'there was no evidence that Tatkier had been shot at'. The evidence given in court differed substantially from that in the signed statements given to Sievwright. Refusing to heed protests from the Crown Prosecutor, James Croke, Willis advised the jury that they must acquit the prisoner.[28]

Did the Boldens have a right to drive Aboriginals off runs that were Crown land held under a £10 annual licence? Judge Willis believed so. During the trial he pointed out that Europeans had a right to drive trespassers off their land, as there 'was no reservation in the grant, lease or licence from the Government in favour of the Aborigines'. Superintendent La Trobe disagreed. In a letter seeking clarification from Governor Gipps in Sydney, La Trobe expressed his belief that it was illegal for squatters to behave in this manner, and pointed out 'the manifest inhumanity of following such a course'. He also asked Gipps to include in the squatting licences a provision that Aboriginals must not be excluded from their traditional hunting grounds. But Gipps, who was already at odds with the landholders in the New South Wales Legislative Council, refused to act in Bolden's case.[29]

In early 1842 Sievwright, accompanied by 210 Aboriginals, moved from the Lake Terang area to Mount Rouse, where land had been reserved for the permanent Western District Protectorate station. A large area was set aside for the station, which included the present site of Penshurst. Aboriginals were invited to move there, and others were driven there. The Native Police, for example, 'drove a party of between two and three hundred Aborigines from Lake Boloke (Bolac) and the River Hopkins' to the station in mid-October.[30]

Racial conflict increased across the district, including the territory of the Kon.ne.wurt, reaching a climax in the area west of Mount Shadwell in 1842. James Blair, Police Magistrate at Portland, wrote to La Trobe that there was a 'general move among the Aborigines'.[31] Virtually the whole western region was caught up in a wave of Aboriginal attacks. In early 1842, the 'Settlers and

Inhabitants of the Port Fairy District' sought urgent government help in a petition to La Trobe, complaining that the Aboriginals were attacking by day and night. Among those who had suffered were Captain Webster of Mount Shadwell, Claude Farie of Merrang, and the Bolden brothers, all on or near Kon.ne.wurt land. Webster's losses were listed as 250 sheep taken and a man wounded; Farie, 50 sheep taken; and the Boldens, 10 cows and 40 calves killed, a hut attacked several times and a man severely wounded.[32]

Relations deteriorated further during winter. In September 1842 attention was again drawn to the behaviour of Europeans in the Hopkins River area when the Police Magistrate at Hamilton received a report that an Aboriginal had died at the Mount Rouse Protectorate Station from wounds inflicted in a 'collision' at the Hopkins. He investigated and discovered that Webster and Farie had clashed with some Aboriginals 'about the 16 September'. Webster claimed that the previous night Aboriginals had taken some sheep, and the next morning he had gone to Merrang to ask Farie for assistance to recover the stolen property. The two men made the following statement:

> We found them roasting sheep at their encampment. When we rode up to them and told them to go to Mt. Rouse as we could not allow them to remain there to steal our property, they then made off in different directions. Most of them towards the river to which we had followed them— When one stopped and called out to the others to stand and come on and then threw several spears at us, we found ourselves nearly surrounded from all quarters, we then cried out to them, not to throw their spears or we should be obliged to fire on them, they however continued throwing so as to endanger our lives, when we were obliged to fire in self-defence. We fired either two or three shots—but did not see anyone fall. They continued throwing their spears till we got out of their reach. We were induced to drive these natives off our runs in consequence of their carrying on a regular system of plundering our sheepfolds by night for a considerable period, having lost about 100 sheep between the two stations in about three weeks.[33]

Driven off the runs by the use of whips and guns, the chief of the Mount Shadwell tribe and members of the Kon.ne.wurt clan had to find somewhere near by to live. Many Aboriginals investigated what the government was offering at the Mount Rouse Protectorate Station. There was much coming and going there in the early 1840s, with numbers peaking at more than 300. Most of the time, however, there was little to gain at the station. Food was often in short supply, and clothing for distribution to those in need was limited. Dr Watton, the man who replaced Sievwright, declined even to prepare a report for the government on the station's operations during 1846, claiming that he was 'not paid enough to supply one'.[34]

Aboriginals at this time were still using their tribal names. At Mount Rouse a record similar to a school register was kept, listing each person's Aboriginal name and the days on which he or she attended. This register provides a marvellous record of the Aboriginal names used in the region, and makes it possible to check who was on the station and for how long.

It appears King David attended for the last three days of October 1842. He would therefore have drawn his own conclusions about how useful the station was. He obviously decided that it was not the place to stay for any length of time, as he didn't return.

But he did find a home on Kangatong, the property owned by James Dawson and Patrick Mitchell, near present-day Hawkesdale, south of the Protectorate station. There he was not only warmly welcomed but given paid employment as a shepherd and general worker at the same rate as other district workers. He worked there for about twenty years except for short breaks to carry out tribal business.[35]

King David had a close relationship with both Patrick Mitchell and James Dawson. Isabella Dawson, who was widely regarded as King David's daughter, was in fact the daughter of Patrick Mitchell and an Aboriginal woman whose name was recorded as Mary.[36] This is one of very few Western District cases where the records give the name of a white man who had fathered an Aboriginal child in the early years of contact. Who was King David's wife in the years he was at Kangatong? Was she the 'Mary' named as Isabella's mother? If so, this suggests that the special relationship between King David and Patrick Mitchell in these years might have extended to King David's sharing his wife.

King David was also close to James Dawson. Dawson's daughter Isabella (after whom King David's daughter was named) learnt local Aboriginal languages from the Aboriginals working on Kangatong and began to record their languages and customs. Her work, first published in the *Australasian* in 1870,[37] eventually led to James Dawson's book, which was published in 1881.

While Kaawirn Kuunawarn was working at Kangatong, he was involved in events that appear to have led to the murder of a fellow Aboriginal, Smiley Austin. The Austins, Smiley and Lilly, 'belonged to Austin's Green Hills'—in other words, their 'country' was in the area that became the Austin family's Green Hills pastoral run. A coroner's inquest into Smiley's death was held at Spring Creek on 17 February 1859.

In the early years of colonisation there had been debate as to whether Aboriginals should be held accountable to British law for crimes against other Aboriginals, but in 1837 the Supreme Court of New South Wales decided that they should.[38] A trial for murder would therefore follow if the coroner's inquest was able to name those alleged to have committed murder.

At coroners' inquests, as in the world outside, those who had power and made official decisions were all Europeans, and males at that—the coroner, the doctor who performed the post-mortem and announced the physical cause of death, and the jurors selected from the general community and entrusted with the verdict.

Inquests were motivated by a concern to establish a rational, ordered framework for colonial life. The colonial authorities early implemented procedures for recording basic information about the population: births, deaths and marriages. Coroners' inquests were part of the same apparatus. They were held to establish the cause of unexplained death. Death was to be understandable, its cause an obvious physical one that could be put in the register of deaths. Death caused by violence should be identified as such, and proceedings immediately instituted to bring the perpetrator of the deed to justice.

Coroners' inquests into cases involving Aboriginals revealed the existence of another way of viewing the world, of another set of customs and laws, another view of justice. They also confronted the Europeans involved with their inability to gain evidence of what took place and why. At such times the great gap between the two cultures living side by side became most starkly apparent. In the words of John Hyland, a local trooper, it was 'very difficult to make the blacks tell you anything of the death of one of themselves'.[39]

In the case of Smiley Austin, Lilly Austin told the coroner's inquest that the violence had begun on Christmas Day, when she and her husband had come from the Austins' and were setting up camp at Spring Creek. She named King David and Johnny Dawson as those who began the attack on her husband, but said others had joined in with them. The first attack had started about sundown and peace was made. But a great row broke out again in the evening. On the following day her husband had gone somewhere in the morning, returned at midday, stopped in the mia-mia for the afternoon, then left in the evening to go to Austins. She never saw him alive again. She named One-eyed Billy, Irish Mickey, Jemmy Ware, Jim Crow and Little Johnny as having also been involved in the fighting.[40]

No evidence was given about the cause of the fighting, nor about how Smiley came to die. There was no mention of alcohol being involved in any way. The jurors' verdict was death by violence, but they were unable to offer any suggestions as to how the death occurred or who was responsible. The authorities were not satisfied and asked that further inquiries be made. As a result King David, Blind Billy and Jim Crow were arrested on a charge of murder. At the time of King David's arrest, according to the *Warrnambool Standard*, he had said, 'White fellow give me nobbler, and make me mad'.[41]

For many years after European contact, Western District Kooris continued to enforce their own laws without reference to the white system of justice.* Those who had extensive dealings with them soon realised that the Aboriginal idea of what constituted murder differed greatly from that of the European community. As the Reverend Tuckfield from the Buntingdale Wesleyan Mission at Birregurra put it, 'murder is not always so among the Aborigines'.[42] In 1852 William Thomas, Guardian of the Aborigines, when asked to explain Aboriginal behaviour for the benefit of the Colonial Secretary, began by stating: 'the aborigines have laws as well as civilised nations to meet all crimes'. Those concerning the taking of life were as follows:

1st Every murderer (that is of his own tribe—in no other case is murder considered a crime) is punished with death inflicted by the family and nearest of kin to those who have been murdered, should the family be extinct the tribe may save the life of the murderer but he must undergo a certain number of spears being thrown at him by his tribe

2. It is considered laudable to kill any other black found in or brought to their district without a previous understanding and consent of the tribe

3. As a religious superstition, when one has lost one dear to him, his tribe (a number being deputed by a regular council) seek the [life] of a stranger to appease the spirit of the departed, and assuage the grief of the mourners†

4. When one kills another accidentally ... he is not punished with death but by a number of spears being hurled at him according to the sentence he being debar'ed from returning the same tho' permitted to have his shield to ward off the spears[43]

'As our laws now stand Your Honour must perceive how lamentably the Aborigines are positioned', Thomas wrote. Those who

* One of the last recorded large-scale meetings of Aboriginals to settle grievances regarding the killing of Aboriginals by Aboriginals was held in the Colac area in September 1848. Many clans attended, including the Kon.ne.wurt gunditj (*Geelong Advertiser*, 16 September 1848).
† Killing for this purpose, according to Dawson, was regarded as a sacred duty.

perpetrated homicides 'in obedience to laws and customs known only to the natives themselves' were being held accountable to the laws of the colonisers, even though their own laws were still in force and it would have been unreasonable to expect anything different.[44]

By the 1850s there was no longer any threat from Aboriginals to European lives or property, and officials were increasingly perturbed by their inability to stop the killing of Aboriginals by Aboriginals. They were also concerned that the implementation of the British judicial system was not neutral but brought additional danger to Aboriginals in custody. There was, for example, the case of Jemmy Suter and Tommy Ritchie 'of the Fitzroy River tribe', who were arrested for the murder of an Aboriginal man called Neddy at Yambuk on 30 January 1860. This appeared to be a case of disembowelment, with death being the result of haemorrhage. The doctor's post-mortem report stated that:

> A circular incision had been made through the integuments of the abdomen and a circular piece about five inches in diameter removed, the external organs of Generation had been removed ... the cranium had been entirely stripped of the scalp and the lower jaw had been removed ...
>
> In my opinion the injury caused by the removal of the organs of generation would be sufficient to cause death by subsequent haemorrhage which mutilation I think was inflicted while life remained.[45]

What did Neddy do, I wonder, that he was punished in such a specific and cruel way? The case was to be heard at the Court of Petty Sessions, Belfast (Port Fairy), on 30 November 1861. The prisoners were remanded several times until 24 December 1861, when the two men were discharged from custody, 'there not being sufficient evidence against them to get a conviction'.[46] They were reluctant to leave the safety of the jail and asked to be allowed to stay there until the steamer left for Portland, as otherwise they had to cross the territory of the dead Neddy and they feared his relatives would kill them. The Superintendent of Police was sympathetic. Yambuk Aboriginals had been watching the jail throughout the time the two had been held there. It was arranged that the two men stay in custody until the steamer arrived.[47] Thus the Superintendent's sympathy for the prisoners' increased vulnerability to attack led him to aid alleged killers to evade what he, and they, saw as a likely result of their earlier action. The representative of the 'law' not only did not punish the men initially because of the lack of an interpreter or witnesses, but actually intervened to save the prisoners from the consequences of their actions by Aboriginal custom and law.

There was also concern about the effects of Aboriginals' spending long periods of time in jail. In the case of Old Man Billy and Young Man Billy, who were found guilty of the murder of Johnny on 25 October 1858, the jurymen wrote to the Executive Council asking that the Governor show mercy and recommending that the sentence not be carried into effect.[48] His Honour Mr Justice Williams, who tried the case, agreed. In an accompanying note he stated: 'The Jury recommended the prisoners to mercy on the ground of their ignorance of our customs and the peculiar nature of their own ... I am altogether disposed to concur in this recommendation.'[49]

Early in its life the Central Board expressed its appreciation that the Governor had intervened and brought about the release of Aboriginals imprisoned for murder, as 'close imprisonment is not the kind of punishment to which an Aboriginal should be subjected'. It asked for similar mercy to be shown in 'all cases where the character and conduct of the criminal are such as to admit of his being set at large'.[50]

Thus it appears that the criminal justice system was reluctant to use the full weight of the law against Aboriginals for offences against other Aboriginals from the late 1850s onwards. If King David had been brought to trial, these factors would have operated to make sure that he did not lose his life. But the case did not proceed to trial, because no evidence could be discovered. After two of the accused had been remanded twice and one of them

SCHEDULE D.

186*7*.   Marriages solemnized in the District of *Warrnambool*

No. in Register	When and where married.	Name and Surname of the Parties.	Condition of the Parties.				Birthplace.
			Bachelor or Spinster. If a Widower or Widow, Date of Decease of former Wife or Husband.	Children by each former Marriage.			
				Living.	Dead.		
92	July 19th 1867. aboriginal Station Framlingham	Joseph Erskine	Bachelor				Penshurst Victoria
		Isabella Dawson	Spinster				Spring Creek Victoria

I, *Thomas Raston*, being *Wesleyan Minister* do hereby certify, that I have this day, at *the Aboriginal Station, Framlingham* duly celebrated Marriage between *Joseph Erskine of Aboriginal Reserve, Framlingham Farmer* and *Isabella Dawson of Aboriginal Reserve, Framlingham* after Notice and Declaration duly made and published, as by law required (and with the written consent of *Daniel Clarke, Master of Aboriginal Station Framlingham*). *(Signature)* *Daniel Clarke*
Dated this *Nineteenth* day of *July* 186*7*.
Signature of Minister, Registrar-General, or other Officer *Thomas Raston.*

| 93 | July 19th 1867 aboriginal Station Framlingham | Albert Austin | Bachelor | | | | Chatsworth Victoria |
| | | Rosanna Francis | Spinster | | | | Wannon Victoria |

I, *Thomas Raston*, being *Wesleyan Minister* do hereby certify, that I have this day, at *the Aboriginal Station, Framlingham* duly celebrated Marriage between *Albert Austin, of Aboriginal Reserve, Framlingham Farmer* and *Rosanna Francis, of Aboriginal Reserve, Framlingham* after Notice and Declaration duly made and published, as by law required (and with the written consent of _____).
Dated this *Nineteenth* day of *July* 186*7*.
Signature of Minister, Registrar-General, or other Officer *Thomas Raston*

| 94 | July 19th 1867 aboriginal Station Framlingham | Barney McLean | Bachelor | | | | Framlingham Victoria |
| | | Katty | Spinster | | | | Warrnambool Victoria |

I, *Thomas Raston*, being *Wesleyan Minister* do hereby certify, that I have this day, at *the Aboriginal Station, Framlingham* duly celebrated Marriage between *Barney McLean, of Aboriginal Reserve Framlingham Farmer* and *Katty, of Aboriginal Reserve, Framlingham* after Notice and Declaration duly made and published, as by law required (and with the written consent of _____).
Dated this *Nineteenth* day of *July* 186*7*.
Signature of Minister, Registrar-General, or other Officer *Thomas Raston*

THREE ABORIGINAL MARRIAGES ON ONE SHEET. NOTE THE WEALTH OF
INFORMATION THAT CAN BE GLEANED FROM THIS SOURCE

SCHEDULE D.

in the Colony of Victoria.

Rank or Profession.	Ages.	Residence.		Parents.	
		Present.	Usual.	Names. (Mother's Maiden Name.)	Father's Rank or Profession.
Farmer	24	Aboriginal Reserve Framlingham	Aboriginal Reserve Framlingham	Mr Brown Mrs Brown	(aboriginal) (aboriginal)
Sempstress	18	Aboriginal Reserve Framlingham	Aboriginal Reserve Framlingham	Patrick Mitchell — Mary —	Squatter (aboriginal)

Marriage, *By License*, was solemnized between us
according to the *Rites and Ceremonies of the Wesleyan Church* { Joseph *his* ✗ *mark* Erskine / Isabella *her* ✗ *mark* Dawson

Witnesses { *Daniel Clarke* / *Isabella ✗ Pilkington*

Rank or Profession.	Ages.	Residence.		Parents.	
Farmer	21	Aboriginal Reserve Framlingham	Aboriginal Reserve Framlingham	— Charlie — — Alice —	aboriginal aboriginal
Sempstress	22	Aboriginal Reserve Framlingham	Aboriginal Reserve Framlingham	— (Unknown) — Mary —	(European) aboriginal

Marriage, *By License*, was solemnized between us
according to the *Rites and Ceremonies of the Wesleyan Church*. { Albert *his* ✗ *mark.* Austin / Rosanna *her* ✗ *mark* Francis

Witnesses { *Daniel Clarke* / *Rachel Clarke*

Rank or Profession.	Ages.	Residence.		Parents.	
Farmer	30	Aboriginal Reserve Framlingham	Aboriginal Reserve Framlingham	— Detka — Kaapjaami —	aboriginal aboriginal
—	35	Aboriginal Reserve Framlingham	Aboriginal Reserve Framlingham	Corobewarra Mokemokecobwin	aboriginal aboriginal

Marriage, *By License*, was solemnized between us
according to the *Rites and Ceremonies of the Wesleyan Church* { Barney *his* ✗ *mark* McLean / Katty *her* mark

Witnesses { *Job Francis* / *Jane Burston*

three times, Sergeant Archibald of Warrnambool reported he had informed the Bench that 'no evidence has been or is likely to be obtained except as might arise from one being allowed to give evidence against the others'. The Chairman of the Bench, C. Vaughan, remarked that no reliance could be placed on such testimony and discharged the prisoners.[51]

King David moved to the Framlingham Aboriginal Station when it opened in 1865, as did his daughter Isabella. She was baptised by the Reverend Beamish at the Aboriginal station on 9 May 1866.[52] King David is in one of the earliest photos of the men on the station (reproduced on p. 48 above), and is in the 1876 official list of those required to reside at Framlingham. He lived there until he died in 1889. At Coranderrk on 14 May 1879 he married Queen Mary (Mary Phillips), whose husband, King Billy of Ballarat, had died about three years earlier.

Isabella, his daughter, married Joseph Erskine, son of Mr and Mrs Brown (Aborigines) at the Framlingham Aboriginal Station on 19 July 1867. There were three weddings celebrated that day. The Framlingham manager, William Goodall, was full of praise for Isabella. 'Isabella's ability as a needlewoman, and also as a housekeeper, is beyond praise; in fact, both Mrs. Goodall and myself prefer many of the articles of clothing that she makes before those of European manufacture.'[53] She died without having children on 3 February 1872.

The old Aboriginals were not expected to work at Framlingham, and by the 1870s, when the station was well under way, little work would have been expected of King David. Reverend Thwaites, who was in charge while Goodall was temporarily manager at Coranderrk, wrote to the BPA Secretary, 'I never press the old people to work, what they do they do from choice'.[54] Nor did the old Aboriginals attend church services. They declined to do so, Goodall told Dawson.[55]

Alcohol was sometimes a problem on the station, but King David was not one of those mentioned in this regard, except for an incident in April 1885, when King David, Jim Crow and George

Edwards 'got drunk'. King David struck his wife Mary, and the Reverend Thwaites was called in the night to protect Emily Edwards from her husband. Thwaites handled the situation by bringing the two men before the Warrnambool Bench as a way of indicating to them how seriously he regarded their actions. They promised to sign a total abstinence pledge and the case was dismissed at Thwaites' request. Their wives and Collin Hood joined them in signing the pledge.[56]

Aboriginal ceremonies such as corroborees were frowned on by the BPA and discouraged on the Aboriginal stations. One of the last recorded corroborees in the Western District was held at Camperdown, with Kaawirn Kuunawarn taking part. It was held at Renny Hill, the home of Isabella Taylor (née Dawson), in early May 1884 to celebrate James Dawson's return after two years overseas. Dawson wrote to the manager at Framlingham asking permission for a large number of Aboriginals to attend, but few arrived. Those who took part and entertained an interested and appreciative audience were Tocas Johnson and his wife Mary Anne; King David and his wife Mary; Jim Crow and his wife Helen; Cunningham Jack and his wife Maria; Billy Murray and his wife Alice; and Jacky Kuukunan.[57]

From the beginning of the 1880s the Aboriginal stations were on borrowed time. Once the 'able-bodied half-castes' were forced off the stations by the 1886 Act, the BPA began considering which station to close first. In the event, it was Framlingham. King David died on 24 September 1889, while William Goodall was packing his bags to leave.

It would have been an emotional time for all concerned. Goodall had earlier declined an offer of promotion that involved moving to the Coranderrk Aboriginal Station because of his attachment to the Framlingham Aboriginals. Having associated with Western District Aboriginals 'almost since infancy', he wrote, 'I do not think I could bring myself to the point of voluntarily parting with them'.[58] Now he had no choice. Both he and they had to go in different directions. One of his last tasks was to make arrangements for the funeral of his long-time friend. On 26 September King David was buried in the Aboriginal station cemetery beside the Hopkins River, not very far from Lake Connewarren.

Barely a week after King David's death, the Secretary of the BPA wrote that arrangements should be made to put Queen Mary in an asylum, as she was incapable of caring for herself and there was no one to take charge of her.[59]

Was Kaawirn Kuunawarn a reliable hard worker who never did anyone harm or, as the anonymous 'Warrnambool correspondent' alleged, a wife-bashing alcoholic and murderer? I carried out a thorough search of the records for any evidence that might support the anonymous correspondent's claims, but found little to substantiate the conclusions he drew. Instead, his statements should be seen for what they are—part of a discourse based on a belief in Aboriginal inferiority that bore little relationship to the facts. That the claims were made at all was largely the result of King David's appearance in court in 1885. The Reverend Thwaites believed that he had dealt with that incident satisfactorily by taking King David and George Edwards before the Warrnambool Bench and then withdrawing the charge. He had overlooked the fact that the *Warrnambool Standard* reported details of local court sessions. His action had made the incident a matter of public knowledge. The *Warrnambool Standard* was not told that the men had taken the pledge, so the public was not informed of this part of the story. Left to make judgements based on partial knowledge, some people arrived at adverse conclusions. To those determined to view the Aboriginals in the worst light, the incident simply appeared as a case of alcoholism and wife-bashing.

The evidence undoubtedly points in one direction. King David was a man to be admired. He was an elder who had to deal with the unexpected arrival of strangers who claimed and took his 'country'. No doubt he was involved in attacks on sheep and cattle, and sometimes on the newcomers themselves, but he would also have had to watch his people whipped and run off the local runs and sometimes shot. He survived and demonstrated his willingness

A POSTCARD IMAGE OF KING DAVID

BANJO CLARKE (LEFT) DWARFED BY KING DAVID'S TREE

and ability to earn his living in the new order. He also played an important part in preserving a record of the customs and languages of the indigenous peoples of the district.

Overlooking the Hopkins River, not far from Uncle Banjo's house, there is a very large old tree that is still referred to as King David's tree. It is believed to have been planted in the early days of the mission. Banjo tells a story about King David and this tree. The incident took place in the 1930s or 1940s, when Banjo was living with Grannie Bella:

Terrick Rose was walking past the tree one day when he looked up into the tree and saw this great big possum. He'd never seen such a large possum before. He thought, that's old King David, come back to show himself. The possum stayed for a while, and Terrick lingered by the tree. Then he called in to see Grannie Bella on his way home—she lived not far from the tree. He told her he'd just seen King David himself. I remember the story real well, because I was there when he called to see Grannie Bella.[60]

CHAPTER 8

James Dawson's
Informants

ABORIGINAL INFORMANTS (KING DAVID STANDING) WITH ISABELLA DAWSON
(FAR RIGHT)

In compiling his book *Australian Aborigines. The Languages and Customs of Several Tribes of Aborigines in the Western District of Victoria, Australia,* published in 1881, James Dawson drew his information entirely from Aboriginal informants. He took 'great care ... not to state anything on the word of a white person'. His daughter, who helped with the preparation of the book, had 'an intimate acquaintance from infancy with the aboriginal inhabitants' of the Port Fairy district and 'with their dialects'. 'All the information contained in this book', Dawson wrote, 'has been obtained from the united testimony of several very intelligent aborigines, and every word was approved by them before being written down'.[1]

Who were the Aboriginals who helped him, and what happened to them? I was able to create the list with the help of a lucky find: some photos in the Ritchie family's private papers, which gave both the Aboriginal and European names of some of those involved. In other cases the informants were already known by European names, so it was possible to trace their lives through European records. One of the principal informants was Kaawirn Kuunawarn, chief of the Kirrae wurrung, who is the subject of the previous chapter. The other main Aboriginal informants were Yarruun Parpur Tarneen, 'chiefess' of the Morpor Aboriginals; Wombeet Tuulawarn, her husband; Muulapuurn yurong yaar; Johnny Dawson; Henry Dawson; Weeratt Kuyuut, who was Yarruun Parpur Tarneen's father and chief of the Morpor Aboriginals; and Gnuurneecheean.

I was able to trace five of these informants through the European records, but I have been unable to find out much about Gnuurneecheean and Muulapuurn yurong yaar, whose European names are unknown.

YARRUUN PARPUR TARNEEN AND WOMBEET TUULAWARN

Yarruun Parpur Tarneen was the daughter of the chief of the Morpor or Spring Creek tribe. Her name meant 'Victorious', and was given to her by her father after he had defeated his enemies in a great battle.[2] Her husband's name meant 'Rotten Spear', from an old spear his father carried.[3] Wombeet Tuulawarn's mother was Mary Robinson or Robertson of Caramut, wife of Samuel Robertson, who was her second husband.[4] On Mary's death certificate Rosie Austin is named as a surviving child.

The Ritchie photos provide evidence that Yarruun Parpur Tarneen and Wombeet Tuulawarn also came to be known by the European names of Johnny Castella (sometimes Costello) and

Mrs Louisa Castella. It is thought that the name comes from Paul de Castella, who was on the pastoral run of Quamby in late 1853 and early 1854. The Castellas were often seen around Woolsthorpe.[5] Their names appear on the 1876 list of those required by government to reside on the Framlingham Aboriginal Station.

Dawson repeatedly refers to Yarruun Parpur Tarneen as the 'very intelligent chiefess', but she and her husband were not approved of by the mission managers. In a surviving letter dated 21 June 1882, Johnny Castella wrote asking for building material to improve his hut, which was falling down. He argued that he did his share of the work, and therefore should have a house as good as the others. William Goodall, normally manager at Framlingham but at this time relieving manager at Coranderrk, wrote to Page, the Board's secretary, disputing Castella's claim that he worked as well as the others: 'He spends most of his time wandering from one place to another earning a little money and drinking, and when home does little or nothing', Goodall wrote.[6]

YARRUUN PARPUR TARNEEN

WOMBEET TUULAWARN (CASTELLA),
HUSBAND OF YARRUUN PARPUR
TARNEEN

YARRUUN PARPUR TARNEEN (MRS CASTELLA) AND HER HUSBAND, BOTH IN
EUROPEAN DRESS

Castella died of heart disease on 30 September 1882, aged fifty. He had been in Warrnambool with Wilmot Abraham, and they were on their way back to Framlingham when Castella complained of a headache and decided to stay in a shed at Wangoom. Wilmot went on, and when Castella didn't arrive he went looking for him. He found Castella's body the next morning, near where he had left him.[7] Louisa died shortly afterwards on 19 December 1882 of 'congestion of the liver and exhaustion'.[8]

The Castellas were among four old Aboriginals who died in the last quarter of 1882, the others being Thomas Kidd and King Charlie of Leura. The Reverend Thwaites wrote in his annual report, 'I would have it known that four out of the five who died were old blacks, of wandering propensities and dissipated habits, who would never remain on the station for any length of time'.[9]

Louisa, her husband and his mother are all buried in the Framlingham Aboriginal Cemetery.

WEERATT KUYUUT

Weeratt Kuyuut's dignity and striking looks are familiar to those interested in colonial and Western District art. He is in the centre of the group of Aborigines in the foreground of Robert Dowling's 'Minjah in the old time' (1856). I have always been keen to find more about him but have found only the briefest reference to his life.

The first comes from the details of an inquest into the death of Maria, the wife of 'King Morpor', at Green Hills on 25 November 1867. Jimmy Laughnan, a fellow Aboriginal who was with the chief and his wife the night she died, reported that they had been at the Framlingham mission, but had left to go visiting. They had called at Henry Good's, then walked on to the Mickles' place and requested permission to stay overnight. There, Maria had started complaining of not feeling well. She was treated very well by the Mickles. Mrs Mickle gave her breakfast and some medicine. In

WEERATT KUYUUT

the evening Maria ate some food and then went to bed. The two men chatted for a while before themselves going to bed. Not long afterwards Weeratt Kuyuut called to his friend to say his wife was dying. The inquest verdict was 'death from natural causes'.

The second reference to Weeratt Kuyuut is a note on the back of the accompanying photograph of him, which reads:

> Weeratt Kuuyuut was a great warrior, and so much feared that he travelled alone all over the country unmolested. He was a professor of languages, astronomy, and geography, and teacher of the tribes between Portland and the River Leigh near Geelong, and from the sea coast to the Grampians.
>
> The chief is now about 70 years of age and intends taking a young woman to himself as wife.

Below are the initials J. D. (James Dawson) and the date 1871.

JOHNNY DAWSON

Johnny Dawson was born about 1842. He died in 1883. He lived at Kangatong with James Dawson, and later moved to the Framlingham Aboriginal Station. A photo of Johnny Dawson in possession of Phillip Ritchie bears a note: 'Johnnie Dawson, for many years stock keeper at Kangatong'. He may have worked at Dunmore station as well, though I found no mention of him in the Dunmore diaries. Mr Francis of the Lake Condah Aboriginal station wrote to James Dawson on 14 April 1868, answering a query about the whereabouts of a number of Aboriginals. He said, 'Johnnie Dawson I believe is at Mr. McKnights station near Eumeralla'. This would be Dunmore. He may also have been the 'Black Johnny' who worked for T. A. Browne (the novelist Rolf Boldrewood) at Squattlesea Mere, but one can't be sure of this. Black Johnny worked as a shepherd at Squattlesea Mere in 1862 and 1863, and was paid ten shillings a week in 1862 and twelve shillings a week in 1863.

Johnny Dawson married Sarah Edwards, and they must have moved to the Framlingham Aboriginal Station soon after it was established. There he was regarded as 'one of the steadiest men'.[10] He was included in the photo of the Aboriginals at the Framlingham Reserve in 1867 (see p. 48 above). He was baptised with other members of his family by the Reverend P. Teulon Beamish at the Framlingham Aboriginal Station on 9 May 1866. At this time John's year of birth was given as 1842 and his wife Sarah's as 1846. They had two children with them at the time: James, born 1864, and John, born 1865.[11] A daughter, Rachel, was born about 1868. Another son, Daniel Clarke Dawson, was born a year later. He was to die of bronchitis on 11 July 1875.[12]

The painter Eugène von Guérard came across an Aboriginal artist at Kangatong on 8 August 1855. Von Guérard was impressed, and sketched the man he called 'Black Johnny'. There is no way of knowing for sure whether this was Johnny Dawson or not, but it may have been.[13]

What is known for certain is that the 111-acre Kangatong Reserve, which is mentioned in lists of land reserved for Aboriginal use, became a reserve because of a request from Johnny

JOHNNY DAWSON

SARAH DAWSON, WIFE OF JOHNNY DAWSON

JOHNNY DAWSON IN EUROPEAN DRESS

Dawson. In 1866 R. Brough Smyth wrote to the Assistant Commissioner of Lands and Surveys asking for a specific piece of land for Johnny Dawson. He enclosed a plan marking the land that Johnny was requesting, and asked that another block be set aside if it was not available. The block that Johnny wanted was on Dawson's and Mitchell's licensed run, Kangatong. The request went to the Executive Council and was gazetted on 25 May 1866. Shortly afterwards the allocation was cancelled and another area was reserved for Aboriginal use.

It was a fascinating study to locate the original area Johnny Dawson requested and to visit it to see what was so special. Was this his birthplace? Or a sacred site? One way or another, it was obviously in his country. Unfortunately, as all through the district, there is little left to indicate anything of significance. The block Johnny asked for has been cleared of all vegetation; while there may be some surface water in winter, there was none when I visited. Old maps, however, reveal extensive areas of swamp and marsh land, suggesting that the area would have been rich in various kinds of food.

The land eventually allocated was closer to the town of Hawkesdale than the one requested, and on the edge of the racecourse. On the old maps one can still see words indicating the two blocks that were, one after the other, land reserved for Aboriginal use.

Why did Dawson miss out on the land he wanted? It appears that the squatter Robert Whitehead, interested in extending the area under his control, had applied to lease 268 acres. The lease was dated 7 June 1865. Later Whitehead went ahead and applied for a grant of the land. So in this case the Aboriginals lost the land twice: the first time when Europeans entered the district, and a second time in the early 1860s, when in spite of the encouragement of liberal whites, Aboriginals' requests to be allocated blocks of land for their own use ran up against the European squatters' desire to extend their runs.

There is nothing to indicate whether Aboriginals used the land near the racecourse. It remained Crown land, being only temporarily reserved for Aboriginal use. By the end of 1879, when there were requests for it to be open for selection as a small farm, the Board agreed, as the land was no longer needed for Aboriginal use. There was intense competition for the block, though some prospective buyers' enthusiasm cooled when they realised it was not the original area reserved, which was probably better land. The successful buyer was John Toogood.[14]

Johnny Dawson died of 'pulmonary and abdominal consumption' on 3 October 1883, aged forty-two.[15] On 12 September the Reverend Thwaites had notified the BPA that John had a 'fistula' but was unable to travel to Melbourne for an operation, and would need to be housed in Warrnambool for a few weeks so that the doctor could attend to him frequently. His wife would be with him and nurse him. But on 20 September Thwaites reported, 'Dawson dying; operation no use'. He died shortly afterwards. He was buried the following day at the Framlingham Station with Mr Clarke, the first manager of the station, officiating in Thwaites's absence. At this time his only surviving child was Rachel, who was to marry Henry Albert, as we shall see in chapter 10.

Sarah lived much longer. She moved to Gippsland and married William Thorpe. She died on 20 August 1935, aged almost ninety years, and was laid to rest in the Bairnsdale cemetery. At that time she had one surviving child, Alice.[16]

Henry Dawson, reared at Kangatong.

HENRY DAWSON

HENRY DAWSON

Henry Dawson was born on Kangatong, and worked there for James Dawson. He married Susannah Jerry on 27 May 1876. Both had been married before, but to whom is not indicated.[17] Henry's age at the time was given as twenty-five. They were married at Wurrong, a property near Camperdown that James Dawson leased for a time after the sale of Kangatong. This suggests that Henry had kept in close touch with the Dawson family. Dawson's daughter, Isabella, signed the marriage certificate as a witness.

Henry appears to have been linked to both Lake Condah and Framlingham. He was in the 1876 list of Aboriginals required to reside on Lake Condah,[18] and was also in the list of those who petitioned the Chief Secretary not to close the Lake Condah station in July 1907.[19]

Between these two dates, however, his name appears on a letter of protest originating from Framlingham in January 1898. The occasion of this letter was yet another move by the BPA against the Framlingham community. The BPA had gained an Order in Council to remove three couples—the Gibbs, William Rawlings and his wife, and John Rose and his wife—and a single man, Frank Blair. The residents complained to the Chief Secretary that the government had broken yet another promise:

There are only a few of us old people here now and we would like to be left here until we die we want to be buried here beside our friends. You told us here when you came to see us that the station was not to be broken. Well then how is it that some of our friends Pure Blacks have

been shifted away from here taken off by the police as prisoners is that
right. The old [people] did not see them taken away from here as they
were taken before daylight.

The residents intended to write to the Queen herself to see if she
would intercede on their behalf. They complained that the BPA
had given them no implements to cultivate the land. Even the
houses belonging to the people who had been taken away were
pulled down. At the bottom of the letter, in the same handwriting,
was a list of names: George Edwards, Sam Robertson, W. Johnson,
W. Abhrams (presumably Wilmot Abraham), R. Patterson and
Henry Dawson.

Hagenauer, the BPA General Inspector, justified the decision to
remove the houses, saying that if they were left standing 'they
would only become a harbour for halfcastes and useless white
people'.[20] When Hagenauer and the Board chairman visited
Framlingham to investigate the complaints, the residents all
declared they knew nothing about the letter, and had not autho-
rised anyone to sign for them. Having gone behind the Board's
back in writing to the Chief Secretary, the residents obviously felt
it was politic to be unaware of the letter's existence.

Henry Dawson probably continued to move between the two
stations. He was buried in the Framlingham Aboriginal cemetery
on 2 July 1915. His wife Susannah died in 1880.[21]

CHAPTER 9

'Why are we kept prisoners here?'

These educated blacks are much more difficult to deal with than the old blacks were.

Reverend J. H. Stähle, manager of Lake Condah Aboriginal Station

He is a liar and has always been

Maggie Mobourne, of the Reverend Stähle

This is the story of a passionate and independent woman and a remarkable man whose partnership survived against the odds. It is also the story of their struggle against the control of the Board for the Protection of the Aborigines and its representative at Lake Condah, the Reverend John Heinrich Stähle, who managed the station from 1875 to 1913.

Maggie Turner was a second-generation resident of the Lake Condah Aboriginal Station. Born about 1872, she married Ernest Mobourne, also of the Lake Condah mission. Like many other Aboriginals, they were moved by Order in Council to a distant Aboriginal station for misbehaviour. Their case is exceptional in that they were held against their wishes on the Lake Tyers Aboriginal Mission until they died. Only death set them free.

The story of the Mobournes provides an example of how the BPA used its power to crush the spirit of Aboriginal people. It is a demonstration of what Mick Dodson has recently described as the aspect of white domination that makes him most angry:

> There's still a hangover in the whitefellow systems. They think they can still absolutely dominate us, and not only that, they think they have a right to do it! That's the thing that sticks most in my memory—this total control that the whitefellow system felt that they had to have over us. That's the thing that really gets up my bloody nose.[1]

The same paternalistic attitude was clear in the evidence given by the BPA's station managers to the Royal Commission of 1877, which was charged with establishing whether the Aboriginal people of Victoria had made such advances along the road to 'civilisation' that the Board's stations could be closed and their residents dispersed among the general population.

Predictably, perhaps, the station managers told the Royal Commission that the Aboriginals were not yet ready to take responsibility for their own lives. Reverend Stähle said in his evidence that, while many of the children were better educated than white children, they lacked a 'spirit of courage and independence'. Asked whether Aboriginals who had learnt a trade could carry out the work unsupervised, Stähle said that he believed not. They displayed 'a certain carelessness or thoughtlessness': they were 'capable of learning, but not of carrying their knowledge practically'.[2] The Reverend Hagenauer, manager of Ramahyuck, said that 'their moral status and self-control is not strong enough for scattering them abroad yet ... they would fall back into their old state'. Pushed to specify how long it would be before the Aboriginals could be assimilated, Hagenauer insisted, 'It would want generations'.[3]

The Royal Commission's verdict was that the system of Aboriginal stations should continue for some time, as the Aboriginals were not yet ready to make their own way in the general community. As to when they might be ready, the Royal Commissioners believed that 'so long a period must first elapse, it is unnecessary now to enter into consideration of the subject'.[4]

Despite the condescension of white officials, there were individuals who grew up on the Aboriginal stations who spoke and wrote English well, who were independent thinkers, and who were so confident that they were prepared to press their cases with the BPA, Members of Parliament, the Chief Secretary, the Premier and even the Governor. Such a couple were Ernest and Maggie Mobourne. Their lives demonstrate the lengths to which an Aboriginal station manager could—and did—go to enforce obedience from those under his control.

The Mobournes' story reminds me of some comments made by Captain Reg Saunders, the first Aboriginal to become a commissioned officer in the Australian Army. I was writing the biography of one of his ancestors, Reginald William Rawlings, MM, who died a hero's death on a battlefield in France in World War I. 'Point out how well educated the Aborigines from Condah were,' Reg Saunders remarked. He recalled that the Aboriginals were far better educated than many of the farmers from the surrounding area. This was certainly true of the Mobournes.

Maggie Turner and Ernest Mobourne were married on 24 January 1893.[5] By this time the BPA had implemented the 1886 Aborigines Protection Act, under which 'able-bodied half-castes' were to support themselves outside the stations. Maggie and Ernest were not affected directly by the Act; because they were classified as 'full-bloods', they were entitled to be on the Lake Condah mission, where they continued to live after they were married. On the other hand, the implementation of the Act indirectly fostered a growing independence and willingness to speak out among those still on the mission, and this formed part of the background to the Mobournes' persistent problems with the Reverend Stähle.

Even before their marriage, Stähle had reported Ernest Mobourne to the BPA for disobedience. In October 1892 the BPA instructed its General Inspector to write Ernest an 'earnest letter of reproof', cautioning him that if he did not obey the manager he would be removed to another station.[6] Ernest would be in trouble with Stähle many times in the years to follow, as he was a leader of those who flouted Stähle's authority or were dissatisfied with how he treated them. Many years later Joe Sharrock, who lived next to the mission station property and knew the local Aboriginals very well, recalled Ernest as 'A happy sort. Orator, could speak good English, and once made a speech to the Governor. Very bald, and known as "Shine-eye".'[7]

The sources of the conflict between Stähle and sections of the Lake Condah Aboriginal community can be traced back to the late 1870s. Between 1878 and the mid-1880s the Stähles had to deal with a simmering rebellion, which occasionally erupted into open disobedience. In June 1876 Robert Sutton from the mission took out a summons against Stähle for assault, and the manager had to appear before the court in Macarthur. The case was dismissed, but Stähle found that in law he had very little power. He appealed to the Board 'to invest the missionaries and superintendents of Aboriginal stations with ... power to correct insubordination and refractory blacks'.[8]

A wave of unrest was about to pass across the Victorian Aboriginal stations as residents baulked at the authoritarian style of the managers who controlled their lives. At Condah a group of rebels refused to do as Stähle asked. He reacted by stopping rations, including tobacco, and when this move produced an uproar he called in the police. Stähle also attempted to force obedience by refusing to permit the rebels to apply to the Board for certificates allowing them to work off the station. The men looked forward to getting work outside, where they could earn some money and gain a respite from the restrictions of mission life. Ill-feeling escalated, and the Board at last intervened in late April 1878, banishing seven families for six months—those of Johnny Sutton, Tommy Green, Billy Gorrie, Jackie Fraser, Billy Wallaby, Billy Hewitt and Harry Robinson. The children were allowed to stay on the station, but the families took them with them.

The BPA used similar tactics to quell unrest at Ramahyuck and Coranderrk. The Board instructed the General Inspector to make

THE WALLABY FAMILY—BILLY, KITTY AND CHILDREN

it clear that it would punish insubordination by sending those responsible away from the Aboriginal stations. Offenders would be given certificates to make this legal. These certificates, which had originally been issued as a privilege to allow Aboriginals to work off the stations, were now becoming a means of control.

In early November 1880 a second rebellion broke out at Condah. The protesters included those involved in the earlier unrest, who wrote to the Board explaining their reasons for not obeying Stähle. The Board asked him to respond. The new protest was led by a 'half-caste' called James Scott, who had moved on to the mission. He played on the desire of many of the Aborigines to have control over their own lives. There followed three weeks of worry as the Stähles tried to cope with these 'stiff backed and rebellious people', as they put it, who wanted to manage themselves. Mary Stähle was so troubled by what was happening that, without her husband's knowledge, she wrote to ask the Board for

This Certificate *was issued on the*   *day of*
18   *to an Aboriginal named*   *aged about*
height about   *and known or distinguishable by the following*
peculiarities :

he having represented himself as able and willing to earn a living by his own exertions.

    The effect of this Certificate while in force, is as follows :

It authorizes him to enter into a binding Contract of Service for any time during which this Certificate remains in force.

    It permits a European to harbour him without incurring any penalty.

    It does not authorize any person to sell or give him any intoxicating drink or affect the penalty for so doing, or confer any other exemption from penalties under the said Act.

    This Certificate will not remain in force after the   *day of*
    18   *, unless renewed in the meantime by the date of renewal and signature of some Member of the Board for the Protection of Aborigines, local guardian, or member of local Committee being written thereon, and it will not remain in force after six months from the date of the last renewal.*

         Secretary to the Board for the Protection to Aborigines.

COPY OF THE CERTIFICATE ABORIGINAL MEN HAD TO CARRY TO SHOW THEY HAD
BEEN GIVEN BOARD PERMISSION TO WORK OFF THE ABORIGINAL STATIONS

help. She described Scott as a combination of a 'Jimmy Barker and a Punch', two of the most recalcitrant of the Coranderrk Aboriginals. 'Surely', she begged, 'we are not bound to keep such a man here'. She complained:

> Scott does not rest day or night from doing mischief or sowing the seeds of rebellion and discontent telling the blacks how badly they are treated—and how they all should have land to settle down on and cultivate for themselves and they should not rest until all their wishes are fulfilled, until they become their own masters, not to be led like children any more.[9]

She named Billy Wallaby, Billy Hewitt, Andy McKinnon, Johnny Sutton and Scott as the most active promoters of the rebellion, for which there was widespread support. Mary recoiled from what she described as the 'treachery' around her, branding the Aboriginals 'a generation of vipers for as a viper will turn around and sting one who caresses it so these people'.

The Board ended her ordeal by ordering Scott off the mission, transferring Johnny Sutton to the Ebenezer Mission and making changes designed to end the insubordination. Those who had written letters of complaint[10] were threatened with being removed by Order in Council if they continued their behaviour. It was arranged that the police should visit the station once a fortnight. The Board also decided that allowing Aboriginals to have firearms in their possession was 'very objectionable and dangerous'. They were ordered to hand in their guns. The Board asked the local police to collect the weapons at Condah, so that Stähle would not have to demand the firearms from the Aboriginals. After a period of civilising and Christianising on the mission, Aboriginals who had been using firearms since the 1850s were no longer to be trusted to do so.

Meanwhile, the protests at Coranderrk had gained the attention of the press. In 1881 the government was forced to set up a Board 'to enquire into, and report upon, the present condition and management of the Coranderrk Aboriginal Station'. This Board stated in its report that the Aboriginals 'desire to see the Central Board with its inspector and superintendent abolished'.[11] It was an exasperating time for the Aboriginal Board and for those who had to deal with the restless and dissatisfied among the Aboriginal communities.

By the late 1880s there was a new factor complicating life on the Lake Condah mission. A number of 'half-castes' who had been forced to leave the mission had taken up residence at Dunmore, not far from the station. From there it was easy for them to come and go, visiting friends on the station, providing an example of how it was possible to live independently without having to put up with the restrictions on behaviour imposed by the authoritarian Reverend Stähle. One of the 'half-castes', Angus King, owned land at Dunmore, and if he was prepared to put people up on his property there was nothing Stähle could do about it, as the manager was the first to admit.

In time Dunmore became increasingly attractive to some of the people on the station. Ernest Mobourne, having been warned in 1892 that if he did not become more obedient he would be sent to another station, for a time accepted BPA advice, but he continued to be dissatisfied with the Reverend Stähle's management. The Chief Secretary's papers for 1897 include a letter from John Murray MLA, the friend of Western District Aboriginals, enclosing 'a letter of a trenchant kind' from Ernest. It provides evidence that Ernest was already aware of how to use contacts to inform high-ranking officials of the way the Aboriginals were treated. Murray wrote to the Chief Secretary:

> [The letter] makes definite charges against the management of that Station which should be enquired into. Can you fix the date of your intended visit to the Stations in the district and let me know at once as the numerous complaints that have been made by the suffering blacks should be considered without any further delay and urgently demand your personal investigation.[12]

The Chief Secretary, Sir Alexander Peacock, visited Lake Condah on 30 January 1898 without warning. By chance Stähle was away, and Peacock met the Aboriginals to discuss the charges and gauge for himself the extent of concern. Ernest had alleged that the manager's sons had been wearing clothes intended for the Aboriginals and that the rations were insufficient. Peacock found little support for Ernest's claims, and Ernest asked to be allowed to withdraw his charges, perhaps placated by the level of attention his letter had received and the chance to talk openly with someone in a position of power.[13]

In May 1899 the situation again became tense. Realising that Stähle had turned against him, though not knowing why, Ernest left the station and went to live at Dunmore. There followed a battle of wills between Ernest and Stähle in which neither was willing to back down. It ended with Stähle issuing an ultimatum to the Board: either Ernest went or he would no longer manage the station.

Those who clashed most strongly with Stähle realised the importance of making sure the Board heard their side of the story. There are therefore two accounts of this clash of wills in the BPA records: Stähle's account and that of his opponents.

At first Stähle reported to the Board that Mobourne and Hugh Courtwine had let him know that they were leaving the station to go to Dunmore and earn their own living. He told the Board that the two hoped the station would collapse when they left and the people would be able to live as they wanted, as did the small number of people who were allowed to stay at Framlingham after the station had been closed. Stähle said philosophically that he was sure that with time the two men would return 'wiser but sadder and let us hope better behaving people'.[14]

Others joined the movement to Dunmore. On 5 June 1899 Stähle had to report that the following 'full blacks' had left the station and were living at Dunmore: Peter Hewitt, Billy and Kitty Wallaby, Arthur Green, Hugh and Flora Courtwine, and the Mobournes and their two children. Determined that 'the blacks whom the Board had power to deal with for their own good' should not be allowed to be with the 'half-castes', he asked the

Board to instruct the police at Heywood to notify 'the blacks' that if they didn't 'quit Dunmore' within one week of the notice being served and 'give proof that they mean to earn their own living', they would be 'drafted out' and sent to different stations. He named Billy and Kitty Wallaby as ringleaders: 'Wallaby and his wife have always been at the bottom of the mischief with regards to the blacks who made for Dunmore whenever they became unruly on the station'.[15]

Ernest wrote to the BPA two days after Stähle. In his letter he explained that the Aboriginals living at Dunmore had called at the mission station to discuss the situation with Stähle, only to have him order them off. Stähle defended his action in his next letter to the Board: he hadn't asked them to come and they should wait till he sent for them.[16]

On 27 June Stähle wrote to the Board that the sooner 'the blacks' were removed from Dunmore the better. It was in this letter that he first attacked the character of Maggie, Ernest's wife, though he did not provide any evidence to support his assertion: 'I must also state, though reluctantly that the characters of the two women Flora Courtwine and Maggie Mobourne are such that I could not recommend them to be at large among the white population'.[17]

Constable Gleeson attempted to carry out the Board's orders, but found the Aboriginals refused to return to the station. He recommended to the Board that Ernest be removed to one of the other stations, as he 'appears to be a sort of King amongst them' and 'is a very intelligent and conceited man and has a good deal of influence over the others'. He wrote to Stähle telling him that he had written to the Board recommending that Ernest be removed to another station as 'He is without doubt a Bush Lawyer and the others recognise him as a sort of King or leader'.[17]

Stähle wrote immediately to the Board accusing Ernest of creating 'disaffection among the blacks' and 'slandering' him whenever he had a chance to do so. Ernest, he wrote, 'has all along acted as a leader among the blacks here and at Dunmore and ... has given me more trouble than all the other blacks together'.[19] He

A little starvation might be a good thing for them, only I am sorry the rest of the people would not let it come to that, and even the rabbits are against this resolution, for as long as they are so plentiful no black or white man will starve in this district.

With kind regards

yours faithfully

J. H. Stähle.

The Rev.

F. A. Hagenauer

Gen. Insp. & Sec.

B. P. A.

Melbourne

THE REVEREND STÄHLE TELLS THE SECRETARY OF THE BOARD FOR
THE PROTECTION OF ABORIGINES THAT A LITTLE STARVATION WOULD BE GOOD
FOR THE MOBOURNES

demanded that Ernest and Wallaby 'be removed as soon as possible so as to avoid any further trouble which might end seriously if a firm hand is not laid on them at once'. If Board members had even the slightest suspicion that he had not dealt with the 'blacks' 'in a most forgiving and forbearing spirit', he urged them to hold an inquiry to establish the truth.

Ernest again used John Murray MLA to convey a letter to the Chairman of the BPA. He explained why he and Hughie Courtwine had decided to leave the station. They had asked to attend the sports at Condah on the Queen's Birthday, and Stähle had agreed. Ernest felt they had been back at a reasonable time, but evidently something they had done had upset Stähle. Ernest suspected Stähle had turned against him. On 25 May, when there was an inspection by members of the Board—an important event at the station—Ernest's place had been bypassed. Reading this as a sign of disapproval, he had asked Stähle the reason. Stähle had said he could leave the station, so he had done so.[20]

Ernest ended his letter by justifying his refusal to move from Dunmore and appealing to the Board not to allow force to be used against him: 'I pray gentlemen you will not allow me to be molested in any way, as I am earning a living for myself and family and am much happier than I would be living on the Station'.[21]

But Ernest's letter arrived too late. The Board had decided that Stähle should be supported. By September the Mobournes had returned to the station, though the exact nature of the pressure exerted on them to return is not clear from the surviving records.

In early 1900 the Mobournes were again out of favour with Stähle, who claimed they wanted to roam the countryside 'in defiance of law and order'. He admitted to the Board that they were able to keep themselves without difficulty—'The country abounds with rabbits which find a ready sale at the freezing works so they can easily get along for a considerable time'.[22] This seems to have annoyed him, because it reduced the Mobournes' dependence on him.

The Mobournes were also finding Stähle difficult to cope with. Maggie wrote to the *Hamilton Spectator* reporting that she and the manager had clashed after he had reproved her for not having her husband and children with her at prayers. She had told him to 'speak to the other half of the people who were absent as well as my husband and children, and to his own'. He had then threatened reprisals against her and the children, though he denied he had done so when her father raised the matter with him. In her letter, Maggie overtly sought the support of the newspaper's white readers:

I am quite ashamed to see him handle the Bible and teach us as if he were an earnest Christian gentleman as some of you take him to be. He doesn't practice what he preaches as one sees who knows him every day that passes. He's not a fit person for the position he holds but is dragging us down into hell rather than helping us to rise. What I say here is true and I can take a solemn oath before God and before any Christian people as I have proofs for his falsehoods. If any of you would only know the true state of affairs you would be amazed to see how we put up with his treacherous ways and that he is alive to this very day. We who know his ways often wonder he is not punished by the Master he professes to serve.[23]

Maggie also wrote to the BPA complaining that Stähle 'seems determined to annoy us and to take every opportunity of reporting us to the Board for insubordination'. She asserted that he had stopped their rations and was lying when he claimed not to have done so: 'he is a liar and has always been ... and he doesn't treat us justly'. She ended the letter by calling on the BPA to set up an impartial Board of Inquiry to investigate whether they were being treated fairly. For good measure she included the signatures of eleven people who supported her request.[24]

Taken aback, the Board asked Stähle whether he had stopped the Mobournes' rations or not. He admitted he had when 'they became so unbearable and troublesome and ceased to go to work at the same time'. Since the Board was to consider their situation at the next meeting, however, he had decided to allow them rations providing that Ernest agreed to return to work and the Mobournes understood they would receive rations only until the Board's decision was known. Maggie and Ernest decided to refuse rations: they 'would prefer to starve', they said. [25]

The Mobournes also contacted Mr Duffit Snr, Justice of the Peace at Oakbank, near Heywood. In early March 1900 Stähle heard from Duffit that the Mobournes had come to him with a written complaint about Stähle signed by ten of the Lake Condah men. Stähle's distress was obvious in his letter to the Board: Mobourne, he wrote, must be sent away and 'soon':

> or else I will be obliged to give up my charge ere long ... neither my own or my wife's health could stand the strain of it. What his complaints are, I do not know, for he and his wife have received (besides what the Government allows them) nothing but kindness in every way, from my wife and myself.[26]

The Acting Vice-Chairman of the BPA visited Lake Condah to assess the situation for himself and reported back to the Reverend Hagenauer, General Inspector and Secretary of the BPA:

> We regret ... that Ernest Mobourne and his wife have again given trouble. The man is very cunning and while apparently keeping quiet seems forever to make trouble and mischief among the rest of the people, as for his wife she is reported to be not only grossly immoral but she seems possessed of a most unruly and ungovernable temper for she even attacked us with her vile tongue and her conduct towards Mrs Stähle is outrageous ... we are of opinion that they should now be sent to Lake Tyers station under an Order in Council.[27]

The Order in Council exiling the Mobournes to Lake Tyers in Gippsland, the most distant Aboriginal station to which the Board could banish them, was issued on 26 March 1900. Constable Gleeson was given the duty of reading it to the Mobournes and removing them from Lake Condah. He took Constable McManus along, but still had difficulty:

I thought for a long time we would have to return without them however by partly bouncing and partly coaxing we at length succeeded in persuading them to accompany us to the Lockup after spending the greater part of the day.[28]

On 10 April 1900 Stähle reported their removal. They had been taken away while the Sunday church service was taking place:

The blacks, as is natural, did not like it that Mobourne had to go—but the effect will be for the good, for they not only see what they did not believe viz: that the Board has power *but that they mean to use it when nothing else will bring them to their senses.*[29]

Yet the removal of Maggie and Ernest did not bring the Lake Condah people 'to their senses'. On the contrary, Stähle found that there was still disobedience, which he blamed on Ernest's brother Sam and his wife Bella. He suspected some of the people had decided that if Ernest was sent away they too would try to be sent away, in the hope that this would lead to the closure of the station. In a long letter to the BPA on 13 April 1900, Stähle made it clear how he manipulated food supplies to try to control residents' behaviour. He also disclosed that he was still encountering opposition, and named those who sided with the Mobournes:

[Sam Mobourne] did not come to prayers, so this morning I gave Bella sugar and tea for herself but not for Sam until he should come to prayers like the others . . .

[S]ince I have observed the disaffection among the people, I gave them their rations flour, rice, oatmeal, meat etc twice a week, but sugar and tea each morning after prayers, which is as you know at 8 o'clock. I had to take this course in order to get them out of their beds, as some would have stayed till all hours of the day.

Bella Mobourne called her husband who came to the store in a moment saying, 'Never mind I shall get some sugar elsewhere'. I told Sam not to repeat his former conduct, whereupon he drew a letter out of his coat pocket and shook it in my face saying, 'Look here, here is a letter about you signed by all and you will see what will be done'. I said, 'all

*right, get as many signatures as you can but meanwhile I shall give you
no rations till I hear from the Board'. I then sent for the men and the
following are those who said they gave their permission to affix their
names to the letter*

> *Isaac McDuff*
>
> *William Carter (who is here on a Certificate)*
>
> *Henry Connolly (also here on a Certificate)**
>
> *Tommy Willis*
>
> *James Courtwine*
>
> *Sam Mobourne*
>
> *Thomas McCallum said he would have given his name only he was*
too late.

*I told all those who had signed the rebellious document ... that I
would give them no rations until I would hear from the Board.*[30]

Meanwhile, at Lake Tyers, tragedy struck. Both the Mobournes'
sons died just sixteen days apart in May 1900 of 'acute intestinal
catarrh, diarrhoea and exhaustion'. Arthur was four years and nine
months old and William Robert was six. Maggie blamed the Board
for their deaths.[31]

A new source of tension had emerged on the stations at the
end of 1899. From the time of the 1886 Act, the Board had removed
'half caste' orphans to the Department for Neglected Children,[32]
but in 1899 it gained power to remove any Aboriginal child. In
December 1899 it amended Clause 13 of its regulations to read:

> *The Governor may for the better care, custody and education of any
> aboriginal child order that such child be transferred to the care of the
> Department for Neglected Children or the Department for Reformatory
> Schools.*[33]

The minutes of the Board meeting of 6 December 1899 recorded
that four children—John and Edward Mullett, Dinah Rawlings and

---

* Those with certificates would be people who should be living off the station and providing for
themselves but had been permitted to stay on the station for a time because they were having
difficulties of one kind or another. That such people were willing to sign a document criticising
Stähle when they were dependent on his good will shows the intensity of the feelings he was
evoking.

Charles Mobourne, son of Sam and Bella—had been transferred to the Industrial Schools 'from whence they will be apprenticed out to approved employers'. In September 1900 the Board passed a motion that the children of half-caste parents residing on the stations should if possible be transferred to the Industrial Schools Department at the age of twelve years. At the same meeting it was recorded that William Carter (14), Henry Carter (18) and Laurence Harvey (13) were transferred under Orders in Council to the Industrial Schools. All these children were from the Western District.

By the end of 1900 ten children—eight boys and two girls—had been transferred under the new regulation. The head of the Industrial Schools Department reported that he was pleased to have an opportunity to give a larger number of Aboriginal children 'the advantages of being dealt with in the same way as the other wards of the State'. In 1901 the Board reported that the girls had been sent into domestic service—one directly, the other after a few months training at Albion House. Five of the eight boys were sent to the Bayswater Training Farm, which was run by the Salvation Army, to be prepared for sending out into service, one went directly into service, and one was returned to his family, who had left the mission station and were working to support themselves. The eighth boy, Charles Mobourne, had died.[34]

The Board had allowed Bella to visit Charles when it became clear that he was seriously ill. It seems that she wanted to take Charles home with her, but her request was refused. She returned to Condah when he appeared to be getting better, but wrote seeking assurances that he was improving. She received the following letter by return mail:

Boys' Depot, Park Street, Brunswick
Nov. 20th 1900

Dear Mrs Mobourn,

Yours just received. You will be pleased to hear that Charlie is improving every day ... You may rest assured that everything will be done for him here.

He was hardly strong enough to travel the day you left, if you are coming down he will be pleased to see you as he was very anxious about you.

He is such a good boy, reads his Bible every chance, and I often find him on his knees praying, so do not be anxious about him.

Yours sincerely
M. Johnson[35]

His parents visited again, but Charles, who was suffering from consumption (tuberculosis), passed away on 20 January 1901 in the Austin Hospital.

At Lake Condah the effect of the child removals was immediately apparent. It was with sadness that Stähle wrote on 31 December 1900:

Owing to all the boys (with the exception of one) having been taken away, our station is painfully quiet ... Were it not for some white children, who, along with some half-castes, attend the school, and a few girls who are still left, it would probably have been closed by the Department.

He then told the story of an old man who had recently passed away as the result of a severe bout of influenza, and concluded:

So one by one the older people depart and the young folks are taken away by the Board for the Protection of the Aborigines, and consequently Mission work among the Aborigines of Victoria will have reached finality before many more years have passed away.[36]

While the Board reported that the system of training the boys and girls 'was working remarkably well' and that the children were 'happy',[37] this was not true of the Condah boys. They ran away and turned up at the Coranderrk Aboriginal Station, from which they were promptly returned to the Bayswater Training Farm.[38]

Maggie and Ernest Mobourne were allowed to return to Lake Condah in 1903. Their return was the direct result of the intervention of the Governor, Sir George Clarke. Though I have not discovered the circumstances, it is clear Ernest met the Governor at Kalimna and took the opportunity to speak to him about the family's desire to return to Lake Condah. He then wrote to the Governor formally requesting the cancellation of the Order in Council keeping them at Lake Tyers so that they could return home.[39] A note on the letter states, 'The necessary amendment in the Order in Council ... will be made'. Only later were the Mobournes to realise that, although they were allowed to return home, the Order in Council was not amended.

They behaved satisfactorily in Stähle's view until March 1904, when Stähle complained that Ernest would not work and 'walks out of church in the middle of the service to pay visits to someone who doesn't attend'. He asked Hagenauer to write Ernest a short letter enquiring how he was getting on. Although Ernest was perfectly capable of reading the letter himself, it would be sent via Stähle, who would read the letter to him: 'it might do him good. You know he is a very difficult customer to deal with.'[40]

But it was Maggie, not Ernest, who was to cause Stähle the most trouble in the next few years. In July 1907 Maggie eloped with Henry Albert, whose wife Rachel had died on 30 August 1905.[41] Stähle's letter to the Sergeant of Police at Portland makes clear the enormity of the situation as he saw it: 'a full black married Aboriginal woman who resides here eloped on 23 July with a half-caste widower "Henry Albert" residing at Dunmore, about three miles from here'.

Stähle tried desperately to think of how to bring the situation back under control. He asked the Sergeant of Police to tell the local police that it was of great importance to have Maggie brought back 'for the sake of decency and morality, as well as for the good of the little community of the Blacks who reside here'. He thought the law was on his side:

> Henry Albert is a _pure_ half-caste and is therefore not an 'Aboriginal' within the meaning of the Act, but a _white_ man. Now no white man can

'harbour or engage', far less elope with, an Aboriginal within the meaning of the Act without becoming amenable to the law.

The police suggested that a warrant be issued for Henry Albert's arrest, but both Stähle and Ernest declined to take such a step. Ernest told the Constable that Maggie had said she was leaving, but not that she was going to another man. He stated that this was the third time Maggie had left him; even if she returned he would not live with her, as she would want to leave again soon.[42] Stähle investigated the possibility of having Maggie charged with desertion from the station, but discovered that under the Act Aboriginals could leave 'at their will', although he could refuse to receive them back.[43]

In the midst of all this, the continuing existence of the Lake Condah station came into question, and internal differences were pushed into the background. In the 1890s the effects of the 'Half-caste Act' were blunted by the prevailing depression, because many of those who had left were granted the right to receive rations temporarily on the stations. With economic recovery in the early 1900s, however, numbers on the stations again began to fall. By late 1906 the combined population of the stations was only 275. The Board had already closed the stations at Framlingham and Ebenezer, and in 1907 it announced that it planned to close Lake Condah and Ramahyuck. As at Framlingham in the late 1880s, local pressure and Board plans coincided to promote the closure of Lake Condah. Local whites petitioned the Minister of Lands asking for the resumption of 1000 acres to be leased out in small farms. The Board was also interested in closing stations as the next stage of its long-term plan to close all except Lake Tyers. Lake Condah Aboriginals fought hard to thwart the Board's plans, and in this campaign Ernest Mobourne played a leading role.

Ernest wrote to Mr Campbell MLA on behalf of the Condah Aboriginals. He said that they had seen in the *Portland Guardian* that the Cabinet had decided to do away with some of the mission stations, including their own. He asked Campbell to present the Cabinet with a petition asking the government to reconsider its decision.[44] The petition listed the improvements the residents had undertaken, and mentioned their belief that they were told when they moved to the mission that the place would be theirs for 'their children's children'. It would be 'heart breaking' to be forced to leave:

> They [our fathers] with their loved missionary Mr Stähle whose labours have blessed and who is still with us, then put their minds and hands together fencing in the whole reserve with a good substantial fence, clearing it and have built stone and wooden cottages for our use, a fine church wherein to worship God, a Mission House for their much loved Missionary.

At the same time Ernest, on behalf of the Aboriginal community, wrote an appeal to the 'Ratepayers' of the district asking for their help. Again he emphasised the work the residents had done, and pointed out that the Chief Secretary, Sir Alexander Peacock, had promised them that the station would not be closed while he was in office. From 'the first' they had all understood that the station 'was granted to us by our late most gracious sovereign Queen Victoria, our mother, to let us live and die here'.[45]

The 'ratepayers' responded immediately, and 348 people signed the petition asking the Governor in Council to reconsider the decision to close Condah.[46] The Condah residents' wish to stay was aired in the Melbourne newspapers. It was concentrated lobbying, and the strength of the protest saved the station. Ramahyuck was closed, but Lake Condah was allowed to continue for the time being. 'Ratepayers' who supported the cause were thanked in writing. Years later Henry Pottage told of the appreciative letter he had received: 'We read your kind letter in the paper and we now wish to send you our best thanks for your help and kindness'.[47]

Maggie returned to the station, and to Ernest, in December 1910. She was warned that if she was not obedient the Order in Council used to remove her to Lake Tyers in 1900 would again be used. Stähle was soon complaining of her behaviour, but he had second thoughts about stopping her rations; if he were to do so, he wrote, 'her husband would at once complain to the Premier for he boasts ... that the Premier and he correspond with each other'.[48] The Board, however, made its position quite clear. A Board official wrote on the letter, 'This doesn't affect the principle and he can rely on the Minister supporting his authority in any case of want of discipline'.

In April 1911 Maggie again left the station and went away with Henry Albert. Late in September she returned to her husband, and Stähle reported that she was 'thoroughly ashamed and deeply sorry for her past conduct'.[49]

By August 1912, however, the conflict between Maggie and the station staff had resumed. On 10 August Stähle wrote to tell the Board of an incident that had aroused such intensity of feeling that he admitted his family had shut the door of their house in Maggie's face and left her screaming of her ill-treatment to everyone as she walked back home across the mission. He claimed Maggie had behaved 'outrageously' to Miss Bagnall, the school-teacher, and as a consequence he had stopped her rations. He asked if the previous Order in Council was still in force and could be used again to remove the Mobournes. Two days later Stähle reported that he wanted to remove Maggie alone, because Ernest had said that there was no reason why he should be punished.

Maggie sought the advice of a solicitor and wrote to Stähle:

I am instructed by my solicitor to tell you that it was Miss Bagnall who used the abusive words first.

I am obliged to write to you as you told me not to put my foot near the Mission House and besides you stopped my rations from the day this occurred.[50]

Miss Bagnall supplied an official version of the incident. There had been an exchange in which Maggie, feeling she was under attack, had called Miss Bagnall 'a two-faced crawler'. Miss Bagnall had looked at Maggie, who was holding a baby fathered by Henry

THE LAKE CONDAH ABORIGINAL MISSION GROUNDS ACROSS WHICH MAGGIE
MOBOURNE WALKED TELLING EVERYONE WHAT SHE THOUGHT OF MISS BAGNALL
AND OF THE REVEREND STÄHLE. THE HUTS IN WHICH THE ABORIGINAL FAMILIES
LIVED CAN BE SEEN AT BACK AND LEFT. THE MISSIONARY'S HOUSE IS PROBABLY THE
ONE IN THE DISTANCE ON THE RIGHT

Albert, and retorted, 'Do I hold in my arms what you have there?'
At this, Maggie became 'like a wild hyena', using abusive language
and ordering her out of the house.

Maggie supplied her own version of the clash. She apologised
to Stähle for her behaviour, but explained that she had been very
upset by Miss Bagnall, who had said, 'You're a vile creature. Thank
God I haven't got what you got in your arms.'

Stähle told the Board he had refused to accept Maggie's
apology, because he felt she was still claiming that she was in the
right and Miss Bagnall in the wrong. Miss Bagnall, he told the
Board, says what she thinks 'openly and without reserve'. This was
why she was disliked by Maggie and others. Maggie's conduct was

so very offensive and aggravating in that she broke out just after the
newcomers had settled down ... shouting at the top of her voice she

*invited all the people to come and see 'this double-faced crawler' and
'ugly beast' etc. and there was nothing for it but to keep our family
inside and shut the door on her ... It is my duty to protect members of
my family and household against assaults of that kind.*

Stähle told the Board that he would give supplies to Ernest for
Maggie, but would not allow her to come to the store or Mission
House until she apologised for her 'offensive conduct' to Miss
Bagnall.

For once, surprisingly, the Board sided with Maggie:

*With regard to the correspondence relating to Mrs Maggie Mobourne, it
seems to me that she has furnished as much apology as can reasonably
be expected from her, considering the provocation Miss Bagnall admits
to having given her. The embargo placed on her should be removed and
she should be warned to control her tongue in future.*[51]

Stähle refused. If he was forced to remove the embargo on her, he
told the Board, he would tender his resignation as manager,
retaining only the position as resident missionary. But he asked the
Board to make a full inquiry into the case before he did so. He

enclosed a statement from his daughter about a further incident in which she and Mrs Stähle had gone to the Mobournes' house to dress an injury on Ernest's hand, only to be abused by Maggie:

> Maggie ... started to scream at us as she did at Miss Bagnall before, saying 'that man' referring to my father 'was feeding her on wind and that he was no Christian. She did not want anything from him or the Board either. They were all alike. She would get Henry Albert to keep her and his child ... He had given her two children and could give her more and keep them. You people at the house fatten yourselves on everything and we have to go without. Clear out of my house,' she screamed at both of us ... Janet Turner (her mother) and Ernest Mobourne (her husband) and Harry Rose, were all in the house at the time. Each of them told her she was mad and tried to stop her, but she would not listen to them.[52]

It was time to act, the Board decided. Maggie must be reminded of the Order in Council and asked to provide 'evidence of regret ... satisfactory to you' and 'on doing so' should be restored to the same position as the other residents on the station. If she refused, the Order in Council would be used to remove her: 'Those who are not obedient and respectful must be punished'.[53]

Stähle read the letter to Maggie in Ernest's presence, and about an hour later they both came to apologise. They also told Stähle that they were going to leave the station. This meant, he said, that matters would no longer be in his hands: it was a matter for the Board. He immediately wrote to the Board pointing out that their daughter, Ethel, who was twelve years of age and attending school, should not be allowed to leave the station with them. He asked permission to call the police to bring her back if they tried to take her. 'I must say that these educated blacks are much more difficult to deal with than the old blacks were', he confided to the Board.[54]

The Board issued an instruction that Ethel Mobourne was not to be removed from the station and, if taken, must be brought back.

For the moment the Mobournes stayed at Lake Condah. Maggie 'apologised for her rudeness', but Stähle reported she showed 'a more bitter spirit than before'. She refused to attend devotional meetings or come for her rations as the other women did. On 8 October 1912 Stähle reported to the Board that Ernest had been told he would only be given rations for himself and the child; if Maggie wanted rations, she must come for them. On the first day he tried to implement this policy, there was a scene. When Ernest was refused rations for Maggie, he 'threatened before all the women that if his wife could not get her rations he would go at once for the police to get them'. Stähle's son reminded him that her rations were there, but she had to come to get them. Ernest then went home, and soon afterwards Maggie came to the store, but was very difficult to handle. Then Ernest asked that the doctor be called, because the baby was sick. Stähle wrote: 'I had to tell him that it was a matter for me to decide and not for him, whether a Doctor was required or not'.

Stähle now used his second-last card. He alleged that everyone on the station knew that Maggie was regularly going over to Dunmore to see Henry Albert. Something must be done about it, Stähle announced:

> *Otherwise these people will get beyond all control for they are weak and unstable and one rebellious person among them can do an untold amount of mischief within a short time . . .*
>
> *I am distressed about this woman for her conduct and example cannot fail to have an evil influence over the natives on the station.*[55]

On 24 October he played his trump card, again threatening to abandon his position if Maggie was not removed. He could no longer allow his wife 'to be open to such continual insults', he said. If the Board would not act, 'I cannot possibly manage these people'. The BPA sent a letter, which was read to Ernest on 31 October, whereupon Ernest promised that he and his wife would be better behaved. They had just written to His Excellency, Sir John Fuller, Governor of Victoria, asking for his help to prevent them from being removed from their home. Fuller appears to have intervened, as there was no further talk of invoking the Order in Council for some time.

In mid-1913 Maggie told Stähle that she was leaving the station to live with Henry Albert. Henry was living 'at the foot of the station in a hut which Mr Dashper gave him leave to occupy'. Stähle, eager to have her removed to Lake Tyers, pointed out to the Board that the hut had only one room, and living in it were:

Henry Albert	*48*
Beattie Albert	*21*
Paddy Albert	*19*
Wallace Albert	*12*
Sallie Albert	*10*
Maggie Mobourne	*38*
Dorothy Albert	*1 yr 6 mths*

He asked the Board, 'Could not Henry Albert be summoned for harbouring Maggie Mobourne, full black and ward of the state?'[56]

In November Maggie again wrote, this time saying that she intended to live with Ernest and asking for permission to return. By this time Stähle had retired, and his successor, Sydney Crawford, supported her application. Maggie returned, but in December she again left to be with Henry Albert. Henry wrote to Mr Crawford explaining that Maggie had only returned to the station while he was away shearing. He was now back and she had come to him 'for protection which she has often found and always will'.[57] He also referred to a child on the way. Crawford felt powerless to intervene:

> Is there no law to reach this man, as he seems to have this woman completely under his control. The police appear to be quite helpless, as they state they cannot arrest him for harbouring her, as he tells them he is not detaining her from leaving him, but that she will not go.[58]

On 2 January 1914 the Board decided that the Order in Council was to be used for the second time: Maggie was to be removed to Lake Tyers. A day later the Chief Commissioner of Police in Melbourne

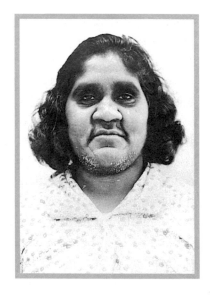

TOP LEFT: ERNEST MOBOURNE IN HIS OLDER YEARS
TOP RIGHT: ETHEL HOOD (NÉE MOBOURNE) AGED 38. PHOTO TAKEN AT LAKE TYERS
IN 1939
ABOVE LEFT: ETHEL HOOD (NÉE MOBOURNE), ORGANIST AND NIGHT NURSE,
IN HER LATER YEARS OUTSIDE LAKE TYERS CHURCH
ABOVE RIGHT: DOLLY STEVENS (NÉE MOBOURNE) AGED 27. PHOTO TAKEN AT
LAKE TYERS IN 1939

was given instructions to arrange for Maggie to be taken to Lake Tyers as soon as possible. Ernest made it clear that he didn't want to go with her.

Maggie arrived at Lake Tyers with her daughter Dolly on 14 January. Barely a month later, Ernest wrote to John Murray MLA complaining about the treatment his wife received at Lake Tyers and asking for help to get Maggie and Dolly back home again. The Board followed this up, but decided to do nothing. A note put on the letter by a Board official stated that Maggie seemed satisfied at Lake Tyers, as she had made no complaints.

In August Ernest requested that he and his daughter Ethel be allowed to join Maggie at Lake Tyers. Permission was given, but it was obvious that the family was intent on returning to Lake Condah. Maggie wrote to the Board asking to be permitted to visit her mother, who was not well. The Board checked and found that her mother was in good health; Maggie, it ruled, should stay where she was. In October Ernest wrote to the Board asking when he could return to Condah. He had believed he was visiting Lake Tyers for about three months. He explained that as he was leaving, 'Captain Crawford says to me, Ernest—when are you coming back and I answered him in three months time, allright says he and bring Maggie with you after you have made it up together'. 'Now', he continued, 'I will ask the Board why should I be forced to remain here'. The Board replied to the manager of Lake Tyers that there was 'no fixed term of residence' for Ernest, but that they thought he should stay where he was for the moment.

By May 1915 Ernest had decided to try again for their return to Lake Condah. He wrote to Mr Murray, who was then Chief Secretary, asking how long his wife was to be kept under the Order in Council and pointing out that others removed by Order in Council had already returned to Lake Condah: 'I consider this is not fair to her or me either. Can't you give her a chance again for the sake of her poor mother who is far advanced in years for she writes always to us to come home.'[59] In November Maggie wrote to Mr Murray asking if she could return home for Christmas: 'I think

BOARD
FOR THE PROTECTION OF
ABORIGINES
Melbourne
892

July 27/1916

Dear daughter

I am very pleased to say I am well. also all the people here at present and trust my letter will find you and dear dad and littlesister dollie well so will close with kind regards to all enquiring friends tell dad to come for me as I am so restless here and don't forget to say your prayers also dollie and pray for our dear ones whereever you are

I am yr loving Mother

Maggie Mobourne

To Miss Ethel Mobourne
Lakes Entrance
Cunninghame P.O.

MAGGIE MOBOURNE WRITES TO HER DAUGHTER ETHEL FROM THE HOSPITAL FOR
THE INSANE, MELBOURNE, 27 JULY 1916

I have behaved myself during the two years I have been here', she asserted.[60] Finally Ernest wrote to the Governor of Victoria, his strong words indicating the couple's growing sense of despair:

> Why are we kept prisoners here and not permitted to return to our friends and our home? This country is free and we understand we are under the British flag, but it seems we [are] slaves in [the BPA secretary] Mr Ditchburn's sight.[61]

Things were unravelling for the Mobournes. On 18 November 1915 Henry Albert married Jessie Lancaster at Framlingham.[62] In July 1916 Maggie was admitted to the Yarra Bend Asylum suffering from 'religious delusions accompanied by insane excitement'. It appears that she had killed Henry Albert's dog, which she had taken to Lake Tyers with her. Ernest wrote asking that Maggie's mother be allowed to come to Lake Tyers, and permission was given. On 27 July Maggie wrote from hospital to her daughter Ethel, 'tell dad to come for me as I am so restless'. Ernest's response was immediate. The manager had difficulty preventing him leaving for Melbourne on the spot; eventually he was persuaded to wait while the manager sought a progress report on Maggie's condition. The response was good news: Maggie was much better. The hospital was arranging for her to leave on probation.

On 26 August she was back at Lake Tyers and her mother was there to help her. Greene, the manager at Lake Tyers, tried to have her removed again, claiming that he could not be responsible for her and that she was likely to injure Dolly or her husband. For a brief time it appeared that Maggie might be indefinitely confined in an asylum. Fortunately the Board asked the advice of the Inspector General of the Hospital, who was adamant that there was nothing wrong with Maggie and insisted that he had no reservations about this. The Board accepted the advice and wrote back to Greene that 'after discussing the case with the Inspector General of the Insane, the Vice-Chairman is satisfied if you are unable to manage Mrs Mobourne, you thereby demonstrate your inefficiency for the position you hold'.

Ernest kept on trying to obtain their return to Lake Condah. He reminded Maurice Blackman MLA that a letter had been written to the Board on the Mobournes' behalf, but there had been no response. Blackman again wrote asking for a reply. It came on 30 January 1917. The Board, totally ignoring the Mobournes' expressed wishes, stated that since Maggie's mother had come to be with them they 'seemed quite content'.

Maggie died two months later, on 30 May 1917, of what was called on the death certificate 'general illness'. She was buried in the Lake Tyers Aboriginal Cemetery.[63] After her death Ernest sought permission to return home to Lake Condah, but his request for passes for himself and the two girls was refused. Ernest must have felt absolutely powerless at not being free to return home even after Maggie's death. He died on 16 May 1918 and was buried in the Bairnsdale Cemetery.[64]

Ann Bon, a great friend to Aboriginals, who was a member of the BPA from 1904 to 1936 and was reprimanded on three occasions for disloyalty to the Board because she complained to the Minister about the injustice and hardship caused to Aboriginals by Board decisions, wrote in an unofficial letter to Mr Bowser of the BPA:

> *Ernest was a leader in his own community [Lake Tyers] during the*
> *management of Howe and Greene who neither could nor would try to*
> *pray—Ernest became their priest by conducting Sunday and perhaps*
> *week-day services his daughter Ethel acting as organist.*
>
> *How sad to think such a valuable life was shortened by neglect. He*
> *went to hospital stayed <u>one</u> day—came home—remained a week prob-*
> *ably [with] lack of attention—he goes back to hospital and in two days*
> *died and was buried away from his wife and relatives—such a blot on*
> *our escutcheon! I want a copy of the certificate of his death.*

Ernest's days of protesting and fighting were over. He would hardly have endorsed the praise of the Stähles with which Ann Bon concluded her letter:

> *Any well-behaved superior Aborigines you meet at Tyers hailed from*
> *Condah and were instructed in religion by Mr and Mrs Stähle.*[65]

The official records contain one further letter about Ernest. It is a reply to Mrs Bon, who appears to have asked for the right to exhume Ernest's body and have it taken back to Lake Condah:

I have to inform you that ... under existing law a body must remain where originally buried for 12 months before being exhumed. The Board cannot therefore take any further action in the matter of exhumation until that period has expired.[66]

Stähle knew full well how great was the punishment he had inflicted on the Mobournes by banishing them. In 1907, when he was arguing with the Board that the Lake Condah station should not be closed, he wrote:

My thirty-five years' experience is, that although natives like to go away for a change, they invariably return after a while to their own home, and those who had once or twice to be sent away for correction and for the good of the little community, were never at rest until permission was given to them to return.[67]

Yet he did nothing to help the Mobournes return home.

Maggie was by no means the only Condah resident of whom Stähle complained to the Board. Nor were the Mobournes the only Aboriginals to be removed by Order in Council. Why the Mobournes stand out is that they fought back so strongly all through their married life. Even when they were having personal differences, Ernest sprang to Maggie's defence and did his best to help her against the tyranny of the Board and its officials. In this they were truly remarkable. The Mobournes' official file includes their letters to Members of Parliament, the Chief Secretary, the Premier and the Governor, as well as to the BPA. It is a considerable collection, providing testimony of their ability to make their voice heard at the highest levels in the State. Their failure to gain permission to return home demonstrates the power of the Board and its insistence on imposing its own agendas, regardless of the wishes of the Aboriginal people it had been appointed to protect.

CHAPTER 10

'The old ones, they wouldn't tell us nothing'

MRS CONNIE HART'S MEMORIES

Mrs Connie Hart (née Alberts), born in 1917, was one of the oldest Gunditjmara Elders when I interviewed her in June 1993. Her mother grew up on the Lake Condah mission and became personal maid to Mrs Stähle. Her father, Angus Alberts, was the son of Henry Albert (or Alberts)* and Rachel Dawson. After finishing school at fourteen, Connie helped her father and brothers in their rabbiting business for two years, then for forty years she joined the white workforce:

She constantly held jobs first as a housemaid and cook on large Western District properties such as Weerite and Hexham Station. Then 'after looking Melbourne over a few times I thought I would work there', she says. So during World War II she lived in a flat in Fitzroy and worked in a munitions factory. Later she was a wardsmaid in St. James ward at St. Vincent's Hospital and finally worked for 25 years making shoes in Dummett's Shoes factory in Fitzroy.[1]

A friendly, outgoing person, Connie died shortly after this interview. She left a wonderful legacy for anyone interested in Koori

---

* Apparently at this time the surname was spelt Albert as opposed to Alberts. Henry signed as Henry Albert when he married Jessie Lancaster in 1915, but the surname used by the hospital where he died was Alberts.

culture: a large collection of grass baskets made in the traditional style. She began making these late in life. After her mother died in 1983, she wondered if she could make the baskets she had watched being made as a child. I remember when she made her first baskets, small ones to see if she could do it. Then, as her confidence grew, she tackled much larger tasks. Her work has been collected by several institutions, including the Koorie Heritage Trust.*

I interviewed Connie on 26 June 1993 and began by asking about her grandfather Henry Alberts, son of Jeanie (Jennie) Green and an unknown father. Henry was born about 1860, several years before the Lake Condah and Framlingham Aboriginal stations were established.

Jan:

Connie, you have memories of your grandfather. Where was he living at the time?

Connie:

More or less at Framlingham, because we used to go and stay there and go to school while Dad was shearing up there, and he [Grandfather Henry] used to preach, have service in the Church—have service in his house in the mornings, then over to the Church and have service in the morning, back home, then back again in the afternoon. This was all happening on Sundays.

---

* The Koorie Heritage Trust Inc. collection will be on display at its new centre at 35–41 Lonsdale Street, Melbourne, from March 1999.

Jan:

Which church was this?

Connie:

It was the church that is up there now on the Framlingham mission. It's only a little church.

Jan:

Who was he living with? His wife Jessie?* I think you said once before that your sister Louie lived with them also.

Connie:

Yes, she was the favourite, Louie. She is younger than me.

A daughter of the Soil.

JENNY GREEN SMOKING HER PIPE

Jan:

Did she live with them for any length of time, or just for holidays?

Connie:

Holidays and that . . . but she was spoilt. They spoilt her.

Jan:

I'm wondering what kind of house they had.

Connie:

It was a weatherboard house. That photo you had of them standing outside a house the last time you came here, remember? That's the type of house, a weatherboard one.

Jan:

What do you remember of Jessie?

Connie:

Well, she was elderly when I knew her. She'd never come out of the room. She'd sit in there and make her baskets and she was stout, very big. But she was a kind-hearted woman. She used to play a concertina

---

* Henry's second wife was Jessie Lancaster. When they married on 18 November 1915, he gave his age as fifty-three and she gave hers as fifty: Marriage Certificate no. 11908/1915.

THE ALBERTS WERE CLOSE FRIENDS OF LIZZIE AND HENRY McCRAE
(SEE CHAPTER 5). HERE LIZZIE McCRAE (REAR LEFT) IS PHOTOGRAPHED WITH
HENRY ALBERTS (HEAD CUT OFF); IN FRONT, JOSEPH (JO) ALBERTS, JESSIE
(HENRY'S SECOND WIFE), AND HIS GRANDDAUGHTER LOUIE ALBERTS. JO WAS
CONNIE HART'S 'FIRST COUSIN AND GREAT FRIEND', AND LOUIE HER SISTER.
THE HOUSE IS TYPICAL OF HOUSING AT FRAMLINGHAM IN THE LATE 1920S

for the church services and that like, in the house—for Sunday School
for us. She was a quiet-living person.

Jan:
*Returning to the baskets—she would have been making them with
the Framlingham grasses and making them the way they do at
Framlingham rather than the way you do?*

Connie:
Yes, the Framlingham grass, the flat grass, what they call walritch.
She used to make lovely strong baskets.

Jan:

Have you any favourite memories of your grandfather?

Connie:

Oh, yes. He was a churchgoer and all that, but he was very strict with us kids. He wouldn't let us touch a tennis ball on Sunday—we wasn't allowed to play with it or anything like that, because he was that strong—religion. Then he had to go to a nursing home and that's where he passed away 'cause he was more or less going off his head through the religion.

Jan:

Had Jessie died by this time?

Connie:

She'd died. She'd gone. Yes, he was on his own. Granny Jessie died before him.

Jan:

Did he live alone, or did he live in another household after she died?

Connie:

No, he still lived there at that house and he had a daughter. She was looking after him. There were two girls, Sally and Beattie. But Auntie Effie had already gone over to Lake Tyers. Only had those three girls.

Jan:

Did he ever tell stories of Peter Hewitt?*

Connie:

No, he never told us nothing but my father did, 'cause Dad used to go amongst and see all the old people on the Lake Condah Mission. I knew Peter Hewitt because he cracked me with the walking stick! [She laughs at the memory.]

I was only a young girl, you know. I was going to school—I'd probably be about just a little after seven, because I started at seven

---

* Peter Hewitt was a Lake Condah Elder noted for his knowledge of the traditional customs and language of his people.

years of age—and the mission manager's house on the mission at Lake Condah, he lived there see, by himself, in this big house.[2]

Jan:

Can I just intervene there? I talked to Amy Lowe about this, too. Amy said your mother took her to visit the house that Peter Hewitt used to live in. You'd said you thought it was the mission manager's house, but Amy said it was a bluestone house, she could remember it quite clearly. She took some of the bluestone home with her because it was from the house that Peter Hewitt lived in [Connie laughs], but she said she didn't think it would have been the mission manager's house as it wasn't big enough.*

Connie:

No, that was it. Yes, it was quite big inside and where they had the study they had a few steps going down, see, before you get into the drawing room, what they called the drawing room, and old Peter Hewitt was in the front and he had his walking stick and then came the rest of us behind him. There was my mum, my dad and a few of my brothers and sisters. He started to sing in his language, an Aboriginal native song, and I started to mock him. I didn't know one word he was saying, but I was mumbling away behind him and he just reached around [without looking] and cracked me hard on the arm, so I never liked him after that. I was really glad when he died [she laughs] and followed his body up to the cemetery. I never went in that house again while he was there. He was a little old man and he had a long beard on him, grey hair, but he was a witchdoctor, see.

Jan:

You said that on the day of his funeral an old horse and buggy was used to take him to the cemetery.

Connie:

Yes, a dray, old horse and cart taking the body up to the cemetery, everyone walking behind it. I must have been the proudest one there, walking up behind. [She laughs.]

---

* Amy, daughter of Mrs Mary Clarke and sister to Banjo Clarke, was a contemporary of Connie's. Good friends, they had gone to the Purnim school together at times when Connie had stayed on the Framlingham mission.

Jan:

What do you mean, proud?

Connie:

Because he hit me, see. I didn't like him. Poor old Peter. Yes, he's buried in the Lake Condah cemetery.

Jan:

You've also previously told me about how he used to go ahead of people, that he'd tell people he would see them when they arrived at an occasion that they were going to, such as the football, and they would wonder how he was going to do it. And he would be there just as he said he was going to be.

Connie:

He'd send them. He'd say, 'Don't wait for me.' He'd say, 'All you others go ahead,' he said, 'I'll be there before you.' He used to turn himself into a big bird, they used to say, and it was called a gungul.* He'd turn himself into this big eagle and he'd fly, and he'd be sitting on the log there when they got to the football ground. Dad often talked about him. He'd be there before them.

Jan:

I asked Amy if she remembered Peter Hewitt and she said yes, she had seen him at Framlingham, and I said, 'How did he get there?' She said, 'He flew!' I said, 'How do you know he flew?' She replied, 'I saw him come.' I said, 'What did he look like?' She answered, 'A bird, it could be an eagle, a duck or even a big dark cloud.' She said he could come as a cloud!

Connie:

Yes, he moved around. He got to places. Yes, just like that, that's what he done. He told them all to get ahead to the football ground and he'll be there before them and he did too.

Jan:

Would he be the last of the people to have those special skills and the knowledge?

---

* Connie had never seen this word recorded in written form; she sounded it as 'goongle'.

Connie:

Yes, he was. They were all like that at the mission: they handed nothing to us. What we wanted to know we had to learn.

Jan:

Why do you think that was?

Connie:

Well, as my mother told me, coming into the white people's way of living you must forget, forget everything. But Dad went right in amongst them all—and he didn't live on the mission—and he learnt a lot more than what my mother did from them, yet she was born on the mission. Dad would go right in amongst those old people and that's what I tried to do when I grew up, go in amongst them and sit and listen to them and learnt the basket weaving. The only way I could learn was to just sit and watch them and don't ask any questions. They wouldn't tell me, no, not a thing.

Jan:

And yet it's not that long ago, is it? You remember your grandfather Henry Alberts and Peter Hewitt, and you've heard the language of your own people being spoken, haven't you?

Connie:

Yes, that's right. They used to talk it all the time and you'd want to know what it meant. No way would they tell you, see. Oh yes, I've gone right back to those old people.

Jan:

How many people do you think there would have been in your lifetime that could still speak the language?

Connie:

Oh they spoke it right up. There was an old couple there, they were real full-blood Aboriginals. They were tall, thin people and they used to wear the red dotted scarf around their neck—those old red dotted scarves they used to get from the government, like a big handkerchief—and they would wear that around their neck and they used to smoke the white clay pipes and they were very tall people. There was another family on the mission there, too—they were still living in those houses at the mission, some of them.

Jan:

How old would you have been at the time? That's probably our best way of pinning down the date.

Connie:

I must have been seven or eight, just started school.

Jan:

And you're almost seventy-six now?

Connie:

Yes, in October. I started when I was seven years of age. I was born in 1917. I started seven years on from then and finished when I was fourteen ...

Jan:

So you remember them speaking their language on the mission in 1924–25?

Connie:

Yes, they spoke it right up, and yet they wouldn't teach us.

Jan:

It's less than seventy years ago. So close—it seems so bad to have lost the language when it was so close to surviving as a living language.

Connie:

I am so close to it! See, they wouldn't tell me. If they'd told me I'd have kept it in my mind. Dad tried to tell us things but Mum, she was down on us. She'd say, 'No, you're not learning nothing!' She wouldn't because she was born on the mission, see, she's gone through it all. She was the personal maid to Mrs Stähle ... I suppose she was sick of it, sick of the mission like, because they were strict, they were brought up strict—too strict, I reckon. Yes, she was the personal maid to Mrs Stähle ... You know, every time Mrs Stähle rang the bell she had to go attend to her, whatever she wanted done—the strokes of her hair with the brush and all that sort of nonsense. I tell you, they wouldn't get any of the young ones today to do that, and that's why Mum was down on us, us kids, wouldn't tell us nothing. We had to learn, so I learnt the hard way with the [basket] weaving.

Even with the Framlingham Aboriginals from up there, the old ones, they wouldn't tell us nothing. Those people up there now, the young ones, they don't know nothing. You can ask them things and they won't tell you because they don't know. They never been taught. I think if we'd had a teacher coming into the school teaching us the Aboriginal language we would've been better off, but no, not them. Yet my father picked it up, and he wasn't born on the mission. He was a half-caste.

Jan:

Why do you think he managed to learn things?

Connie:

He used to go over to the mission—in his time there he'd go amongst the old people and they used to talk to him and tell him everything. He learnt. That's what I was trying to do, too, when I grew up. I wasn't taught as much as what he was. He was taught everything. How they took the kidney fat and all that sort of thing. Yes, he knew the lot. Dad was good.

Jan:

Yes, you've told me one of your father's stories about Peter Hewitt and the taking of kidney fat. Will you tell me again?

Connie:

Yes. He sat down by a little fire, see, just a little fire to make the smoke, way over in the forest on the side of the hill, in the mission station but across the swamp. This bloke he was after was on a horse out in the paddock. He sang his native song, his Aboriginal song, and made the smoke and brushed the smoke now and again. And this fellow came right up to him on his horse, and his horse stood over the fire, this little weeny fire, and that's when he got him. He just fell off the horse, and

Peter Hewitt he done his job with the bones and that—bruised his kidney and made a hole and scraped the fat out—and just gave him two weeks to live. And that's all he lived. Two weeks and he was gone.

Jan:
Was it a white man that he did this to?

Connie:
No, an Aboriginal bloke.

Jan:
Do you know the reason?

Connie:
No. I think he might have been on with one of the women, see. That's what they were down on. So Peter Hewitt put him away—he was no good. I guess there's a lot up in that cemetery been done like that. They had their rules and they kept their rules . . .

Jan:
Do you know if Peter Hewitt had a wife and children?

Connie:
I suppose he'd have a lot of wives, Peter Hewitt . . .

Jan:
And this kidney fatting went on right up into your generation, because you were telling me about your brother and the problem he had.

Connie:
Yes, over in South Australia, I think it was Point Pearce or Point McLeay. He went over there, and of course, being a stranger on the mission, they got him too, and he went to Adelaide Hospital. My mum told them to have a look at his kidneys. 'If it's bruised,' she said, 'he's been done.' So they did, too, and he come all right. They got him in time, the white doctors. Oh yes, they could do it, and I believe they can still do it too. Yes. It was their way of killing, murdering people, and they had their way of making them better. They had their own ways, their own cures.

Jan:

Have you heard any stories of how they made people get better?

Connie:

No, not really. All those medicines, you know, from out in the bush and that, that's the only way they made them better. But they were determined people, very determined, the old people. I wish I had learnt more, but they wouldn't tell me. I was interested in it, but the old people must have thought, You're smart, you're not going to learn anything. They got down on me.

Jan:

Henry Alberts would have had to move off the Aboriginal stations after the passing of the Half-Caste Act in 1886 and support himself. Do you know where he worked and what kind of work he did?

Connie:

He lived over at Little Dunmore. That's where Dad and them lived. My father went to school there in the bush. There was a little school there.

Jan:

Where was Little Dunmore and what was there?

Connie:

It's part of the mission. A lot of houses were built for them over there. There was bluestone and lime and weatherboards, mostly weatherboards. There must have been about seven or eight houses over there for the people from the mission to go there. That's where I was born, at Little Dunmore.

Jan:

Where is it in relation to the present buildings at Lake Condah?

Connie:

Sitting in the lounge, the recreation room, you can look out straight across the stones [towards the Princes Highway and the sea]. That's where Little Dunmore is, on the other side of the stones. Across those stones is Little Dunmore, all clear country. You cross the creek. There

used to be a bridge over the creek, but the flood took it. Grandfather
Alberts used to live there too ... That's three-and-a-half miles across
there. That's what we had to do, to walk that three-and-a-half miles to
school and three-and-a-half miles back. It didn't seem far to us,
because there was about forty children at school but there must have
been about twenty or more of us going from Dunmore and other places
across there. Every time anybody went, gone ahead, they'd stick a fern
in the post to let us know that person had gone ...

Jan:
What about Henry? How did he support himself?

Connie:
He probably would have went rabbiting or stone crushing or working
on the roads. All that stuff they done.

Jan:
*Are there any stories in the family of a pastoral property that he may
have worked on, perhaps shearing?*

Connie:
It would be all the farms around them, the big sheep stations. My dad
was a shearer, and a brother of mine was a shearer. He worked all up
round Mortlake, Hamilton, Branxholme, all round there, shearing for
the farmers. He was a good shearer. One of my brothers took it up—
Angus—but the other one, Roderick, he was just a rouseabout ...

Jan:
*He's the one who had the problem with the kidney fatters. What was his
nickname?*

Connie:
Mookeye. Mookeye was his nickname. That stuck to him till he died,
too. He died in Ballarat in a nursing home. I'm the only one left, but I
wished I'd known more, because I'd have kept it in my head. Because I
was interested in the Aboriginal people, the old ones. I really was, but
they seem to look through me and send me off to play with the other
kids. [She laughs light-heartedly, but is serious in her regret that more

was not shared with her.] And that's what happened up at Framlingham now, all the girls up that way. They've never been taught nothing, not a thing.

Jan:

Sad, really, isn't it, as there is such growing interest in it all. Everyone wants to know and there's nobody left to teach them the language. They're trying to set up language classes down at the Gunditjmara Co-op. If only the language was still being spoken it would be so much easier.

Connie:

You go to other States, they all know, they can talk their language good as anything. All the young ones. But us Victorians, we know nothing about the language.

Jan:

Back to Jessie—did she have children from an earlier marriage?

Connie:

No, I don't think she did. She had an earlier marriage beside Grandfather Alberts. I never seen any or heard of any. But her sister who married the Couzens had family . . . They married just for company, those old people. All been married twice or more . . .

I remember the old black plug tobacco they got. I used to see my dad chopping it up, rubbing it in his hands and filling his pipe up with it. They got—what they got?—they didn't get much. Golden syrup, treacle and all that sort of stuff. Brown sugar. I don't reckon they were ever looked after properly. And as they died out at the mission station, the older people, that was it. It just played right into the government's hands—close it down, instead of letting the young ones stay there and keep it going. It would have been OK.

Jan:

It's quite clear in the records that they believed the race was dying out, and that was something which they would take into account and make plans for, so that finally there'd be no land reserved for Aboriginal use.

Connie:

Yes, and that's what happened over here at Lake Condah. There was a lot of young people willing to stay there and live there. Oh no, it had to go, the government says so. But that could have been in full swing all the time. They've got [some of the old mission land] back now. People are living there . . .

Jan:

Did Grandfather Alberts have an Aboriginal name?

Connie:

No, he never had an Aboriginal name because that name he had, Alberts, that come from a big station home where these people took him when he was only a little boy, and they gave him Alberts. Whether it was the station what he was on, their name, I don't know, but it must have been, because I can't find any other Alberts. There must have been a family with the name Alberts around the district.

There must have been one somewhere round the district and they must be gone. I can't find them at all. I can't find them. Whether he had a brother, whether he had a sister or an aunty, you know, all that sort of thing, there's nothing—nothing of him, just Alberts. So I don't know what they were, foreign people or what. They took him and looked after him and gave him that name . . .

I haven't discovered the answer to Connie's question about where the name Alberts comes from, but I have found that in their youth Henry Albert and Rachel Dawson fell in love and were so determined to be together that they eloped from Framlingham mission.

AN ELOPEMENT AT FRAMLINGHAM

RACHEL DAWSON AND HENRY ALBERT

On the night of 3 February 1885, while her mother was visiting a dying relative at Condah, Rachel Dawson eloped with Henry Albert. She was seventeen.[3]

They had made their plans carefully. They would leave Framlingham Aboriginal Station in the evening, then make their way by train to Ballarat, where they would be married before anyone could intervene.

It was an unusual and brave thing to do, but Henry and Rachel could see no alternative. Rachel's mother, Sarah, had refused them permission to marry. She wanted Rachel to wait until she was at least a year older. When the lovers persisted in seeing each other, Rachel was 'severely chastised' by her mother on several occasions. Rachel's friends told the Reverend Robert Thwaites, who was temporarily managing Framlingham, that after the last beating she had told them she intended to run away from home.

All this came as a surprise to Thwaites, who was aware of the couple's desire to marry and had no objection. He regarded Henry as 'steady and industrious', 'very attached to Rachel' and believed he would make her 'a good husband'. He had recently been in Melbourne and had been unaware of Sarah's opposition to the marriage.

Things went as Rachel and Henry had hoped. It wasn't until 9.30 p.m. that Thwaites was told that Rachel appeared to be missing. She had in fact left the station about an hour and a half earlier, and by the time he had checked and found her clothes missing he realised he had no chance of catching the coach to Camperdown, so he made no attempt to follow her.

Thwaites assumed the 'fugitives' were bound for Melbourne and could be intercepted there by someone from the Board for the Protection of the Aborigines. Next morning he sent a telegram to the Board Secretary:

> *Rachel Dawson, half-caste eloped (aged 17) from station last night with Henry Alberts—will arrive Melb. today.*[4]

But the lovers had gone in a different direction. They had booked their seats on the 4.55 a.m. train from Camperdown to Geelong. From Geelong they travelled to Ballarat, where they were married soon after they arrived.

As station manager, Thwaites was responsible for controlling the movement of Aboriginals on and off the station. He now found himself in a dilemma. He wrote to the Board seeking some advice. Did he have the power to compel Henry and Rachel to return, he asked the Board, and would it be wise to do so? Henry Albert belonged to Lake Condah rather than Framlingham. Rachel was nearly eighteen and was his wife.

Central to Thwaites' uncertainty was the new policy the Board was about to introduce. In 1884 the BPA had foreshadowed its intention of forcing 'able-bodied half-castes' to move off the stations and provide for themselves. Though there had been some delay in passing the legislation, the BPA was determined to make the change. In effect, the Board was in the process of redefining who would be officially regarded as Aboriginal. Both Rachel and Henry were 'half-castes' in the Board's view, and would therefore be forced to live off the stations. Was there any sense in pursuing them, the Reverend Thwaites wondered, when shortly he would have to order them to leave? Hence his question about the wisdom of forcing them to return. At the end of his letter he requested the Board to send him a copy of the Act: 'I've never had one and I need it,' he said bluntly.[5]

From being classified as Aboriginal, Henry and Rachel were about to become 'white' by the stroke of a pen. As such, they would be responsible for supporting themselves, and would have no further claim on the government. They were about to be able to go wherever they desired without asking anyone's permission.

Thwaites decided to do nothing. After their honeymoon the young married couple returned to the Lake Condah area, where Henry had work on McCarthy's farm. By June 1885 they were back at Framlingham. Thwaites reported to the Board that Rachel had been sick, and her mother had written to the young couple requesting them to return to Framlingham. The new Act did not become law until 1886, and even then there was a phasing-in period. The couple's first two children were born at Framlingham.[6]

The plight of young 'half-caste' families during the economic depression of the 1890s is well illustrated by reference to the Alberts. The 'times were hard even for white people', let alone for 'half-castes'.[7] When almost one-third of the workforce was unemployed, there was not much casual work on offer for the likes of Henry Albert. At the same time, the screws were being tightened on 'half-castes' at the Aboriginal stations, particularly at Framlingham. Having disestablished the station, the Board wanted to prevent numbers increasing once again. It therefore decided to refuse rations to those who harboured 'half-castes' at Framlingham. Emily Edwards, who was helping the Alberts, was ordered to send them away. But she stood by her Aboriginal principles. Rather than turn her back on her own people, she went without Board rations and clothing, determined to share what she had. Sergeant Akeroyd reported:

> Old Emily Edwards informed me that Alberts was going to work for a man named Bell and that Alberts was then building a house to take his wife to. I told George and Emily that I would have to stop their rations while they kept Mrs. Alberts on the station, both George and Emily said they would not turn Mrs. Alberts and the children out into the cold and I could stop the rations they said they could beg for their living and Mrs Alberts could stop with them until Alberts finished the house. I gave instructions to Mr. Lewis not to allow them any more rations.[8]

Several months later the Alberts sought to obtain Board rations to tide them over for a short time. It was a dangerous thing to do, as soon became clear. Board policy prescribed that 'half-caste' orphans should be removed to the Industrial Schools for what the Board regarded as their own good. Any parent who admitted having difficulty supporting the family was seen as allowing his children to fall into the same category. The Board replied to D. Slattery, who had written on behalf of the Alberts:

> The Board cannot grant rations to Henry Albert and family, as they are half castes, but every assistance will be given to place their children

into the Industrial Schools and get them boarded out to respectable families.[9]

The Alberts kept their children, and made their own way as best they could, with the help of friends and relatives.

Rachel died on 30 August 1905,[10] but Henry lived until 1934, working on properties around the Lake Condah area. He lived off the mission, but maintained contact with the Condah people. His presence near the station and his freedom from the constraints of mission life played a key part in the saga of the Mobournes' struggle with the BPA and the domineering Reverend Stähle.

CHAPTER 11

'Breaking the cycle is the hard thing to do'

A STOLEN CHILD: GEOFF ROSE

1928–1989

GEOFF ROSE PHOTOGRAPHED WHEN HE CAME BACK TO VISIT THE FRAMLINGHAM MISSION IN 1951. THIS WAS THE FIRST TIME HIS PEOPLE HAD SEEN HIM SINCE HE WAS TAKEN AWAY AS A CHILD

About 1935 the welfare authorities took a young boy named Geoff Rose from the Framlingham mission. The events of that day are recalled here by three Koori Elders: a playmate at the time, Henry Alberts, grandson of the first Henry Alberts; Geoff's cousin Maisie Clarke, who lived near by; and Banjo Clarke. Their testimony is followed by that of Mark, Geoff's son, who talks of the consequences of removal for his father's life and his own.[1]

HENRY ALBERTS' STORY

This was out on the mission, out there on the Black Flat, where Geoff Rose was playing as a kid. He had just gone six years old when he was playing in the water beside his hut, where his auntie was inside. I was up with Mum, playing just outside Mum's hut on the 'Island' there, when I was called inside and told to stay there, because there was a car down the road. Then Mum said, 'It's all right now, you can go outside and play now, the car's gone.' When I asked about the car, she said 'No, it's gone.'

That's when there was yelling and screaming going up the road in this old car, you know. Welfare officers had come and just plucked him out of the drain, playing with boats, and put him in the car and just took him away while his auntie was still inside. His name was Geoff Rose. He was about six years old, just gone six anyway. His mother was in Melbourne at the time, working. His auntie was looking after him. He was just my age. We were young school kids, we had just started school, six-year-olds.

Jan:
And eventually you met his son?

Henry:
I did meet Mark—Mark's his son, yeah, Geoff Rose's son. I wanted to ask a few questions there. He told me then that his father's papers said he was an orphan, which I know he wasn't, because he had a mother working in Melbourne and was being looked after by his auntie, so you can't call him an orphan. As far as I'm concerned it was abduction, which you go to jail for things like that now, but then they were able to

do anything because he being half-caste they could do what they wanted to do with the kids, irrespective of what the people say— parents, you know.

Jan:
Did the aunt appeal to the police or anyone?

Henry:
Well, I was a bit young to know then what happened. I don't know what happened there. I know he was brought up in the homes and that's all I know. It's a long time ago.

MAISIE CLARKE'S STORY

Geoff and I were first cousins. My dad [Jim Rose] and Geoff's mum [Emily] were brother and sister. I was a little older than Geoff.

He was living with Auntie Gracie [Winter, sometimes Winters, later Collins], who was also a sister to my dad and to Geoff's mother, Emily. I was there, but I didn't live near to Auntie Gracie's hut. I lived across the road, and I didn't hear till later that they had taken him.

Jan:
Did you go to school with him?

Maisie:
I did go to school with Geoff. One thing that always stands out in my mind is that he was very good at maths. He was excellent really, top of the class, and our teacher then was Mr Arthur Meadows.

Jan:
Can you remember how you learnt what had happened?

Maisie:
My aunt came across and told my mum and dad. They told me later. We were all very sad to hear that.

Jan:
It would be really frightening, wouldn't it?

Maisie:

Yes, it was, because we knew they could come out at any time and take the other children as well, so we always had that fear.

Jan:

Did you talk later as an adult to your aunt about how she felt on that day? Or what her reaction to it was?

Maisie:

When it happened and she came across to see us, she was very upset, very sad. She felt that for a long time. We all felt it really, even at school, our class at school. We thought a lot of Geoff.

She went with Geoff and the Social Welfare people in the car. She said they said they were going back to Melbourne by train and she went with them. They came to a shop and she said, 'Stop here for me and I'll get Geoff some lollies he can eat on the train.' She went into the shop, bought the lollies, and when she came out the car was gone. She didn't see him any more. She didn't know what happened or where he went, what home he was in.

Jan:

Did she ever talk about how Geoff's mother learnt what had happened? Did somebody ring Geoff's mother?

Maisie:

I can't remember.

Jan:

Where was the hut in which Geoff lived?

Maisie:

He lived with his aunt and their hut was situated between the two roads as we know them today, amongst scrubland. Newnham Avenue didn't exist then. The only road was from the Four Corners to the bush, like it is today. The huts were in the bush off to the side of that main road.

Jan:

Did Geoff ever come back?

Maisie:

Yes, he did find his way back to Fram. He came by bus to the Purnim store and he asked if the Roses were still living at Fram, and they told him yes. They drove him down where we were, and that was the first time we met him since he was taken away. He came back on three occasions to see us. The first time was in 1951. I took a photo of him, and I've still got that photo today.

I wasn't sure who he was till he told us, and then we got talking. My dad told him Auntie Gracie was living in Terang and to go up and see her. He said he would but I don't think he got around to it.

Jan:

Did he come just for the day?

Maisie:

Yes, just for the day.

Jan:

What kind of employment did he have?

Maisie:

He was in the navy.

He came back about two years later and a third time another two years later. He got married and never came back any more.

Jan:

But then you received a surprise, didn't you? His son came back.

Maisie:

His son rang up looking for his relatives. He didn't even know he was an Aboriginal. It was in 1993 when Mark got in touch, and he said, 'I'll be down in a fortnight's time to see you, Maisie,' and he did come down.

Jan:

How did he find his relatives?

Maisie:

Someone in Warrnambool knew. They told him to ring Libby [Clarke] and that Libby would be able to tell him everything. So he rang Libby and Libby gave him my phone number and after they had a chat, then he rang me.

Jan:

Then he came to visit.

Maisie:

Yes, we talked for nearly two hours that night.

Jan:

Was he convinced that he had found his relatives?

Maisie:

Yes, because I told him about his dad and I said I had a photo. He said 'I'll bring some photos down to show you of my dad', which he did. He also brought his dad's marriage certificate. Him and his wife came down, and his aunty, and we talked and talked. We put our stories together. He knew then, and I knew, he was one of us. It was lovely.

I still see Mark. He still comes to visit me. His dad died about six years before Mark came to find me.

Jan:

Then Mark left it for a while after his dad's death before coming to find you?

Maisie:

Yes, he didn't know who he was or what he was but his wife and auntie said to him, 'You look like an Aboriginal. Why don't you start there?' He has Aboriginal features, especially the nose. So that's how he started. He didn't know he was an Aboriginal till he met me.

He invited us to Melbourne and we went down and his brother was there and his wife and little boy.

BANJO CLARKE'S STORY

Years after Geoff Rose was taken away, my old auntie used to think about it all the time because we was talking one day—we wasn't talking about children being taken away, just talking about common things that happened around the place—and all of a sudden she said,

'I'll never forget that little boy's crying.' I said, 'What little boy's crying?' She said, 'Geoff Rose that was taken away.' I said, 'Yeah, was it here?' She said, 'Yes, I heard him.' She said that as he was going away in the car she could hear him screaming out for help, crying and calling out to his mother's people, and they had him in the car going away over Bell's Hill, that's the hill about a mile away from the mission, he was calling out. She said, 'I can still hear his voice', she said, 'calling out to the people, he must have been in that much fear at these strange people taking him away. That poor little boy, I'll hear that poor little boy's crying', she said, 'till the day I die. It's the most horrible thing I ever heard, a little child crying the way he was.' That's the words she said. It just came out of the blue: it must have been on her mind. It might have been on her mind for years, eh?

MARK ROSE'S STORY

Geoff Rose was my father.

Jan:
When did you discover that you were Koori, Mark?

Mark:
It was about four to five years ago. That would put me about thirty-nine. It's one of those things that you never question, who you are or where you've come from, and to a degree it was somewhat of a shock. However . . . there is that blind side—or what other people know that you don't know, so there was evidence and hints along the way.

It was probably an auntie of mine and my wife, Tanya, who sort of pushed it. They had an inclination that I was Koori. As we have discussed before, Dad always said he was an orphan. He didn't know who his father and mother were, and when you get that sort of story from a young age you tend to believe it. But in fact he did. He told us he was an orphan, and every time you pushed him on it, it became a very negative experience.

Jan:
Did you actually ask him the question?

Mark:

From time to time, yes, I did, but he was a very secretive person. In later years, his work in Intelligence, it was a skill I guess he picked up on. Officially he worked for Customs, but in the later parts of his career he was working in the Intelligence area. At his funeral there were members from ASIO and the Federal Police, so he must have had interaction with them. So he was a man who kept a lot of secrets, and I guess that probably helped him in his later career move. A very insular, very secretive person, who walked around with the knowledge of who he was, because, as Maisie has said—and Maisie gave me photos of him coming back to the mission after his orphanage days, yeah—part of his nature would be he would go off for one or two days here and there, and not tell people where he was going and what he was doing. We didn't know whether it was connected with his job.

Jan:

What did your mother think about all this?

Mark:

Well, Mum died when I was in Grade Six. I was already at that time in the boarding school, so the decision was to keep me in the boarding school and my brother Rowan, and at holidays we would come back and live at my grandmother's house, which was around the corner from Dad's. It was thought in those days that a male couldn't act in a single-parent role, and of course Dad didn't object to that. He saw that as being quite [convenient]. Of course, my mum's death was just another one of a whole series of body blows to him so he had time to put that together—again.

Jan:

Did he marry again?

Mark:

Yes. After the obligatory twelve months, he came home and the new wife and the furniture had gone. Yes, he did; yeah, he did. And she got half the house. He had a range of relationships too, but at the back of my mind I think he was trying to replace Mum so that he could get us kids back.

Jan:

But he never said anything like that?

Mark:

No, he wasn't a person who expressed feelings at all. Very cold. Yet there was a warmth there. He would express it in ways that weren't normal or typical of a father-figure.

Jan:

Can you give me an example?

Mark:

My mum died under tragic circumstances. She was in fact trying to apply for a job at a local factory, Ericssons in Broadmeadows. It was a hot day, thirty years ago this year [1997]. She was an epileptic and she was walking across a paddock when she took one of her turns and hit her head on the only rock in the paddock. Bled to death. Wasn't found till eleven o'clock that night. Fairly tragic.

I remember going home. My brother and I were left at the local shops, and Mum [said she] would be back in an hour or so—gave us money. This was about eleven o'clock in the morning. When she didn't return at six, we went home to wake Dad up and say, 'Look, Mum's missing.' His comment was, 'Oh, shit, the TV's broken too.'—'The TV's on the blink too'! In hindsight it was pretty hard to compare the two. But I guess one of the things in our relationship was that I was pretty tough on him for those kind of comments. But given what I now know was his upbringing, his life, it all falls into place.

Jan:

What of the warmth you sensed in him? What kinds of things happened that made you realise that there was something more there?

Mark:

Probably very few. Through reflection—he would express his love by money. I remember going back to boarding school and being given a pound note, and that was the biggest. Playing sport was another way— taking us out kicking the footy or playing cricket, that was an area that he felt he could empower us as sons. Apart from that there was no other areas, or very few. Fundamentally I believe there was a warmth there, but by hell it was a huge obstacle course to get to it.

One of the few times ... When my grandmother, who brought me up for the rest of my life, died and we viewed the body, he put his arm on my shoulder for the first time and said, 'Look, I'll be there for you.' That was the only time he'd ever actually said that or expressed that. I think he was intimidated by people who could show love, and he felt very insecure. So I'm saying that there was a warmth there in terms of, I believe that there was, but I didn't see too much signs. However, talking to work colleagues—some of my friends actually became his juniors in the Customs Service—they said he was a great guy, and I've taught kids whose parents worked with him and they referred to him as a gentleman, as kind—

The money thing is an interesting one. On his death, going through his papers, he was very, very generous. Every charity that you could think of he gave money to. Perhaps that was part of his psyche.

Jan:

I just yesterday watched again the tape of the Four Corners *programme on the life of Rob Riley, the West Australian Aboriginal activist brought up in an orphanage. Sue Gordon, brought up in the same orphanage, Sister Kate's, was asked in the programme where the love came from in such a situation. She said there was no love, no love at all. There was friendship with the other children: that was it, full stop. That was all you got, and many of the people from the orphanage went into the army. Rob Riley does for a while and so does Sue Gordon. She said, 'We fitted in.' She said all over Australia one can find Aboriginal people who went into the army—what they changed was one institution for the next. The best thing about the army, she said, was that you got a second serve at meals, whereas in the orphanage you didn't. 'We fitted in,' she said, whereas ordinary people didn't—because of the orphanage experience, it was like coming home. That's saying much the same thing, isn't it—denied all love, the children grow up used to institutional life and know how to behave in an institutional setting, but they can't do what they have never known.*

Mark:

That sums it up perfectly: the same scenario. Dad went straight from there to the navy. I can still remember. He was a shocker. Everything had a place. He was a typical A-type personality, but almost to a compulsive degree. His pyjamas would be folded on the end of his bed. I inherited nothing of that, let me tell you! And in terms of discipline, from a very young age—Grade Four I think it was—I grew up in a boarding school because of Mum's sickness and the domestic violence in the house. I was away at a boarding school, and I recognise from the institutional love I received there where Dad had got his from. Because of a few key people in my life I feel I've moved beyond that institutional sort of . . . in respect to myself. So, while Dad was forcibly removed, I was voluntarily removed. His discipline was a very paramilitarist sort of discipline.

Jan:

Where did you go to boarding school?

Mark:

I went to one in Ballarat East called Villa Maria College run by the Mercy nuns to about Year Eight. Then I went to St Vincent's in Bendigo for two terms, and there was what I interpreted as attempted sexual abuse, and I gave the person involved a very strong non-verbal message by punching him in the face. That person was a priest and I got expelled. So then I came back and lived at my grandmother's house around the corner from Dad for the last couple of years of my education, so I had that safety net around the corner. So I guess that it would be a pretty atypical story that you've come across. I sometimes remark that Dad was forcibly institutionalised but I was voluntarily, that somehow in the whole thing, the whole assimilative process, that he presumed that was best for me.

Jan:

The dominant society has much to answer for, doesn't it? A society known for the strength of its kinship ties had family and other ties disrupted and broken, generation after generation, and the Aboriginal people were left to deal with the results.

Mark:

Breaking the cycle is the hard thing to do. This is my second marriage now. In both I'm attempting to break the cycle, but I'm probably making a better shot of it now, knowing my background, whereas in my first marriage I didn't have a clue.

Jan:

What made you follow up on the suggestion of your auntie and Tanya that you should try to find out whether you were Koori?

Mark:

For some reason I wasn't convinced that they were right, and virtually they took the move. I think they were in collusion with each other, on reflection. It was Tanya who phoned up and made the enquiry of Link-up or one of those organisations.

The key point was Dad's death, because Dad said he didn't know who his mother was and we never saw a birth certificate, but after he died we found his birth certificate. His mother's name was Emily, so that gave us a piece of the jigsaw to work on. With that and the Warrnambool location given on the certificate, Tanya rang up Link-up and the girl there said, 'Without a doubt he's Koori and he's got aunties still alive down there,' and gave us the direction to look at. I don't know who she was, but she must have known.

In the mean time my auntie, who was a teacher in Warrnambool—Mum's sister—her son was involved with some Koori kids, one of them was Roslyn,* as a friend. Her son through her gave us the name of a person to ring, Libby Clarke. So I thought I'd put all the speculation at an end by ringing this woman. Libby was positive, but then gave me Maisie's phone number. So I rang Maisie. She and my dad were very close on the mission. She knew the story. It was very clear.

I asked the question, 'How many children did Emily have?' and she said, 'She had one out of wedlock, and his name was Geoff.' I said, 'That was my dad,' and then everything fell into place. In two weeks we went down to visit Maisie and in her photo album was the youngest picture of Dad I had ever seen, because there's no pictures of the

* Maisie Clarke's daughter.

orphanage. He was standing on the mission, dressed up in a suit, visiting the place. However, in saying that, there were also other people that encouraged me along the way and other indicators.

I was teaching at Assumption College and one of the teachers there, her brother works in the Koori community, and on the front of the [school] annual was all the pictures of the teachers, and her brother said to her, 'How come you've got a Koori on staff?' She said, 'No, he's not.' From the picture this guy had said, yeah, he's Koori, without any doubts. So that was an indicator.

Walking around Collingwood/Fitzroy, often Kooris would nod to me. I just thought it was the face I had, or that they were just friendly, saying 'Hi.' I was with my wife in Sydney leaning against a shop window and this family of Kooris walked past and said, 'How are you going, brother?' I go, 'Gidday, how are you doing? I'm from Melbourne.' No inclination I was Koori.

Two other very strong indicators—I went to Ayers Rock with an American friend, a teacher. Not knowing I was Koori, I climbed the thing, and when I was on it I felt something special. This was over ten years ago. I said to him, 'Do you feel this?' We were both Catholic teachers. I said to him, 'Do you feel this?' and he couldn't recognise. I said, 'I've been around churches all my life, and I've never had a feeling like this inside a cathedral.' He goes, 'It's probably the altitude, or the air, or something like that.' It's something that goes to the back of the mind, OK.

Growing up in the northern suburbs at Jacana, there was an Aboriginal family who were fairly well known for being 'hoods', a pretty aggressive sort of gang. I used to get off at the railway station in my school uniform—this is when I was living with my grandmother and going to St Bernard's, Essendon—I was a day student for the last four or five years of my education. This gang used to terrorise the northern suburbs. All my schoolmates were terrified of them. Get off at Glenroy in private-school uniform, and instead of terrorising me they would come up and just chat to me. My inclination is they recognised something in me I didn't recognise myself.

My friends would say, 'How come they scare the shit out of us and yet they just talk to you?' I go, 'Well, perhaps they're friendly people,

I don't know.' It's something you don't process and order, but it goes to the back of the mind. It is probably just a strong indication that for a long time people recognised the Aboriginality in me but I had not recognised it.

Jan:

Why do you think your aunt and Tanya were anxious that you did establish whether you were Koori?

Mark:

Probably a range of things, from just satisfying a dying question to wanting me to fully know who I was and, in the case of my wife, probably to understand that our daughter actually has different roots and so break that cycle. You are colliding with a whole range of issues here, such as changing an attitude. I can imagine in my family, being a very middle-class, very white, on my mum's side of the family, the white thing, the question was never asked I guess out of, 'We won't talk about those things', whether they had a blackfellow in their family. I'm not saying that they were prejudiced, but I suspect they always wondered, or knew, or thought about it, but were always too frightened to ask, to find out. I don't think that came from a racist perspective: it was just a reflection of the time.

Jan:

So when you realised you rang Libby, then Maisie, and visited Maisie. That's when you knew for sure.

Mark:

Yes, for a person in Warrnambool to have a picture of my father in her photo album and it was a picture that I had never seen and from an age I'd never had access to, as I said, it was the youngest picture I had ever come across, so that was empirical evidence.

Jan:

It was odd, wasn't it, because you were already a teacher and had been working in the Western District. You'd actually been in Warrnambool quite a few times without knowing that you had Koori relatives there.

Mark:

Oh, absolutely. Two or three years earlier I was principal at Casterton and I had principals' meetings in Warrnambool. On reflection—you don't process these things at the time—but people would say, 'I've seen you before', or 'Hi, how are you going?', obviously confusing me with Daryl Rose or whatever. And Dad came up to Casterton when I was principal, and I remember on a hot day getting into the car and taking him down to Portland for a swim. He knew damn well he was going through his land. He had relatives there. It must have been a bit scary if he was trying to keep a secret.

Jan:

How many times did he go to Casterton?

Mark:

Four or five, in my two years there as principal. Now in hindsight, you know the Roses—Daryl, Damien Bell and Auntie Laura—and passing through Heywood to get to Portland, he must have known [that he might be recognised]. Part of me asks the question, 'Did he want to get caught out?' because there was a perfectly good swimming pool in Casterton, but he wanted to go and swim down at the beach and that was obviously Portland, an hour's drive away.

I'd love to be able to get into the psyche of the man to find out why. After finding out I've gone through a great range of feelings, anger with him—but, talking to people, it was perhaps a sign of love, perhaps a protective thing. I don't know. I really can't process it.

Jan:

Where do you work, Mark?

Mark:

I'm at the moment acting principal of KODE, Glenroy, which is Koorie Open Door Education. It's a State government initiative, a five-year pilot programme to establish a number of KODE schools whose brief it is to deliver the best of Western and the best of Indigenous knowledge to kids, both Koori and non-Koori, in the State of Victoria. Through a lot

of accidents of history I've ended up as the acting principal for a couple
of years.

KODE is about reconstructing culture and for me, who grew up
outside it, it has advantages and also disadvantages. The advantage is
that I have to go out and find out what it means from Elders, and I'm
learning a package educationally. The very product that I am I'm trying
to undo, first of all for myself, then for the kids I work with in the school.

Jan:

How did they find you to offer the position to you?

Mark:

I'm not too sure myself. I left teaching about a year after I found out I
was Koori, so about three years ago. I took up full-time study at RMIT
for a Ph.D. My topic was looking at an indigenous person in Alaska
called Ray Barnhardt, who devised a concept known as organisational
autonomy within educational contexts for indigenous people. I used
his conceptual framework and looked at the educational offerings to
indigenous people in the State of Victoria.

I was studying that when the position became available and was
advertised. I applied, but then withdrew. I just thought I wasn't
qualified enough in terms of community knowledge, so I withdrew
before going to interview. However, my experience was recognised. The
KODE Task Force had my CV, and I was invited in to have a talk anyway.
Then Lionel Bamblett offered me work at VAEAI [Victorian Aboriginal
Education Association Inc.] in order to create—he probably saw some
potential—a community knowledge and a community profile. I was a
Higher Education Rep. for VAEAI for twelve months as a part-time
consultation thing, which was part of my study. There were a few
concerns at the end of the first year of the KODE project on its
direction, and I was invited to take up an acting principal position
there, which I have held for two years.

One of the unique things about KODE which I can't intellectualise,
which I think must be spiritual, is the fact that many of the kids out
there are blood relatives of mine. So it has been a great experience for

me, because it means I have been able to make up a lot of the community interaction I missed out on. So that's been an exciting part for me. A lot of interesting experiences!

Even the year I found out Maisie gave me Bobby Egan's card and said, 'Oh, look, this fellow wants to come and talk to you,' and she goes, 'He's actually got a son that goes to a boarding school outside Melbourne.' I looked at the card. I go, 'Troy Egan. Uh huh. Yeah.' I was teaching him at the time. On Monday after finding out, I called Troy to my office and said, 'Troy.' He goes, 'What d'ya want?' And I go, 'Troy.' He goes, 'What have I done?' I go, 'Troy, it's not what you've done—it's what our ancestors have done, mate. It looks like we're relatives.' He goes [Mark makes a noise of mock, or perhaps real, disgust], 'A teacher in the family, that's all we need!' It was pretty unusual. I found I was teaching a cousin, and a fairly close one too.

That's another thing in the whole picture. When Mum died . . . Although from Mum's side there is a large family with a great history, a 'typical' family, when Dad died there was just my brother and I. I thought my side of the family was getting very, very small. But not so these days!

Jan:
What about your brother? How does he fit into all this?

Mark:
Because I guess essentially the looking came from my side, he acknowledges now, I'm not too certain how well he has embraced it. When I started looking, because I was the driver—or Tanya or Auntie Gail were—my state of readiness was there. His reception of it has been different from mine, but I don't want to go any further into that. It's more appropriate he does.

I found it exhilarating and exciting and it answered a lot of questions I had and also gave me a lot of meaning. I understand myself better, and it's not just working out of stereotypes and things like out. I have always, always felt out of nearly every group I belonged in. I've never felt right, and I've sought to fill that void, that vacuum, with success. I didn't only have to have a teaching degree, I did another degree, then a Master's. I was made principal after four-and-a-half years of teaching, which is fairly young to be made principal. I've filled any void with success. That was like a drug to me.

But the drug never quenched that void I felt. I always felt I didn't belong, to the point that when I married Tanya, who is a very strong Macedonian, I sort of somehow latched on to their culture a bit, by accepting it and by being fascinated. I always felt that void, that vacuum in me. And the moment [I found] out about the Koori heritage, that was gone. It has given me a lot more self-confidence. I understand myself and I understand my father better. The grave disappointment is that he isn't around to share the benefit of that understanding.

Back in the '70s I'd be fighting for the end of the Vietnam War, for every cause, because I felt very isolated. I felt I could achieve, whether it's sport or whether it's education, with the best of them, but it never satisfied me. There was some hunk missing. That night I spoke to Maisie, from that night on, it's not missing. I know who I am and where I've come from. It's a pride. So whether I get the Ph.D finished I don't know. It probably isn't necessary.

Jan:

Have you anything else you want to say?

Mark:

Just one thing which I covered earlier. I guess it's a phenomenon which describes the intensity of my father's will to keep it a secret. Remember back around 1967, when Lionel Rose became the toast of all Australia? I remember sitting in the lounge at Jacana with my dad on a very '60s vinyl lounge watching the black-and-white TV, watching Rose and Harada, and the trip through Melbourne, and being swept up in the euphoria of that time—and there's my father two yards away in the same room, not saying a word: not saying, 'He's my cousin.'

Now, every person at that time related to Lionel Rose, and yet my father sat there. I'm glad he didn't, 'cause it would probably have got me into a few fights going to tell people I was related to him. But that was the intensity of his desire not to tell people. Everyone I knew said, 'I was in a pub with Lionel Rose' or 'I drove past Lionel Rose' or 'I saw

Lionel Rose' or whatever. He was such a legend and my father was a blood relation and he didn't. He was excited with his win, sure, but not to the level where he disclosed that he was blood. That speaks volumes of the intensity of his desire, for right or wrong reasons. Yeah.

Also, I've got my mum and dad's wedding certificate, and in the place where you put down 'father', he put down his own name rather than a father's name: the place where you put 'mother', he put down Auntie Gracie, who was bringing him up at the time he got stolen— Grace Winters. I thought that was fairly interesting.

To conclude, one very grave irony. I know Dad went back to the mission from time to time. He used to disappear fairly often, whether that was to do with work or going back to the mission. One really severe irony is the fact that when he died his mother, who had died a year earlier, had been living less than six kilometres away, and for all that time to my knowledge they may or may not have seen each other. They could have been on the same tram, in the same shop, or waiting at the same railway station, and weren't able to recognise each other—a mother-and-son relationship! It's a pretty severe irony that through stolen generation policy a mother and son could die a year apart within a stone's throw—six kilometres—of each other and not know each other.

Jan:
Mark, you were saying that the only personal things of your father's that you have are his war medals.

Mark:
As I said, his past and his childhood were always a mystery. There were no photos of him as a kid. The only things that I guess you'd see hanging up on the walls or he held in esteem were his war medals from Korea. He was in the navy and served in the Korean War. Memorabilia, pennants from the ships that he served on—the *Melbourne*, the *Anzac*, the *Quickmatch*—they were the only personal items he had. Nothing to do with schooling, nothing to do with upbringing.

Jan:
Did he ever talk about the war experience?

Mark:

No. I think it was a fairly nasty experience for him also. If you look at it, his life was in boxes. It was the mish [mission] when Maisie would have known him, the abduction by Welfare about eight, Menzies Boys' Home which I understand he was at—I understand that he was never adopted, but there is some evidence of him being rented out or leased out to work on a dairy farm somewhere along the line. Very young into the navy, served in Korea, came back and worked in the Post Office for a very short time, then went to Customs, where he made some very large 'busts', as we would now say. He was on the Striking Squad, a tactical response squad, and moved through all facets in Intelligence.

There are also questions that he may have been working in other areas in that field by virtue of the type of people who attended his funeral—Federal Police, ASIO, Victoria Police and of course, Customs. The comment was that it would have been a very good day to bring drugs into the country, because most of the key players were at his funeral.

So that was his life. Then his personal tragedies: his abduction, his growing up institutionalised, his marriage to a white person of a respectable family, marriage problems, domestic violence—all symptoms—tragic death of his spouse, trying to put his life back together, loss of his kids. Although we lived around the corner and there was contact, we never lived as family from that day onwards; then a second marriage that failed.

He served in Customs over forty years I think it was, a very long time in one place.

Jan:

How did he die?

Mark:

He retired from the Customs at sixty, took a pension for life. Lasted six months. Heart attack in the flat, and because we thought he was away on holidays it was probably a week before he was found. So, yeah, fairly tragic.

James Dawson,
Camperdown George
and the Obelisk

(CAMPERDOWN GEORGE)

1818* OR EARLIER–1883

WOMBEETCH PUYUUN IN TRADITIONAL DRESS

* R. D. Scott, who had known George for thirty years, said that he must have been about sixty-five
to seventy years old when he died (*Camperdown Chronicle*, 28 February 1883).

There are no headstones marking the final resting place of most Aboriginals buried in Victorian general cemeteries. The outstanding Western District exception is the grave of Wombeetch Puyuun, also known as Camperdown George, which is marked by an imposing obelisk in the Camperdown cemetery.

In the Warrnambool cemetery, down on the Hopkins River side, in the corner closest to the mouth of the river, lie a number of unmarked graves. Near by is the grave of Penelope Selby, who came to Australia on the same ship as James Dawson and his wife. The two couples became lifelong friends. Penelope died in 1851, aged forty, leaving behind a husband and two boys: seven other children, six boys and one girl, were born dead in Australia. The Selbys had emigrated to escape bankruptcy and poverty, but failed to gain the financial security they hoped for. During the economic depression of the 1840s they were forced to move several times, each time to a hut worse than the last one. In 1845 they were living at the Dawsons' Port Fairy Melting Down Establishment. Belfast (Port Fairy) was at that time 'a few scattered houses close to the sea'. Penelope reported that she was embarrassed to see naked Aboriginals in the streets of the village. She wrote to her sister, Mary, in England:

> I am not surprised at the want of what we consider proper delicacy of feeling when all classes are constantly coming into contact with men and women in a state of complete nudity. I must say I have felt my own cheeks burn when I have seen ladies in company with gentlemen talking and laughing with savages in that state.[1]

Now, ironically, she lies next to the 'savages' whose presence in the town so perturbed her. Beyond her grave there is grass only, the final resting place of many of the area's original inhabitants who died during the late nineteenth century.

Among the Western District's white population there were only two men who consistently put the Aboriginal case on various matters to the general community throughout the late nineteenth century and into the twentieth. They were John Murray and James Dawson.

JAMES DAWSON IN OLD AGE

In 1909 Canon Gason, Superintendent of the Church Missionary Association's mission to Victorian Aboriginals, wrote of John Murray, 'The Natives all regard the Premier as their friend'. He added that Murray had once said to him, '[I]f ever you want anything for the Aborigines come to me, and I will do what I can'.[2] It was Murray as Premier in 1910 who had the 1886 Act amended so that the Board could provide permanent assistance to needy 'half-castes', who were again recognised as 'practically Aboriginals'.

Murray was clearly aware that he and James Dawson were in a small minority within the white community. In 1896 he made an impassioned plea in Parliament for more to be done for the Victorian Aboriginals. Murray wasn't feeling well at the time, and he expressed his fear that, once he and James Dawson—who was then about ninety years of age—died, 'he did not think there would be anyone left in the colony with a particle of sentiment for the poor Aborigines. He would like to have the attention of the public properly directed to this matter before they were both taken away.'[3] The fact that Dawson's was the only other name Murray cited shows how highly Dawson ranked among those who had the interests of the Aboriginals at heart.

Camperdown George's Aboriginal name was Wombeetch Puyuun, which meant 'decayed kangaroo'.[4] The earliest mention I have found of him in European records was in the lists of those attending the Mount Rouse Aboriginal Protectorate station, where he stopped for a few days in late January and early February 1843.[5] Like the large number of other Aboriginals who visited the station, he appears to have stayed only long enough to see what was on offer. He is also in the photo of the Aboriginal men gathered at Framlingham Aboriginal Station in 1867 (see p. 48).

CAMPERDOWN GEORGE IN EUROPEAN DRESS

The best-known fact about Wombeetch Puyuun's life is his preference for living in Camperdown and being free to come and go when he pleased. He refused to move to the Framlingham Aboriginal Station, despite pressure to do so, and continued to camp in Camperdown, where it seems his every move was noted and reported. In this white man's town, George's friends made too much noise when they visited. Having a few drinks led to court appearances and punishment. The ups and downs of his life were all recorded, and even the state of his health, but what stands out is the superficial nature of this mass of information. There is no mention of a wife or family, or of his tribal past, or what he thought about anything—just a record of the ways in which he infringed the white man's rules about how he should live, and a series of indignant protests by James Dawson at George's treatment.

On 3 January 1871, for example, George was charged with being drunk and disorderly. He was discharged with a caution as it was 'holiday time', but he was ordered to leave the township. In early 1872 George, who had recently been sentenced to two months imprisonment in Portland jail, escaped from the Camperdown prison but was quickly caught and returned. In 1876 the *Hampden Guardian* ran a tongue-in-cheek story reporting that George was facing a 'time of temporary retirement' in Geelong 'with a letter of introduction from Mr. Wm Adeney, J. P., to the governor of the gaol at that place, and we understand that the old gentleman does not contemplate a return for the space of six months or so'.[6]

George had been sentenced to six months imprisonment in Geelong jail with hard labour, the severest punishment a Justice of the Peace could impose. And for what?, Dawson asked angrily:

Attempting to chop up a wife? Smash up a policeman with a brickbat? No! but simply because he is black, gets drunk on spirits supplied to him by his Christain [sic] white brethren, makes a noise in imitation of men who under similar circumstances would be admonished by the Bench, and considered wronged by the infliction of a quarter of George's sentence, without the hard labor. If this sentence is carried out on the poor old man to the extent, and in accordance with the fiat of the magistrate ... the Camperdown public will be rid for ever of the presence of nearly the last local representative of ... [the] race, for six months imprisonment with hard labor will finish him.[7]

In mid-1876, after the Camperdown whites complained about the noise made by the Aboriginals gathered in the town—Mr and Mrs Crow and family, Kitty, Charlie and Camperdown George—James Dawson, who was at that time the BPA's Local Guardian, applied to the government for a small sum of money to build a hut for Charlie and George in a paddock just outside the township. The aim was to move the Aboriginals out of town and so prevent 'the nuisance of people supplying the blacks with intoxicating drinks'.[8] The hut was built, and Dawson provided it with everything they needed to be comfortable. On returning a few days later, though, he was 'astonished' to find they had 'forsaken' the hut and returned to their old camping place under a paling fence.

In mid-1882 the *Camperdown Chronicle* again reported that the town Aboriginals were living in 'a miserable mia-mia': their only overhead protection was a 'few sticks resting against a fence and covered with a few rags dripping with rain', while 'underneath' there was 'nothing but a pool of water'.[9] A report in the Melbourne *Argus* about their plight brought a response from William Goodall, manager of the Framlingham Aboriginal Station, who explained how difficult it was to keep such people on the Aboriginal stations. He was not simply making excuses, for he was widely regarded as supporting the Aboriginal point of view.* The Camperdown Aboriginals were not neglected, Goodall explained. Their way of living was one 'of choice ... not of necessity':

> *These blacks have on many occasions been brought by me and also by the aborigines on the station to Framlingham, and everything has been done by me and my people to make them comfortable and happy ... but after a few weeks they would get up in the middle of the night and wander off, taking their warm clothes and blankets which had been given to them ... with them, to be found in less than a month near some township in ... [a] wretched condition ... I have many times ridden after them and induced them to return, but only to remain a few days, and then start off again as before. In fact to keep any of these old people who have a tendency for wandering on the station would require a constant attendant night and day, and then they would elude his vigilance.*[10]

R. D. Scott, acting as Local Guardian of Aborigines while James Dawson was overseas, attempted a novel solution to the problem. He employed Messrs M'Crae and Fullarton to build the Aboriginals a structure that was as close as possible to a mia-mia in form, next to Mr Robertson's bakery. Apparently the Aboriginals approved, and occupied the new mia-mia. Charlie, however, became sick with a severe bout of bronchitis and was moved to the Framlingham Aboriginal Station, where he died before the end of 1882. George was soon to follow, dying also from bronchitis but after an illness of only three days on 26 February 1883.[11]

In the *Chronicle*'s report of George's death, he was referred to as 'a universal favourite'. 'He had a kindly nature, and was possessed of none of the worse qualities of his race.' He was buried in the Camperdown Cemetery 'in the portion set apart for the burial of the aborigines'. Immediately the suggestion was made that his last resting place should be marked in an appropriate way:

---

* A year later he was sharply rebuked by Captain Page, the BPA's General Inspector, for 'trying to serve two masters'.

As the last remnant of his race in this locality has passed away in 'Camperdown George', it has been suggested to commemorate the circumstance by raising a tablet to his memory in the cemetery . . . we commend it to . . . the public.[12]

James Dawson was visiting Scotland at the time. On his return in 1884 he was horrified to discover that his friend was buried at the cemetery in what was pointed out to him as the burying ground of the Aboriginals, a 'boggy, scrubby spot . . . outside the area assigned to white people', and the grave itself was merely 'a hole among the scrub, wherein the hind legs of a horse got bogged'. 'I expressed myself very strongly', Dawson said. Apparently nothing had come of the idea of raising a tablet to George's memory.

Shortly afterwards he sent a circular to squatters throughout the local area soliciting subscriptions towards the cost of an obelisk to be raised over the grave of Wombeetch Puyuun in memory of the extinct tribes. At the same time he drew a sketch of what he envisaged and submitted it to Mr Nash, a sculptor in Geelong.

Although he gained little financial help, Dawson went ahead largely at his own expense, erecting a twenty-foot-tall granite obelisk, which still stands near the centre of the cemetery. At the top was engraved the date 1840, which marked the beginning of the extinction—'extirpation would be a more appropriate word' according to Dawson—of the local Aboriginals. Below were the boomerang, the liangle or club, and the message stick or letter. At the bottom was the date 1883, which saw 'the total extinction of the local tribes' with the death of Wombeetch Puyuun. On the polished face of the base, in gilded letters, are the words:

In Memory of
the
Aborigines
of this district
Here lies the body of the chief,
WOMBEETCH PUYUUN,
and last of the local tribes.[13]

Last of the Tribe: Aborigines' Obelisk, Camperdown, Victoria.

THE FAME OF WOMBEETCH PUYUUN'S MEMORIAL TRAVELLED BEYOND VICTORIA'S
BORDERS. THESE ILLUSTRATIONS ACCOMPANIED A REPORT IN THE *TOWN* AND
COUNTRY JOURNAL (SYDNEY) IN 1886. TOP INSET IMAGE: KING DAVID. MAIN
IMAGE: KING DAVID STANDING BY THE OBELISK ERECTED IN THE CAMPERDOWN
CEMETERY IN MEMORY OF THE ABORIGINES OF THE CAMPERDOWN AREA. BOTTOM
LEFT: WOMBEETCH PUYUUN (CAMPERDOWN GEORGE), THE MAN WHOSE BODY
DAWSON PERSONALLY RAISED FROM ITS RESTING PLACE OUTSIDE THE CEMETERY
AND PLACED AT THE BASE OF THE OBELISK

Camperdown George's body is actually below, as is stated on the obelisk. Dawson applied for permission to raise his friend's remains, and with his own hands moved them to the foot of the obelisk.

This monument is on the Register of the National Estate, the list of places regarded from a heritage point of view as significant not only for the present community but for future generations as well. It is there 'as a solemn reminder of the massive impact of white settlement and a reflection that while most settlers were uncaring, genuine humanitarian concern existed amongst a minority', writes Emeritus Professor John Mulvaney. As he points out, the dates 1840–1883 are less than a normal life span, but they mark the period in which every Aboriginal person in the Camperdown area died.[14] Dawson estimated the original population at 120 persons, but the figure may have been larger.[15]

Aboriginals died as a result of the introduction of European diseases to which they had no immunity, the effects of loss of 'country' and the consequent disruption of their lifestyle and food sources, the effects of alcohol, and the increased killing of Aboriginals by Aboriginals in a world where old certainties had no part and alcohol clouded judgement. Among the Camperdown people, at least according to official records, European violence played no part. The latest publication dealing with massacres and killings in the Western District, Ian Clark's *Scars in the Landscape. A Register of Massacre Sites in Western Victoria, 1803–1859*, shows no officially reported incidents in which Aboriginals occupying the Camperdown area were killed by Europeans. For the area from Mount Emu Creek to Lake Corangamite and north from Lake Elingamite to Derrinallum, which included Camperdown (Djargurd wurrung/Jarcoort territory), Clark lists only Frederick Taylor's alleged massacre of between thirty-five and forty men, women and children from the Mount Emu Creek–Mount Noorat area in 1839. According to information Dawson gathered from local Aboriginals, the Camperdown people were a different group.

Thus there is apparently no record of any of the Camperdown Aboriginals dying as a result of European violence. For the larger area stretching from the Hopkins River east to Lake Corangamite and from the coast north to Lake Bolac, Derrinallum and Cressy (the territory of the Girai/Kirrae wurrung and the Djargurd wurrung) the register lists three incidents only: the killing of one Aboriginal, and possibly two, on the Bolden Brothers' property, as described in chapter 7; an incident at Webster's Mount Shadwell station, in which one Aboriginal was killed; and the alleged massacre by Frederick Taylor.

In the nineteenth century some commentators argued that the Aboriginals simply 'melted away' at 'the very breath of European approach'.[16] The evidence, however, suggests that violence played a significant part. The numbers killed or seriously wounded in each 'affray' or 'outrage', as the settlers called their clashes with Aboriginals, need not have been large. Clark's register of massacres and killings provides clear evidence that the typical incident was one in which one or two Aboriginals were killed. Such incidents accounted for more than half of those reported (53 out of less than 100).

In the Western District it was widely believed that killing Aboriginals was necessary. Niel Black of Glenormiston, for example, wrote to his partner, 'A few days since I found a Grave into which about 20 must have been thrown. *A Settler taking up a new country is obliged to act towards them in this manner or abandon it*' [my italics]. As for Aboriginal women, Black commented, 'it is no uncommon thing for these rascals to sleep all night with a Lubra— and if she poxes him or in any way offends him perhaps shoot her before 12 next day—I am certain it is a thing that has frequently occurred'.[17] The editor of the *Hampden Guardian*, writing on 12 September 1876, asserted that the history of the Western District would never be written, for it 'would be such a long record of oppression, outrage, wrong, and cold blooded murder on the part of the "superior race" that it dare not be, and, therefore, never will be written'. He suggested by way of illustration that:

were it possible for free selectors to use the same kind of 'persuasion' now, in the occupation of the land, as was used to the blacks by ... 'the early pioneers' there would not be many 'squatters' left ... in the course of two or three years.

The fact that the register lists only three entries highlights the wide gulf between popular knowledge and the official record.

The Western District was also an area in which squatters closed ranks to protect each other. Take, for example, their response to the Muston's Creek massacre, in which Europeans murdered three defenceless Aboriginal women and a child while they were sleeping, and a fourth woman later died from wounds received that night. Charles Joseph La Trobe, Superintendent of the Port Phillip District, called on settlers 'to come forward in aid of the authorities'.[18] He was incensed when, instead of endeavouring to discover those guilty of the crime, prominent settlers concocted a story for which investigation revealed there was no supporting evidence. Anxious to clear their names, settlers had claimed that both Aboriginal men and women had been shot, possibly as the result of an affray between settlers and Aboriginals when the settlers endeavoured to force Aboriginals to give up plundered stock. La Trobe wrote to those such as Niel Black who had put forward the story stating that they must not consider themselves 'hardly dealt with' if he held them 'personally and individually' accountable for the contents of the letters to which they had added their signatures.[19] George Gipps, the Governor of New South Wales, saw the matter as a very grave one. He decided that, if attempts to find the murderers were unsuccessful, he would have to resort to extreme action and close the district. He instructed the Colonial Secretary to write to La Trobe and inform him that:

Should all exertions to discover the Murderers fail, it will become His Duty to consider whether it may not be proper to cancel all Licenses in the District, (or at least refuse to renew them) and to convert the whole into an aboriginal Reserve and that He will not shrink from the performance of such a Duty, if Justice and Humanity seem to require it at His hands.[20]

He ordered that a copy of this letter be sent to those settlers who had signed the letter to La Trobe of 23 April in which the false explanation was offered. Claude Farie and Niel Black, on behalf of those signing the letter, wrote an apologetic reply to La Trobe:

We beg to remind your Honour that we did not state it as a fact, nor even as a rumour but merely as a probable supposition that the women killed were attached to a marauding party ... we can only regret now that your attention was ever called to it.[21]

European settlers took such solidarity for granted on the Western District frontier. They expressed reservations in writing about only one man. Writing of the Eumeralla War that raged between Aboriginals and settlers in the stony country around Mount Eccles from 1845 until May 1847, Rolf Boldrewood expressed relief that James Dawson's property, Kangatong, was some distance away: it was 'just outside of the ... hereditary district of the Children of the Rocks, or matters might not have continued so pacific, my old friend being of a temper singularly intolerant of injustice'.[22]

Dawson received many sympathetic replies and small donations in response to his request for help with the cost of the obelisk, but was outraged that some of those who had benefited most at the Aboriginals' expense refused to help:

I had refusals such as—(verbatim)—1. 'I decline to assist in erecting a monument to a race of men we have robbed of their country.' 2. 'Your proposal does not meet with my sympathy.' 3. 'I have always looked on the blacks as a nuisance, and hope the trustees will forbid its erection.' 4. 'Have a strong dislike to hand over any portion of my hard-earned increment for another to spend.' 5. 'I cannot see the use of it.' 6. 'My wife wants her drawing room papered.' 7. 'May subscribe a little out of respect for you.' 8. 'Fail to see the use. The obelisk will point for all time to come to the treatment of this unfortunate race—the possessors of the soil we took from them, and we gave in return the vices belonging to our boasted civilisation. I decline to assist.' From owners of fourteen fine

estates in this district, estimated at a value of £2,200,000 sterling, in
answer to my applications I did not receive one penny, and in many
instances I got no replies from men holding the position of gentlemen,
although they were twice written to by me in a friendly spirit.[23]

According to his friend Louis Bayer, composer of the opera
Muutchaka or The Last of His Tribe, Dawson was so angry that he
went at once to Melbourne, taking with him a bundle of manu-
scripts for the *Argus* editor, F. W. Haddon. These contained 'the
story of some dealings of the Squatters with the Blacks, the exact
nature of which I never could find out, but I had a good idea as I
know that Camperdown George and Charlie . . . never would visit
certain stations'. Bayer reported that:

> *Haddon point blank refused to publish . . . Dawson insisted and when*
> *Haddon ordered him out of his room, old Jimmy Dawson went for him*
> *with his umbrella . . . Dawson threatened to go to the 'Age' . . . but better*
> *counsel prevailed. I received a promise to inherit said M.S. and certain*
> *instructions, but never heard any more about it since.*[24]

Dawson also confided to Page, General Inspector of the BPA, that
most of the wealthy landowners of the district refused to donate
even a 'trifle' towards the obelisk. He wrote:

> *You would be amused if you read some of the letters I hold from some of*
> *those who are powerful in prayer as they are mean in charity and good*
> *deeds, their excuses are contemptible, and in two or three instances*
> *accompanied with religious advice. Religious advice from men holding*
> *Magnificent Estates from which the Aboriginals were expelled and*
> *massacred wholesale.*[25]

I often wondered who had refused his request. Local people of
the day would have known. Recently I came across a letter Dawson
wrote to the local paper after the death of a well-known local
squatter, John Thomson of Keilambete. Dawson hadn't forgotten
what had taken place in the frontier period, and he was not about
to let anyone else forget, either. He wrote:

Sir, I read in the Chronicle *of today that the late John Thomson, of Keilambete, by his will left one hundred and twenty two thousand pounds sterling... money... made chiefly at Keilambete by his occupation of country the legitimate property of the Aborigines, who were disinherited by him without the slightest compensation, except an occasional 'Bite and Buffet'. It is truly pitiable that the owners of such large sums of money, chiefly derived from such a source, do not remember in their old age the condition and half-starved state of the evicted Aborigines.*[26]

Few Europeans of his time would have seen matters this way. Now, more than a hundred years later, we are again confronting the matters about which James Dawson felt so strongly. He would be proud of the High Court of Australia's 1992 Mabo decision recognising that the doctrine of 'terra nullius' was a legal fiction and asserting that at the time of 'settlement' the native title rights of Australia's Indigenous peoples were recognised by British common law. He would probably support the native title claims now existing over Crown land throughout the Western District of Victoria.

But in one respect Dawson's attitude showed him to be a man of his time. In early 1994 I was privileged to be present at a burial ceremony at which members of the Framlingham Aboriginal community put to rest the spirits of some of their ancestors, whose skeletal material was taken overseas in the nineteenth century. This material from the Western District was collected by the *Challenger* Expedition of 1873–76 for the purpose of scientific study and housed in the Department of Anatomy, University of Edinburgh. Records show that one of the skulls, with skeletal material from the same skeleton, was donated by James Dawson.[27]

The last of the Camperdown Aboriginals was laid to rest in 1883, but the obelisk in the Camperdown cemetery and its history remain, a symbol of the attitudes and behaviour of those who colonised this country, both those who took without giving and those, like James Dawson, who fought for the rights of the Aboriginals.

This examination of our history reveals the extent to which Aboriginal people, even the strongest who made their feelings known to those at the highest level of government, often had their requests ignored or refused. They suffered without understanding why. A 'meanness of spirit', to use Mick Dodson's phrase, has too often characterised official government policies, and certainly the implementation of them.

Many non-Aboriginal Australians now know of the conflict and dispossession of the frontier period, the heartbreak of the second dispossession brought about by the closing of the Aboriginal stations, and the devastating effects of child removals during the twentieth century. Less well known is the extent to which the Aboriginal communities of the 1860s were fractured and bruised by forced relocations and the breaking up of families that was suffered generation after generation. There were so many forced removals that few Koori families can have been untouched—thirty young Western District people to Coranderrk between 1863 and 1877; the removal of able-bodied 'half-castes' under the age of thirty-five from the beginning of 1887 (including twenty-eight 'half-caste' girls into service, several boys to apprenticeships and the removal of half-caste orphans to the Orphanage and Industrial Schools between 1887 and 1890)—up to a total of 233 people, according to the Board, out of the 556 Aboriginals residing on the stations in 1886; ten Aboriginal children transferred to Melbourne in late 1899 or early 1900 for training before going into service;[28] plus all those who were required to leave the Aboriginal stations for disciplinary reasons and those taken to distant stations under Orders in Council. The Board ruthlessly implemented its 'half-caste' policy despite the deepening economic depression; by late 1892, according to the Board's annual report, 224 out of the 233 had left the stations.

Board records provide evidence of the motivation behind these policies. The Board avowedly took 'half-caste' orphans away so that 'from the earliest period of their recollection they may be accustomed to regard themselves as members of the community at large' and not 'carry with them through life the impression of the indolent habits and manners of their original black friends'.[29] Although in 1882 the station managers, including Stähle of Lake Condah, argued against sending girls into service because they would not be 'able to protect themselves from the advances of a class of white men into whose way their duties may throw them', the Board went ahead, no doubt influenced by the views of the Reverend Friedrich Hagenauer, the Board's Inspector and Secretary. Hagenauer had come to believe that the girls were 'exposed to greater danger on the stations' with their own people than when 'living with respectable families'.[30]

Behind the relocation of a significant proportion of this captive population one can see the exercise of power built on a conviction that Indigenous people had no option but to be absorbed into the general population. In this view, firmness was essential in the long-term interests of the Aboriginal people. The ruthless implementation of policy was meant to ensure that the Aboriginal population would cease to exist as such. This was the 'finality' Stähle foreshadowed in 1900 as he listened to the silence that had descended on Lake Condah after the children had been taken away.

But even in south-eastern Australia Aboriginality never receded to the extent the authorities hoped, despite the battering inflicted on it. Ties to 'country' survived dispossession and displacement, and new bonds of kinship were forged among Aboriginal people from disparate parts of the continent. Indigenous Australians have increasingly found a common voice, insisting on respect for themselves as the first Australians, compensation for past wrongs and just treatment now and in the future. In the late 1990s unresolved matters between Aboriginal and settler Australians, for so long of marginal concern to the general population, have moved to centre stage.

At the core of these debates—whether they be over native title, compensation for the 'stolen generation' or the inclusion of Indigenous peoples' special claims in the Australian Constitution—is the problem that each in its own way asks settler

Australians to confront a radically different view of the past from the comforting one learnt in childhood, in our homes and schools and at church. Peaceful occupation becomes the taking of land from those who in many places fought to protect what was theirs. Indigenous title rights, an idea so preposterous that it never surfaced in what my generation was taught at school, we now find were protected from the beginning by British common law, which was imported into Australia at the time of arrival of the Europeans. The 'protection' offered to Aboriginal people on Aboriginal stations and in missions we now discover involved the taking of children from families as policy in the hope of obliterating Aboriginality. Accepting such a changed view of the past forces a fundamental reassessment of who we are as a people and the nature of the colonising enterprise. Such rethinking does not come easily, and outdated ideas and old prejudices rise time and time again from places buried deep in the subconscious.

For many there is also the disincentive that accepting a revised version of the past will inevitably lead to a redistribution of resources in favour of Indigenous peoples at a time of economic downturn in rural Australia and increased insecurity of employment. There is a reluctance to admit that Aboriginal people are the most disadvantaged in Australia, and that the circumstances of Indigenous Australians have been substantially affected for the worse by the policies and practices of settler Australia. And yet, as Kooris often state, it is this very basic realisation and understanding that matters most to them. When the Mabo judgment of 1992 laid to rest the legal fiction that Australia was 'terra nullius'— no one's land—before European occupation, it gave a new urgency to the task of taking another look at our past, admitting the injustices suffered by Indigenous people and accepting their right to redress.

As the biographies in this book make plain, Australia's Aboriginal history is alive in the present and actively shaping the future. When Banjo Clarke told his stories and pointed out the places associated with them, I saw a landscape enriched by new layers of meaning—King David's tree; the waterhole where Old Pompey kept his eels, just inside the property-owner's fence, with Warrnambool on the horizon; the culvert where the car that killed Pompey came to a stop; the places where the eel-traps were renewed year after year; the cliff-face where Pompey's helpers climbed eels up the slope, just near Banjo's home. As I looked at these sites and saw them through Banjo's eyes, land and water acquired meanings not part of the experience of the non-Aboriginal community among which the Aboriginals live. The stories also revealed two worlds inhabiting the same geographical space, but with little respect for each other, rarely touching, and sometimes colliding.

It is time for us to face the past, seeing it for what it has been, accepting the 'true history', an account that includes what Kooris know as having happened to their people. To do so is not to be forced to accept guilt, as conservative politicians often claim, but to face the present free of the strongly held beliefs about race and culture that shaped past policies and attitudes. In this freedom lies the opportunity to build new bridges between Indigenous and other Australians, and at last give Indigenous peples a respected and central place in our national life. In doing so we will not only empower Australia's Indigenous people but also alter and enrich what we mean when we say we are Australian.

Appendix A:
The Hood family

Collin Hood and Nora (maiden name given as Villiers on certificate of baptism, and as Ageebonyee on the birth certificate of the twins Rachel and Alice) married on 1 November 1855 at Conawarren in a Christian service presided over by the Reverend William Hamilton. Their children were:

Julian	Born 1856, died 17 April 1870 at the Geelong Hospital and buried in the Geelong Cemetery (Death Certificate no. 4215/1870).
Rachel and Alice	Twins born 23 December 1857 at Dunmore (Birth Certificate nos 7486 of 1858 and 7487 of 1858). (A correction note states that the year of birth was 1857.)
Julia	Mentioned on Wallace's Birth Certificate (see below).
Alice	Mentioned on Wallace's Birth Certificate (see below).
William	Born 1859 at Conawarren, died aged sixteen on 6 September 1875, buried at the Framlingham Aboriginal Cemetery (Death Certificate no. 11568 of 1875).

Nora died on 28 March 1871 and was buried in the New Cemetery, Melbourne, on 30 March 1871 (Death Certificate no. 1948/1871).

Collin and Louisa Lutton (née King; at another time her maiden name was given as Tappoke, the Aboriginal name for Mount Napier; gave her birthplace as near Mount Rouse) married on 6 August 1872 at the Framlingham Aboriginal Station (Marriage Certificate no. 3315 of 1875).

At the time Louisa had three surviving children from her previous marriage to James Lutton, who died in February 1871. They were:

Collin	Died 7 July 1883 aged fifteen (Death Certificate no. 7204 of 1883).
Alfred	Died 14 April 1874 aged six (Death Certificate no. 6561 of 1874).
Susan	Married Frederick Murray on 30 July 1879 (Marriage Certificate no. 3481 of 1879).

Collin and Louisa's children were:

Leah	Born 1 October 1875, birth registered at Purnim (Birth Certificate no. 25148 of 1875).
Unnamed male	Born 26 February 1878 at the Framlingham Aboriginal Station, died the same day and was buried at the station cemetery (Birth Certificate no. 4603 of 1878, Death Certificate no. 3008 of 1878).
Wallace	Born 13 January 1879 at Framlingham Aboriginal Station; died 30 September 1881 and was buried in the Aboriginal cemetery (Birth Certificate no. 11300 of 1879, Death Certificate 11604 of 1881).
Minna Martha	Born at the Framlingham Aboriginal Station on 11 April 1883 (Birth Certificate no. 13788 of 1883).

Louisa died on 7 September 1890 and is buried in the Framlingham Aboriginal cemetery (Death Certificate no. 13441 of 1890).

Collin and Helen (or Ellen) Rivers, daughter of Larry Johnson and Kitty Perry (Kurnai), married on 17 March 1898 at Lake Tyers Church (Marriage Certificate no. 8 of 1898). Their children were:

Jack	Born 1897 at Lake Tyers (Birth Certificate no. 29248 of 1897).
Minna	Born 1899 at Lake Tyers (Birth Certificate no. 4130 of 1899).
Lara Johnson	Born 1900 at Stratford (Birth Certificate no. 14744 of 1900).

Alexander Stewart	Born 1902 at Stratford (Birth Certificate no. 6285 of 1902).
Julian	Born 1905 at Lake Tyers (Birth Certificate no. 19433 of 1905).
Daisy Leah	Born 1906 at Lake Tyers (Birth Certificate no. 27868 of 1906).
Clive Colin	Born 1908 at Lake Tyers (Birth Certificate no. 28183 of 1908).

Collin Hood died on 3 May 1914 at Lake Tyers (Death Certificate no. 6187 of 1914) and was survived by six children—Martha, Jack, Minna, Alexander Stewart, Julian and Clive. Helen died in September 1915.

Appendix B: The Mobourne letters

The sources of the letters reproduced here are as follows:

Maggie Mobourne to D. N. McLeod Esq. MLA, 27 February 1900: Australian Archives (Victoria): Series B337, 507, 1900.

Ernest Mobourne to the Hon. Members of the Cabinet, 2 July 1907: Public Record Office of Victoria, VPRS 3992, Unit no. 1457, A5318. Reproduced with the permission of the Keeper of Public Records.

Ernest Mobourne to H. J. M. Campbell Esq. MLA, 2 July 1907: Public Record Office of Victoria, VPRS 3992, Unit no. 1457, A5318. Reproduced with the permission of the Keeper of Public Records.

Typed copy of Ernest Mobourne's Appeal to the Ratepayers, 2 July 1907: Public Record Office of Victoria, VPRS 3992, Unit no. 1457, B5755 with A5318. Reproduced with the permission of the Keeper of Public Records.

The Ratepayers' Petition: Public Record Office Victoria, VPRS 3992, Unit no. 1457, B5755 with A5318. Reproduced with the permission of the Keeper of Public Records.

Maggie Mobourne to Reverend J. H. Stähle, 12 August 1912: Australian Archives (Victoria): Series B337, 507, 1912/704.

Ernest Mobourne to the Secretary of the Board for the Protection of the Aborigines, 31 October 1914: Australian Archives (Victoria): Series B337, 507, 1914/1101.

Ernest Mobourne to His Excellency Sir Arthur Stanley, Governor of Victoria, 6 March 1916: Australian Archives (Victoria): Series B337, 507, 1916/T2448.

Mission Station
Lake Condah
February 27ᵗʰ 1900

D. N. McLeod, Esqre. M. L. A.
and Vice Chairman

Sir

Having returned in September last to the Mission Station, with the object of endeavouring to live in peace and in accordance with the rules of the Station. I am sorry to inform you that Mr Stähle seems to take every opportunity to find fault with us, and it seems as if our efforts to live peaceably are of no use here because Mr Stähle seems determined to annoy us and to take every opportunity of reporting us to the Board for insubordination.

On the 19ᵗʰ inst Mr Stähle spoke in a threatening manner to me and stopped our rations, which he denies and I say that he is a liar and has always been (See full particulars in another letter). and he doesn't treat us justly. I would ask you to get up an impartial Board of Inquiry to investigate and see fairness and justice.

I am prepared to substantiate my statements to be true and also can get the majority here as witnesses to prove that we have been living peacefully.

I am
Sir
Yours respectfully
Maggie Mobourne

(We the following corroborate the statements given above)
Signatures

Ernest Mobourne
Robert Turner   his X mark
Thomas Willes   his X mark
James Cortwine   his X mark
Jenny Green   her X mark
Albert White
Fred Carmichael
Louisa White   her X mark
Edward Cortwine

Isaac McDuff   his X mark
Bella Mobourne

MAGGIE MOBOURNE TO D. N. McLEOD, MLA, 27 FEBRUARY 1900

A 5318

Lake Condah
Mission Station
July 2nd 1907.

To The Hon Members of the Cabinet
Gentlemen

We the undersigned
Aboriginese of the Lake Condah Mission
Station noticed in the columns of the
Portland Guardian and Argus with very
great sorrow that the Cabinet had decided
to dissolve two of the Mission Stations in
Victoria. one of these being Lake Condah on
which we reside, and the other Lake Wellington.
We the Aboriginese residing at Lake Condah
would earnestly pray the Cabinet to reconsider
their decision and allow us to remain at
Lake Condah. Our fathers were brought
here some forty years back to form a
mission Station here and were then informed
that if they built houses, fenced in and
cleared the reserve, that the Mission Station
would remain theirs for them and their
childrens children. They with their loved
missionary Mr Stahle whose labours have
blessed and who is still with us. then put
their minds and hands together fenceing
in the whole reserve with a good substantial
fence, clearing it and have built stone
and wooden cottages for our use. a fine
church wherein to worship God. a Mission House
for their much loved missionary
a schoolroom wherein our children are
taught to read and write. It would be
very heart breaking to us if after

these promises by the then Government, the present Government would still retain their decision, and transfer us to another station. Our fathers have passed peacefully to rest and we would wish to live and work and be buried beside them. Praying that you will grant us our request.

We are:

Gentlemen

yours respectfully,

The Aboriginese of Lake Condah

Peter Hewitt *his mark*	Lizzie Carter
William Carter Senior *his mark*	Fanny McDougall 8
James Cortwine *his mark*	Joseph McDougall 7
Isaac McDuff *his mark*	Louie McDougall
Henry Rose *his mark*	Ethel Mobourne 6
Jocas Johnson *his mark*	Elizabeth Carmichael 10
John Dutton *his mark*	Leslie Johnson 4
Edward Cortwine	Fanny Carter
Albert White	Anthony Johnson 12 months
Daniel James Cortwine	Ernest Mobourne
Annie Turner 10	Annie Harrison 22
Donald Turner	James Young
Maria McDuff *her mark*	Jennie Green
Agnes Carter	Lawrence Young
Louisa Carter	William Carter
Louisa White *her mark*	Sam Mobourne
Janet Turner *her mark*	Flora Stewart
Dinah White	Jackson Stewart *his mark*
Catherine Cortwine	Hughie Cortwine
Bessie Johnson	Henry Dawson *his mark*
Maggie Mobourne	Ellen McCallum
Jessie Carter 10	Eddie Mullett 21
Wallace Carter 6	Elsie Florence Evelyn White
John Mullett	

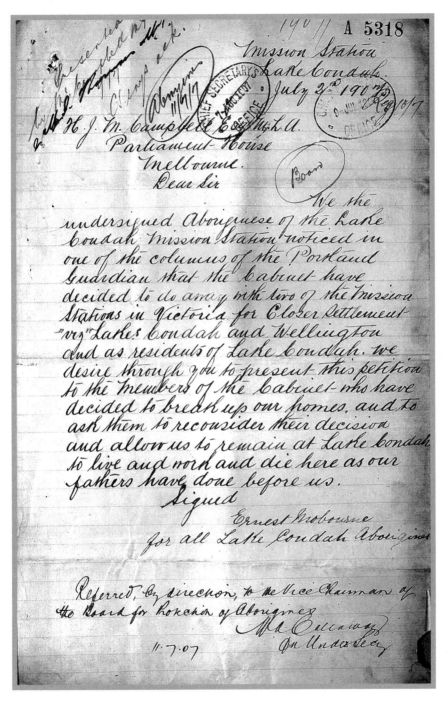

A 5318

Mission Station
Lake Condah.
July 2nd 1907

H. J. M. Campbell Esq MLA.
Parliament House
Melbourne.
Dear Sir

We the
undersigned Aboriginese of the Lake
Condah Mission Station noticed in
one of the columns of the Portland
Guardian that the Cabinet have
decided to do away with two of the Mission
Stations in Victoria for Closer Settlement
"viz" Lakes Condah and Wellington
and as residents of Lake Condah we
desire through you to present this petition
to the Members of the Cabinet who have
decided to break up our homes. and to
ask them to reconsider their decision
and allow us to remain at Lake Condah
to live and work and die here as our
fathers have done before us.
Signed
Ernest Mobourne
for all Lake Condah Aborigines

Referred, By direction, to the Vice Chairman of
the Board for Protection of Aborigines
M. d. Callaway
On Under Secy
11.7.07

ERNEST MOBOURNE TO H. J. M. CAMPBELL, MLA, 2 JULY 1907

B 5755

C O P Y.

Duplicate

AN APPEAL.

Mission Station, LAKE CONDAH
July 2nd. 1907.

To the Ratepayers,

Ladies and Gentleman,-

Having seen in the Portland Guardian on Saturday, the paper that was lent to us, that the Cabinet has come to a decision to dissolve our home, Lake Condah, and disorganise us to Coranderrk or Lake Tyers Stations, which is very heartbreaking to us because we love our home. When first this mission station was formed, our forefathers, fathers and ourselves understood that it was our own to live on while life lasted, and now we are sad indeed to see it taken from us. This is very hard indeed, after working and labouring all these years in putting up fences, clearing ground, building houses &c, besides a nice lovely Church and a school, where we and our children receive instruction. Had our fathers and ancestors been spared to live to see this our mission now, they would feel very proud of it, but they had not that opportunity as they had to obey to the call to step on the other side of time and rest in our little Cemetery till we meet them again by and by on the other shore when our turn comes. So dear ladies and gentlemen we ask you to do your very best for us, and see that our home is not all taken, but leave some portion for us. We ask you also to recall to the memory of the Chief Secretary, Mr Peacock, that he told our men here some years back, that as long as he would be Chief Secretary he would never let this Lake Condah Mission Station be taken from us. There are some older aborigines here who are unfit to travel far distances, so we think it is very unkind of the Government to take our home from us and our children, but should reconsider their decision and let us retain our station again as before, for we all understood at the first that it was granted to us by our late most gracious sovereign Queen Victoria, our mother, to let us live and die here.

ERNEST MOBOURNE

For all the Lake Condah aborigines.

ABOVE: ERNEST MOBOURNE'S APPEAL TO THE RATEPAYERS, 2 JULY 1907

FACING PAGE: THE RATEPAYERS' PETITION OPPOSING THE CLOSURE OF
LAKE CONDAH

B 5755

IN THE MATTER of Protection of Aborigines

And

IN THE MATTER of the LAKE CONDAH ABORIGINAL STATION.

TO/

His Excellency

The GOVERNOR -IN - COUNCIL

of the State of Victoria.

May it please your Excellency,

THE HUMBLE PETITION of the undersigned RESIDENTS and RATEPAYERS OF THE SOUTH-WESTERN DISTRICT OF VICTORIA sheweth as follows:-

1. THAT it appears from certain paragraphs in the newspapers that it is the intention of the Cabinet of the State Parliament or of the Minister of the Crown administering the "Aborigines Act 1890" to disband the Mission Station at Lake Condah and to transfer the Aborigines from the said Station to a distant part of the State.

2. THAT if this proposal is carried into effect very great hardship will result to the Aborigines in that:-

(a) They will be compelled to give up the place which has become dear to them as the home of their ancestors and themselves

(b) The burial ground in which have been interred the remains of their deceased relatives will be wrested from them and probably will be upturned by the plough of the Settler, and by their residence in a distant part of Victoria the survivors will be debarred from visiting the tombs of their fathers.

(c) The dwelling houses, school, church and other buildings which have been erected either by or for them and which have been occupied by them and their ancestors for nearly half a century will be compulsorily taken from them

(d) The crops they have sown will be lost to them, the improvements in fencing, clearing and draining will benefit the Crown, as owners of the land, for which no compensation will be made to the actual improvers

(e) The older members of the Settlement will be subjected to the severity of a long journey to a distant part of the State which they in the frailty of their old age may be unable to withstand

(f) A promise was made to them by The Hon. The Acting Chief Secretary

(1).

Lake Condah
Mission Station
August 12th 1912

Mr. Stähle

Dear Sir

As you have been so kind to point out to Ernest the error I have made in coming to the Mission House in the manner I did, when I wanted to go and see Mrs. Stähle and tell her my troubles about Miss Bagnall, last Tuesday, and that you wanted me to apologise, I do, because at the time I could not control my feelings as I was hurt very much indeed at Miss Bagnall's remarks which was this, "You're a vile creature"

"Thank God I haven't got what you got in your arms." When she finished I said, I know I am vile, but I never thought it was in you to speak as you have just spoken, I took you to be a lady, a Christian, and my friend.

No more was said between us, the Almighty being my witness as well as my sister.

yrs respectfully
Maggie Mobourne.

ABOVE: MAGGIE MOBOURNE TO REVEREND STÄHLE, 12 AUGUST 1912

FACING PAGE: ERNEST MOBOURNE TO BPA SECRETARY, 31 OCTOBER 1914

1101

Mission Station, Lake Tyers,
October 31st 1914

To The Secretary of The Board,
Sir,

May I kindly ask you, do you remember asking me in your office how long Ethel and I was going to stay at Lake Tyers, and I plainly told you only three months, as I asked the manager at Lake Condah for the same. How is it then that Captain Howe tells me that there was nothing said in the correspondence he got about three months holiday. Before leaving Milltown, Ry. Stn when he was there to see us off, Captain Crawford says to me, Ernest — when are you coming back, & I answered him in three months time, allright says he, and bring Maggie with you after you both have made it up together. Previous to this he expressed himself to me on the Condah mission station before the men to that effect —

Now I will ask the Board why should I be forced to remain here.

. I am, sir, respectfully Yours
Ernest Mobourne

I. 2448

Mission Station
Lake Tyers
March 6ᵗʰ 1916

To His Excellency
Sir Arthur Stanley K.C.M.G.
Governor of Victoria.

Sir,

May it please your Excellency. I am Ernest Mobourne the first-colored native who met you at Lake Tyers as soon as you came of the launch, and had the previlege of shaking hands with you & escorted you with Mr Cameron M.P. & the other members on to the Mission. Sir, I have a request to ask you, & I trust you will kindly favor me your help in the matter. Ten or Twelve years ago myself, wife & family was transferred to this Station by the Board. until I referred the matter of our transport-ation to Sir George Sydenham Clarke then Governor of this State & he helped to get us back to Lake Condah which is our home, besides

ERNEST MOBOURNE TO THE GOVERNOR OF VICTORIA, 6 MARCH 1916

I 3448

giving me an Order which I have in my possession that it is Cancelled, and how is it that the Board Mr Ditchburn should have my wife transferred here on the same Order (Ten or Twelve yrs) I think this is very unfair indeed for Mr Ditchburn to do such an underhand thing. Mr Ditchburn as done this just for spitefulness to the Mobournes I also have a letter as well of Mr Murray who was then Member in the Legislature in which he says The Country Would not tolerate any harsh treatment of your people, (the blacks,) as it now recognizes that the original owners of the whole of the State have claims that cannot be disregarded. Why are we Kept prisoners here & not permitted to return to our friends and home? This country is free & we understand we are under the British Flag, but it seems that we are slaves in Mr Ditchburn's sight. Respectfully your

Ernest Mobourne

Abbreviations

AV	Australian Archives, Victoria
AIATSIS	Australian Institute of Aboriginal and Torres Strait Islander Studies
BPA	Board for the Protection of the Aborigines
CSIL	Colonial Secretary Inward Letters
ML	Mitchell Library, Sydney
PROV VPRS	Public Record Office of Victoria, Victorian Public Records Series
RCA	Royal Commission on the Aborigines, Victoria, 1877
VPD	*Victorian Parliamentary Debates*
VPP	*Victorian Parliamentary Papers*

Notes

INTRODUCTION

1. Royal Commission into Aboriginal Deaths in Custody, *National Report*, pp. 4–5.
2. Royal Commission into Aboriginal Deaths in Custody, *National Report*, pp. 7.

CHAPTER 2
'AN OLD HAND': JIM CAIN

1. Richard Osburne, *The History of Warrnambool*, p. 198.
2. Details of Magisterial Inquiry, 12 November 1882, PROV, VPRS 24, Unit 445, 1302/1882.
3. Details of Magisterial Inquiry, 12 November 1882, PROV, VPRS 24, Unit 445, 1302/1882.
4. *Camperdown Chronicle*, 30 August 1882.
5. Deborah Bird Rose, *Nourishing Terrains. Australian Aboriginal Views of Landscape and Wilderness*, pp. 7, 9.
6. *Warrnambool Standard*, 30 November 1877.
7. Jan Critchett (ed.), *Richard Bennett's Early Days of Port Fairy*, pp. 67–9.
8. Proceedings of Inquest held 16 June 1862 at Terang, PROV, VPRS 24, Unit 22, 340/1862. The Allan brothers, William and John, took up land in the Allansford area in 1839 (Allansford 125th Anniversary Celebrations Committee, *Allan's Ford Allansford 1855–1981*, p. 9).
9. Aldo Massola, *Journey to Aboriginal Victoria*, p. 38.
10. Interview with Banjo Clarke, 5 February 1996.
11. Rolf Boldrewood, *Old Melbourne Memories*, p. 17. Thomas Alexander Browne used the pseudonym Rolf Boldrewood.

12 Aborigines (Australian Colonies), *House of Commons Sessional Papers*, 1844, vol. 34, no. 627, pp. 213–14. Names are provided in the *Geelong Advertiser*, 4 April 1842.

13 Boldrewood, *Old Melbourne Memories*, pp. 57, 69–70.

14 See Jan Critchett, *A distant field of murder*, Chapters 6 and 7 for a detailed treatment of interracial conflict.

15 Colonial Secretary to La Trobe, 17 June 1842, CSIL Port Phillip 1843, Part 1, 4/2626, in accumulated file 42/2847 (Archives Office of NSW). For details see Critchett, *A distant field of murder*, pp. 118–19.

16 Sievwright, Proceedings from 1 March to 31 May 1842, 42/5708, Archival Estrays, CSIL/11 (Dixson Library).

17 A. S. Kenyon, 'The Aboriginal Protectorate of Port Phillip', p. 145.

18 Kenyon, 'Aboriginal Protectorate', p. 145.

19 Ian D. Clark (ed.), *The Port Phillip Journals of George Augustus Robinson: 8 March–7 April 1842 and 18 March–29 April 1843*, p. 23.

20 Geoffrey Blainey, *Triumph of the Nomads*, p. 225.

21 Blainey, *Triumph of the Nomads*, p. 228.

22 Robert Burke, Mount Shadwell, Reply to Circular, in Report of the Select Committee of the Legislative Council on the Aborigines together with Proceedings of Committee, Minutes of Evidence and Appendices, *VPP*, 1858–59, D8, p. 84. See also comment by J. M. Allan, p. 68.

23 First Report of the Central Board to Watch over the Interests of the Aborigines, *VPP*, 1863, no. 39, Appendix 2, p. 15.

24 Rolf Boldrewood quoted in J. W. Powling, *Port Fairy. The First Fifty Years*, p. 62.

25 'The Late Richard Rutledge of the "Briars", Farnham', *Warrnambool Standard*, 10 November 1887.

26 *Geelong Advertiser and Intelligencer*, 7 February 1854.

27 PROV, VPRS 937, Unit 32, Bundle 1, Letter from Inspector Lydiard, Belfast, to the Chief Commissioner of Police, Melbourne, 18 July 1854, enclosing the letter dated 15 July 1854 from two gentlemen to Inspector Lydiard.

28 Charles Flower, 'Reminiscences', undated manuscript. Copy in possession of Mary Hamilton of Geelong. See also court details in *Warrnambool Examiner*, 15 May 1855.

29 Report of the Select Committee of the Legislative Council on the Aborigines, 1858–59, p. 54.

30 For details see Critchett, *A distant field of murder*, p. 183.

31 W. N. Gray, Crown Land Commissioner, Aborigines in Portland Bay District—Return December 31st 1853, in T. F. Bride (ed.), *Letters from Victorian Pioneers*, p. 414.

32 1881 Census of Victoria, *VPP*, 1883, no. 39, General Report, Item 316, and Table LXV, p. 179.

33 Select Committee of the Legislative Council on the Aborigines, 1858–59, Replies to a Circular Letter, pp. 35–6.

34 Select Committee of the Legislative Council on the Aborigines, 1858–59, Replies to a Circular Letter, p. 36.

35 Robert Burke, Select Committee on the Aborigines, Replies from gentlemen to whom 'Circulars' were sent, p. 84.

36 *Warrnambool Examiner*, 10 December 1867.

37 *Warrnambool Examiner*, 31 December 1867.

38 Osburne, *History of Warrnambool*, p. 198. Richmond Henty's version of the visit is given in *Australiana or My Early Life*, pp. 24–5, 217–27.

39   *Warrnambool Examiner*, 22 May 1857.
40   *Warrnambool Standard*, 6 October 1876.
41   *Warrnambool Standard*, 23 May 1877.
42   Report of the Select Committee of the Legislative Council on the Aborigines, 1858–59, p. 33.
43   Philip Chauncey, First Report of the Central Board, *VPP*, 1863, no. 39, Appendix 2, p. 19.
44   Annual Reports of the Board for the Protection of the Aborigines (BPA). In addition there is evidence of one offence that is not in the Board reports. For this see Warrnambool Petty Sessions Register, PROV, VPRS 699, Unit 2, Assault on his 'lubra', sentence of one month with hard labour, 20 August 1867.
45   *Warrnambool Examiner*, 30 January 1877.
46   Details are in the Annual Reports of the Central Board (later Board for the Protection of the Aborigines).
47   E. Eggleston, *Fear, Favour or Affection: Aborigines and the Criminal Law in Victoria, South Australia and Western Australia*, p. 13. See also C. D. Rowley, *Outcasts in White Australia*, p. 355.
48   Original seen in the Pennycuick family newspaper cutting book in possession of S. Pennycuick, Hamilton.
49   Osburne, *History of Warrnambool*, p. 198.
50   *Warrnambool Standard*, 30 November 1877.
51   *Warrnambool Standard*, 27 November 1879.
52   Death Certificate no. 999/1880.
53   Osburne, *History of Warrnambool*, p. 61.
54   Proceedings of Magisterial Inquiry, PROV, VPRS 24, Unit 445, 1302/1882; *Warrnambool Standard*, 14 November 1882.
55   *Warrnambool Standard*, 17 March 1886.
56   Warrnambool Cemetery Records.

CHAPTER 3
'I'M YOUR HALF-BROTHER, AND I'M HERE TO STAY': WILMOT ABRAHAM

1   'Mr Arthur Jordan Revives Old Memories of W'bool', *Warrnambool Standard*, 24 September 1953.
2   List of Aborigines at Framlingham in November 1889 with place of birth, *Warrnambool Standard*, 29 November 1889, p. 3.
3   *Nullawarre School Centenary and District History*, 'Back To' Celebrations, Easter 1975, Souvenir Booklet, no date, no author.
4   Rex Mathieson, interview 14 October 1996.
5   Alice Goldstraw, *The Border of the Heytesbury*, p. 13.
6   Goldstraw, *Border of the Heytesbury*, pp. 13–14.
7   *Warrnambool Standard*, 27 May 1891.
8   *Warrnambool Standard*, 27 May 1891.
9   *Warrnambool Standard*, 2 October 1889.
10   'Mr Arthur Jordan Revives Old Memories of W'bool', *Warrnambool Standard*, 24 September 1953.
11   *Hampden Guardian*, quoted in *Warrnambool Standard*, 12 September 1873, p. 2, col. 7. I am indebted to Michael Sturmfels for drawing my attention to this article.
12   James Dawson, *Australian Aborigines. The Languages and Customs of Several Tribes of Aborigines in the Western District of Victoria, Australia*, p. lxxxiii.

[13] Paper entitled 'Early History of Peterborough by M. E. MacKenzie', chapter headed 'My Mother's Talks at the Fireside', pp. 7–8, written 7 June 1934. Ann Wilkinson of Peterborough kindly drew this information to my attention.

[14] Interview with Reg Grauer of Allansford, 8 December 1996.

[15] *Warrnambool Standard*, 24 September 1884.

[16] *Warrnambool Standard*, 8 July 1916.

[17] Framlingham Manager's Letter Book, pp. 88–90, Report of the Rev. Thwaites for September 1884. Personal copy of notes made by the late Dr Diane Barwick.

[18] Fifteenth Report of the BPA, *VPP*, 1879, no. 68, Appendix XIII, p. 13.

CHAPTER 4
THE THREE POMPEYS

[1] Death Certificate no. 8537/1889.

[2] Marriage Certificate no. 2622/1867. Rosie's death certificate is no. 14408/1907. On it her parents are named as Mary Caramut and Samuel Robinson, though on the marriage certificate her mother is given as Mary (Aboriginal) and father as European, unknown. On her death certificate the children are listed as Walter (deceased), male child (deceased), Christopher, Ada and Lena (twins).

[3] Michael Cannon, *Who Killed the Koories?*, p. 54.

[4] Letter from H. M. Matson cited in W. G. Manifold, *The Wished-for-Land. The Migration and Settlement of the Manifolds of Western Victoria*, p. 238.

[5] Manifold, *The Wished-for-Land*, p. 66.

[6] Quoted from Rodney Hall, *J. S. Manifold. An introduction to the man and his work*, p. 12.

[7] Cited in Manifold, *The Wished-for-Land*, p. 128.

[8] Quoted from Hall, *J. S. Manifold*, p. 17.

[9] *Star*, 6 January 1934, p. 6.

[10] Colin Tatz, *Obstacle Race. Aborigines in Sport*, p. 367.

[11] I interviewed Banjo on 15 September and 21 September 1997.

[12] His son said he was 65 years old in 1939 (PROV, VPRS 24, Unit 1382, File 970, Proceedings of Inquest into the death of Christopher Austin, 28 July 1939).

CHAPTER 5
'WHY DID THEY TAKE THEM AWAY?': LIZZIE AND HENRY MCCRAE

[1] Interview with Henry (Banjo) Clarke, 29 April 1996. Banjo was not at Framlingham at the time, but the incident so shocked the community and was talked about so much that he tells the story as though he were present.

[2] Percy Leason, *The Last of the Victorian Aborigines*, p. 8.

[3] Leason, *Last of the Victorian Aborigines*, pp. 16–17.

[4] *Warrnambool Standard*, 20 November 1936, 2 May 1938, 3 May 1938, 12 May 1938, 9 August 1938.

CHAPTER 6
IN DEFENCE OF FRAMLINGHAM: COLLIN HOOD

[1] On the earliest written record I have, that registering the birth of his twin daughters (Birth Certificates nos 7486 and 7487 of 1858) his age is given as twenty-one.

[2] Marriage Certificate no. 8 of 1898.

³ He discussed his totem with Rev. John Bulmer at Lake Tyers Aboriginal Station and Bulmer recorded his totem as jallan (whipsnake); see Alastair Campbell (comp.), *Victorian Aborigines. John Bulmer's Recollections 1855–1908*, p. 6. But jallan is the Djab wurrung word for boa snake according to Dawson, *Australian Aborigines*, p. lviii. Maybe boa snake and whipsnake are the same snake.

⁴ Dawson, *Australian Aborigines*, p. 26.

⁵ Campbell (comp.), *Victorian Aborigines*, p. 6.

⁶ G. Presland (ed.), 'Journals of G. A. Robinson March–May 1841', p. 54.

⁷ See Leason, *Last of the Victorian Aborigines*, pp. 6–7 and R. Brough Smyth, *Aborigines of Victoria*, vol. 2, 1878, p. 261.

⁸ 1881 Census of Victoria, VPP, 1883, no. 39, General Report, Item 160, p. 28.

⁹ Interview with Banjo Clarke, 1 May 1996.

¹⁰ On the twins' Certificates of Birth Collin's name is given as 'Colin alias Merang' (7486 of 1858).

¹¹ Merrang pastoral station records in possession of the Hood family, Merrang.

¹² Robert Hood, *Merrang and the Hood Family*, p. 15.

¹³ Rev. James Paton (ed.), *John G. Paton D. D., Missionary to the New Hebrides. An Autobiography*, p. 270.

¹⁴ Paton, *John G. Paton*, p. 271.

¹⁵ See Rev. Hamilton's comment on the twins' Birth Certificates, 7486 and 7487 of 1858.

¹⁶ Dawson, *Australian Aborigines*, p. 41.

¹⁷ Paton, *John G. Paton*, p. 272.

¹⁸ Paton, *John G. Paton*, p. 272.

¹⁹ Paton, *John G. Paton*, p. 270.

²⁰ Paton, *John G. Paton*, p. 275.

²¹ Rough Draft of Minutes of Central Board Meeting, 11 June 1860, Series B335, Item 1 (AAV).

²² Minutes of Central Board Meeting, 12 November 1860, Series B335, Item 1 (AAV).

²³ Listing of topics for discussion at Central Board Meetings 7 June 1860–8 September 1862; Notes for Meeting of 11 June 1860, Series B335, Item 2 (AAV).

²⁴ I am thinking of Nora's comment that they had lost a home through drink (Paton, *John G. Paton*, p. 264) and the Rev. Hagenauer's 1 November 1889 comment quoted in this biography. Also, in the diary of Anthony MacKenzie of Woolongoon, Collin is mentioned as owning stock: 'Collin Hood . . . was in a great way because I had pounded a bullock of his, and he wished me to refund him the Pound fees, 8 shillings, but I would not' (20 July 1869).

²⁵ Domestic Intelligence, 'A Black Charge', *Warrnambool Examiner*, 31 May 1867.

²⁶ See for example Andrew Markus, *From the Barrel of a Gun. The Oppression of the Aborigines, 1860–1900*, p. 8.

²⁷ Bain Attwood, *The Making of the Aborigines*, pp. 20–1.

²⁸ Death Certificate no. 1948 of 1871.

²⁹ Warrnambool Court of Petty Sessions Register.

³⁰ Thwaites to Page, bundled in-letters, 27 April 1885 and Framlingham Manager's Letter Book, pp. 108–9, 4 May 1885, from notes made by the late Dr Diane Barwick.

³¹ John Mulvaney and Rex Harcourt, *Cricket Walkabout*, p. 2.

³² *Warrnambool Standard*, 19 January 1875; 7 March 1876; 7 April 1876; 5 March 1878; 28 December 1878.

³³ *Warrnambool Standard*, 20 February 1875.

³⁴ *Warrnambool Standard*, 7 March 1876.

35 *Warrnambool Standard,* 11 March 1879.
36 Collin Hood to Captain Page, Secretary, BPA, June 1884, Series B313, Item 57 (AAV).
37 *Camperdown Chronicle,* 23 November 1887.
38 *Warrnambool Standard,* Letters to the Editor, 29 October 1889.
39 *Warrnambool Standard,* Letters to the Editor, 1 November 1889.
40 *Warrnambool Standard,* 2 November 1889, pp. 2–3.
41 Hagenauer to Dr Morrison, 1 November 1889, Chief Secretary's Inward Correspondence, PROV, VPRS 3992, N13183, 1889.
42 *VPD,* Legislative Assembly, 25 September 1889, vol. 61, p. 1526.
43 *VPD,* Legislative Assembly, 23 September 1890, vol. 64, pp. 1711–19.
44 Extract from letter from James Dawson read by Mr Bailes, *VPD,* Legislative Assembly, 23 September 1890, vol. 64, p. 1718.
45 Minutes of the BPA, 5 February 1891, Series B314 (AAV).
46 Register of the Common School, Hexham, no. 296.
47 Minutes of the BPA, 1 August 1894, Series B314 (AAV).
48 *VPD,* Legislative Assembly, 1896, vol. 82, p. 1326.
49 Clothing Book, 1882–1907, Clothes distributed at Ramahyuck, 19 April 1887, B1272 (AAV).
50 Hagenauer to Chief Secretary, 9 July 1896, Chief Secretary's Inward Correspondence, PROV, VPRS 3992, Unit 898, C5228 in C7911 of 1897.
51 Hagenauer to Dr Morrison, 1 November 1889, enclosed in Morrison to Chief Secretary, 5 November 1889, Chief Secretary's Inward Correspondence, PROV, VPRS 3992, N13182 with N13183,1889.
52 Thirty-eighth Report of the BPA, *VPP,* 1902, no. 12, Appendix 3.
53 I am not sure I have all ten. I have only one mention of the Alice and Julia listed on Wallace's birth register details. The records mention that the Hood family members allowed to stay at Framlingham in 1890 were Louise, Collin, Sarah and Martha, but I have found no other mention of Sarah and find the lack of mention of Leah at this time odd. I think this is a mistake and should be Leah. The age given is correct for Leah.
54 Magisterial Inquiry into the death of Helen Hood, held at Orbost, 13 October 1915, PROV, VPRS 24, Unit 931, File no. 1102.
55 Colin Tatz, *Obstacle Race: Aborigines in Sport,* pp. 135–6, 370.
56 Tatz, *Obstacle Race,* pp. 259, 274–5, 366.

CHAPTER 7
DOUBLE DISPOSSESSION: KING DAVID

1   It also appeared in the *Camperdown Chronicle,* 26 September 1889.
2   See for example the Vagabond's account of his visit to the Framlingham Aboriginal community in early 1885, *Argus,* 3 January 1885.
3   Twenty-third Report of the BPA, 1 November 1887, *VPP,* 1887, no. 116, p. 3.
4   Hagenauer to Chief Secretary, 11 June 1897, PROV, VPRS 3992, Unit 946, F6503 of 1897.
5   Osburne, *History of Warrnambool,* p. 229.
6   *Warrnambool Standard,* 3 September 1889.
7   *Camperdown Chronicle,* 26 September 1889.
8   *Camperdown Chronicle,* 8 October 1889.
9   Robert Vickers to the Hon. J. L. Dow MP, 27 September 1889, handed on to Chief Secretary. Chief Secretary's Inward Correspondence, PROV, VPRS 3992, Unit 467, N11755 of 1889.
10 *Hamilton Spectator,* 5 October 1889, p. 4.

11 *Camperdown Chronicle*, 15 October 1889.

12 Dawson, *Australian Aborigines*, p. iv.

13 L. Bayer, Letter to the Editor, *Camperdown Chronicle*, 8 October 1889.

14 G. Presland (ed.), 'Journals of George Augustus Robinson March–May 1841', p. 31.

15 Presland (ed.), 'Journals of George Augustus Robinson March–May 1841', pp. 30, 105–10.

16 PROV, VPRS 12, Unit 2, Item 7.

17 R. Brough Smyth, *The Aborigines of Victoria*, vol. 2, pp. 233–4.

18 Presland (ed.), 'Journals of George Augustus Robinson March–May 1841', p. 48.

19 Dawson, *Australian Aborigines*, p. 103.

20 Dawson, *Australian Aborigines*, p. 103.

21 Discussion with Mr W. Weatherly, Mortlake, formerly of Woolongoon, 8 June 1996.

22 G. Soilleux, 'Blackfellow's Mounds'.

23 Dawson, Letter to the Editor, *Camperdown Chronicle*, 15 October 1889.

24 Dawson Scrapbook, p. 159.

25 Presland (ed.), 'Journals of George Augustus Robinson March–May 1841', p. 47.

26 Sievwright to Chief Protector, 5 November 1841, Lake Terang, in PROV, VPRS 30, Unit 185, Criminal Sessions: Port Phillip, Criminal Trial Briefs, 1841, 1842.

27 Statement of the Boldens and the stockmen in PROV, VPRS 30, Unit 185, Criminal Sessions: Port Phillip, Criminal Trial Briefs, 1841, 1842.

28 I. MacFarlane (comp.), *1842. The Public Executions at Melbourne*, pp. 19–20; Law Intelligence notes on the case held in the Aboriginal Cultural Heritage Unit, Museum of Victoria; see also Rev. Orton, Journal, vol. 2, p. 180. A1715 (ML).

29 MacFarlane, *1842*, p. 19 and Cannon, *Who Killed the Koories?*, pp. 60–1.

30 Dana to La Trobe, 22 November 1842, PROV, VPRS 19, 42/2153.

31 Blair to La Trobe, 29 January 1842, PROV, VPRS 19.

32 Aborigines (Australian Colonies), *House of Commons Sessional Papers*, 1844, vol. 34, no. 627, pp. 213–14; names added from the *Geelong Advertiser*, 4 April 1842.

33 Acheson French to La Trobe, 13 October 1842, in French Letterbook, MS 10053, Box 1298/1 (La Trobe Library).

34 Annual Report for 1846, PROV, VPRS 19, Unit 8, no. 716 of 1847. For more details on the Mt Rouse Protectorate Station see Critchett, *A distant field of murder*, Chapter 9.

35 *Camperdown Chronicle*, 15 October 1889.

36 See Marriage Certificate no. 2621/1867, marriage of Isabella Dawson and Joseph Erskine.

37 Letter to the Editor, *Australasian*, 19 March 1870.

38 R. H. W. Reece, *Aborigines and Colonists*, p. 119.

39 PROV, VPRS 24, Unit 31, Inquest no. 116/1856, George, a native.

40 PROV, VPRS 24, Unit 67, Inquest no. 556/1859.

41 *Warrnambool Examiner*, 22 March 1859, p. 2.

42 Quoted in Cannon, *Who Killed The Koories?*, p. 78.

43 William Thomas to Colonial Secretary, 13 September 1852, 52/3540 in PROV, VPRS 1189, Unit 20, Judicial Department, Crown Law Officers, Bundle 3, 52/3999.

44 'The Crown Law Officers respecting enactment of legislative measures to check the crime of murder among the natives', 10 October 1852, in PROV, VPRS 1189, Unit 20, Bundle 3, Judicial Department, 52/3999.

45 Post-mortem examination included in Proceedings of Inquest held upon the body of Neddy, PROV, VPRS 24, Unit 80, Inquest no. 275/1860.

46 PROV, VPRS 1526, Unit 6, Belfast Petty Sessions Record Book, 1 August 1860–3 October 1863.

47 Superintendent of Police, Belfast, to the Chief Commissioner of Police, Melbourne, 24 December 1861, in PROV, VPRS 937, Unit 33, Bundle 2, 1861, murder of Neddy, an Aboriginal.

48 Recommendation of the Jurymen who convicted Young Man Billy and Old Man Billy to be laid before the Executive Council, dated 27 October 1858, PROV, VPRS 264, Unit 1.

49 His Honour Mr Justice Williams to the Clerk of the Executive Council, 26 October 1858, enclosed with the recommendation of the jurymen, PROV, VPRS 264, Unit 1.

50 Second Report of the Central Board, *VPP*, 1862, no. 11, p. 14.

51 PROV, VPRS 937, Unit 32, Bundle 6, 1859. Report on Aborigines discharged, from Joseph Archibald, Sergeant at Warrnambool, to the Superintendent of Police, Belfast, 15 April 1859.

52 Register of Baptisms 1850–1908, Church of England, Parish of Warrnambool. Held at Christ Church, Warrnambool.

53 Eighth Report of the BPA, *VPP*, no. 60, 1872, p. 22.

54 Framlingham Manager's Letter Book, Thwaites to Page, 3 November 1884, Report for October 1884, from notes made by the late Dr Diane Barwick.

55 Information Dawson collected from Goodall, 1886, in Dawson Scrapbook, about pp. 159–60.

56 Thwaites to Page, Bundled In-letters, 27 April 1885; Thwaites in Framlingham Manager's Letter Book, pp. 108–9, Letter of 4 May 1885, Report for April.

57 *Camperdown Chronicle*, 10 May 1884 and Dawson Scrapbook.

58 Bundled In-letters, Goodall to the Secretary of the BPA, 7 March 1882, from notes made by the late Dr Diane Barwick.

59 BPA Secretary's Letter Book, no. 970, 1 October 1889, from notes made by the late Dr Diane Barwick.

60 Discussion with Banjo Clarke, 24 June 1996.

CHAPTER 8
JAMES DAWSON'S INFORMANTS

1 Dawson, *Australian Aborigines*, p. iii.

2 Dawson, *Australian Aborigines*, p. 45.

3 Dawson, *Australian Aborigines*, p. 44.

4 Death Certificate no. 10913/1894.

5 Information supplied by Woolsthorpe local historian, Gwen Bennett.

6 Framlingham Manager's Letter Book, 24 June 1882, from notes made by the late Dr Diane Barwick.

7 PROV, VPRS 24, Unit 444, Inquest no. 1146/1882.

8 Death Certificate no. 2881/1882.

9 Nineteenth Report of the BPA, *VPP*, 1884, no. 1, Appendix 2.

10 Ninth Report of the BPA, *VPP*, 1873, no. 14, Dr Jamieson's Report, p. 10.

11 Register of Baptisms 1850–1908, Church of England, Parish of Warrnambool (held at Christ Church, Warrnambool).

12 Death Certificate no. 11566/1875.

13 See Andrew Sayers, *Aboriginal Artists of the Nineteenth Century*.

14 I am indebted to Marie H. Fels for the detective work which finally revealed the story of the Kangatong Reserve. Details can be found in PROV, VPRS 629, Unit 1044, File 3872/1920 and Unit 26, File 33/4762.

15 Death Certificate no. 10056/1883.

16 Death Certificate no. 15270/1935.

17 Marriage Certificate no. 1908/1876.
18 Chief Secretary's Inward Correspondence, PROV, VPRS 3991, Unit 1104, J9682 of 1876. This is an important file, as it includes lists of Aboriginals required to reside at the various stations.
19 PROV, VPRS 1694, File A5315.
20 PROV, VPRS 3992, Unit 1096, L4155 of 1900.
21 Death Certificate no. 460/1880.

CHAPTER 9
'WHY ARE WE KEPT PRISONERS HERE?': ERNEST AND MAGGIE MOBOURNE

1 Michael Dodson, Aboriginal and Torres Strait Islander Social Justice Commissioner, *Australian Story*, ABC Television, 29 March 1997.
2 Royal Commission on the Aborigines (RCA), Report of the Commissioners ... together with Minutes of Evidence and Appendices, Presented to both Houses of Parliament, *VPP*, 1877, no. 76, Minutes of Evidence, p. 17.
3 RCA, Minutes of Evidence, pp. 36, 39.
4 RCA, Report, p. xii.
5 Twenty-ninth Annual Report of the BPA, *VPP*, 1893, no. 8, p. 6. Marriage Certificate 1693/1893.
6 Minutes of the BPA, 5 October 1892, Series B314 (AAV).
7 J. J. Sharrock, 'Reminiscences of the Lake Condah Blacks', *Portland Guardian*, 11 May 1961.
8 Stähle to Capt. Page, BPA Secretary, 19 June 1876, Series B313, Item 107 (AAV).
9 Mary Stähle to Page, 12 November 1880, Series B313, Item 115 (AAV).
10 The Board had received four detailed letters of complaint about Stähle during this period. They were (1) the Aboriginal Narrative signed by Johnny Sutton, Billy Gorrie and Tommy Green, July 1880; (2) a letter of complaint addressed to the Chief Secretary, 18 November 1880 (3) a letter of complaint addressed to C. M. Officer MLA from Tommy Green, Robert Turner and Harry Rose dated 16 February 1884 and (4) that of Thomas Green to the Chief Secretary, 22 July 1885, in Series B313 (AAV).
11 Report of the Board Appointed to Enquire into, and Report upon, the Present Condition and Management of the Coranderrk Aboriginal Station, *VPP*, 1882, no 5, p. iii.
12 John Murray to Peacock, 27 January 1897, Chief Secretary's Inward Correspondence, PROV VPRS 3992, Unit 898, C7911 of 1897.
13 Report of Chief Secretary's Visit to Lake Condah, Chief Secretary's Inward Correspondence, PROV VPRS 3992, E12789 of 1897.
14 Stähle to Hagenauer, 26 May 1899, Series B337, Item 507 (AAV).
15 Stähle to Hagenauer, 5 June 1899, Series B337, Item 507 (AAV).
16 Ernest Mobourne to the BPA, 7 June 1899; Stähle to Hagenauer, 9 June 1899, Series B337, Item 507 (AAV).
17 Stähle to Hagenauer, 27 June 1899, Series B337, Item 507 (AAV).
18 Constable Gleeson in note to Stähle replying to Stähle's note of 16 August 1899, Series B337, Item 507 (AAV).
19 Stähle to Hagenauer, 16 August 1899, Series B337, Item 507 (AAV).
20 This letter is with that by Stähle dated 26 May 1899, Series B337, Item 507 (AAV).
21 Undated letter to the Chairman and Members of the BPA per favour of Mr J. Murray MLA, Series B337, Item 507 (AAV).
22 Stähle to Hagenauer, 24 February 1900, Series B337, Item 507 (AAV).
23 Maggie Mobourne to Editor, *Hamilton Spectator*, Series B337, Item 507 (AAV).

24 Maggie Mobourne to Mr N. McLeod MLA, Vice Chairman, BPA, 27 February 1900, Series B337, Item 507 (AAV).

25 Stähle to Hagenauer, 3 March 1900, Series B337, Item 507 (AAV).

26 Stähle to Hagenauer, 5 March 1900, Series B337, Item 507 (AAV).

27 Report of Le Souef to F. A. Hagenauer, 6 March 1900, Series B337, Item 507 (AAV).

28 Constable Gleeson to Stähle, 14 April 1900, Series B337, Item 507 (AAV).

29 Stähle to Hagenauer, 10 April 1900, Series B337, Item 507 (AAV).

30 Stähle to Hagenauer, 13 April 1900, Series B337, Item 507 (AAV).

31 Death Certificates nos 6006/1900 and 6007/1900.

32 Twenty-sixth Report of the BPA, 4 October 1890, *VPP*, no. 212, 1890.

33 Minutes of BPA meeting, 6 December 1899.

34 Thirty-seventh Report of the BPA, *VPP*, 1901, no. 42, pp. 4–5.

35 Extract from Stähle's Report dated 31 December 1900, published in *Church Missionary Gleaner*, 1 January 1901, pp. 298–9.

36 Stähle's Report in *Church Missionary Gleaner*, 1 January 1901, pp. 298–9.

37 Thirty-seventh Report of the BPA, 3 September 1901, *VPP*, 1901, no. 42, p. 4.

38 Minutes of the BPA Meeting, 3 July 1901, Series B314 (AAV).

39 Ernest Mobourne to His Excellency, Sir George Sydenham Clarke, 8 May 1903, PROV, VPRS 1096, Inward Correspondence to the Governor, Unit 51, S3275A, 1903.

40 Stähle to Hagenauer, 28 March 1904, Series B337, Item 507 (AAV).

41 Rachel died at the Hamilton Hospital and was buried in Hamilton. Death Certificate no. 9165/1905.

42 Stähle did not know that Maggie had left Ernest before, and he told the Board that this must have occurred while they were at Lake Tyers (Stähle to the Acting Secretary, BPA, 30 August 1907, Series B337, Item 507).

43 Constable Adams, Heywood, to Superintendent Milne, Hamilton, 9 August 1907, attaching a letter from Stähle, Series B337, Item 507 (AAV).

44 Mobourne to Campbell, Chief Secretary's Inward Correspondence, PROV, VPRS 3992, Unit no. 1457, B5755 in file A5318 of 1907. For the petition, see The Aboriginals of Lake Condah to Members of the Cabinet, Chief Secretary's Inward Correspondence, A5318 of 1907.

45 Ernest Mobourne to the Ratepayers, Chief Secretary's Inward Correspondence, PROV, VPRS 3992, Unit no. 1457, B5755 in file A5318 of 1907.

46 Petition to His Excellency, the Governor-in-Council of the State of Victoria, Chief Secretary's Inward Correspondence, PROV, VPRS 3992, Unit no. 1457, B5755 in file A5318 of 1907.

47 Henry Pottage, Letter to the Editor, *Argus*, 8 June 1921.

48 Stähle to Secretary, BPA, 8 December 1910, Series B337, Item 507 (AAV).

49 Stähle to Secretary, BPA, 1 April 1911 and 23 September 1911, Series B337, Item 507 (AAV).

50 Maggie Mobourne to Stähle, 10 August 1912, Series B337, Item 507 (AAV).

51 Vice-Chairman, BPA, to Stähle, 22 August 1912, Series B337, Item 507 (AAV).

52 Statement by Rita Stähle, 24 August 1912, Series B337, Item 507 (AAV).

53 Vice-Chairman, BPA, to Stähle, 27 August 1912, Series B337, Item 507 (AAV).

54 Stähle to Vice-Chairman, BPA, 29 August 1912, Series B337, Item 507 (AAV).

55 Stähle to Secretary, BPA, 8 October 1912, Series B337, Item 507 (AAV).

56 Stähle to Secretary, BPA, 11 June 1913, Series B337, Item 507 (AAV).

57 Henry Albert to Mr Crawford, 17 December 1913, Series B337, Item 507 (AAV).

58 Crawford to Secretary, BPA, 17 December 1913, Series B337, Item 507 (AAV).

[59] Ernest Mobourne to Hon. John Murray, 26 May 1915, Series B337, Item 507 (AAV).

[60] Maggie Mobourne to Hon. John Murray, 3 November 1915, Series B337, Item 507 (AAV).

[61] Ernest Mobourne to the Governor of Victoria, 6 March 1916, Series B337, Item 507 (AAV).

[62] Marriage Certificate no. 11908 of 1915.

[63] Death Certificate no. 4520/1917.

[64] Death Certificate no. 3649/1918.

[65] Ann F. Bon, unofficial letter to Mr Bowser, 11 June 1918, BPA Correspondence Files, Lake Condah, Series B313, Item 138 (AAV).

[66] BPA to Mrs Bon, 8 June 1918, Series B337, Item 507 (AAV).

[67] Forty-third Report of the BPA, *VPP*, 1907, no. 47, Appendix 2, p. 7.

CHAPTER 10
'THE OLD ONES, THEY WOULDN'T TELL US NOTHING':
MRS CONNIE HART'S MEMORIES

[1] Merryl K. Robson, *Keeping The Culture Alive*, unpaged but above illustration 33.

[2] Peter Hewitt died on 1 February 1922 at the Lake Condah Mission Station. His age was given as ninety (Death Certificate no. 1977/1922). There is a surviving word-list of the language of the Kerrup Jmara collected from Peter Hewitt by James Lindsay in 1892. It is owned by his descendant, John Lindsay of Warrnambool.

[3] Bundled In-letters, Thwaites to Page, 4 February 1885, from notes made by the late Dr Diane Barwick.

[4] Sent 4 February 1885, from notes made by the late Dr Diane Barwick.

[5] Bundled In-letters, Thwaites to Page, 14 February 1885, from notes made by the late Dr Diane Barwick.

[6] Twenty-second Annual Report of the BPA, *VPP*, 1886, no. 99, Appendix V, p. 10 and Twenty-third Annual Report, *VPP*, 1887, no. 116, Appendix II, p. 7.

[7] Constable Loftus of the Heywood Police Station to the Board, 27 July 1896, in the Board's incoming correspondence, B313, Item 130 (AAV).

[8] Akeroyd to Hagenauer, 8 May 1897, B313, Item 60 (AAV).

[9] Hagenauer to D. Slattery, 9 September 1897, B329/2, Item 7 (AAV).

[10] Death Certificate no. 9165 of 1905.

CHAPTER 11
'BREAKING THE CYCLE IS THE HARD THING TO DO': GEOFF ROSE

[1] I interviewed Maisie on 8 July 1997, Henry on 20 June 1997, Banjo on 26 August 1997 and Mark on 22 August 1997.

EPILOGUE
JAMES DAWSON, CAMPERDOWN GEORGE AND THE OBELISK

[1] Penelope Selby to Mary, 1 March 1845, Penelope Selby Letters 1839–1851. Copy held by the Port Fairy Historical Society.

[2] Report of Canon Gason, Superintendent for the Mission to the Victorian Aborigines, Eighteenth Annual Report of the Church Missionary Association, Report for 1909. Copy held by the Rev. Dr Keith Cole of Bendigo.

[3] *VPD*, Legislative Assembly, 1896, vol. 82, p. 1324.

[4] Dawson, *Australian Aborigines*, p. 44.

[5] PROV, VPRS 12, Unit 4, Item 17.

[6] *Hampden Guardian*, Local and General News, 23 May 1876.

[7] Letter to the Editor, *Camperdown Chronicle*, 15 May 1876.

[8] *Hampden Guardian*, 16 June 1876.

[9] News and Notes, *Camperdown Chronicle*, 27 May 1882.

[10] 'The Camperdown Aborigines', *Camperdown Chronicle*, 5 July 1882.

[11] Death Certificate no. 577 of 1883.

[12] *Camperdown Chronicle*, 28 February 1883.

[13] *Town and Country Journal*, 7 August 1886, p. 279.

[14] D. J. Mulvaney, *Encounters in Place. Outsiders and Aboriginal Australians 1606–1985*, p. 164.

[15] Mulvaney, *Encounters in Place*, p. 164 and Dawson, *Australian Aborigines*, p. 3.

[16] Samuel Butler, *The Handbook for Australian Emigrants*, p. 15.

[17] Margaret Kiddle, *Men of Yesterday*, pp. 121–2.

[18] La Trobe to the Gentlemen signing a Representation without date ..., 26 March 1842, Aborigines (Australian Colonies), *House of Commons Sessional Papers*, 1844, vol. 34, no. 627, pp. 214–15.

[19] La Trobe to the Gentlemen signing a communication dated 23 April entrusted to the care of Messrs. Claude Farie and Niel Black, 15 July 1842, Archival estrays, Add 87 (Dixson Library).

[20] Colonial Secretary to La Trobe, 17 June 1842, CSIL Port Phillip 1843, Part 1, 4/2626, in accumulated file 42/2847 (Archives Office of NSW). See Critchett, *A 'distant field of murder'*, Chapters 7 and 8.

[21] Niel Black and others to La Trobe, 1 August 1842, PROV, VPRS 19, 42/1418; copy enclosed in CSIL Port Phillip 1843, Part 1, 4/2626, in accumulated file 42/2847 (Archives Office of NSW).

[22] Boldrewood, *Old Melbourne Memories*, p. 145.

[23] 'Last of the Tribe', *Town and Country Journal*, 7 August 1886, p. 279.

[24] L. Bayer to A. G. Stephens, 6 June 1903, Ab 120 Bayer L., catalogued under Dawson, Mitchell Library.

[25] James Dawson to Captain Page, 27 September 1886.

[26] James Dawson, Letter to the Editor, *Camperdown Chronicle*, 25 April 1896.

[27] Sir William Turner, *Report on the Scientific Results of the Voyage of H.M.S. Challenger*, vol. X, p. 28.

[28] These figures have been drawn from the following sources: 1863–77 from Diane Barwick, 'Changes in the Aboriginal Population of Victoria, 1863–1966', p. 298; 1887–90 from Twenty-sixth Report of the BPA, 4 October 1890, *VPP*, 1890, no. 212, p. 3; 1887 figures for 'half-castes' from Twenty-third Report of the BPA, 1 November 1887, *VPP*, 1887, no. 116, p. 4; 1899–1900 from Thirty-seventh Report of the BPA, 3 September 1901, *VPP*, 1901, no. 42, pp. 4–5.

[29] Twentieth Report of the BPA, *VPP*, 1884, no. 1, p. 5.

[30] Stähle's Report, in Twenty-fourth Report of the BPA, *VPP*, 1888, no. 119, Appendix 3, p. 8.

Bibliography

OFFICIAL PRINTED SOURCES

New South Wales

Legislative Council, Votes and Proceedings

1845   Report from the Select Committee on the Conditions of the Aborigines, with Appendix, Minutes of Evidence and Replies to a Circular Letter. vol. 2, pp. 117–358.

1849   Report from the Select Committee on the Aborigines and Protectorate, with Appendix, Minutes of Evidence and Replies to a Circular Letter. vol. 2, pp. 417–75.

Victoria

Legislative Council, Votes and Proceedings

1858–59   Report of the Select Committee of the Legislative Council on the Aborigines, together with the Proceedings of Committee, Minutes of Evidence and Appendices. D8.

Parliamentary Debates

Parliamentary Papers

1861–69   Annual Reports of the Central Board appointed ... to watch over the Interests of the Aborigines, presented to both Houses of Parliament.

1871–1925   Seventh to the Fifty-First Annual Reports of the Board for the Protection of the Aborigines, presented to both Houses of Parliament.

1877   Report of the Commissioners appointed to inquire into the present condition of the Aborigines ... and to advise as to the best means of caring for, and dealing with them in the future, together with Minutes of Evidence and Appendices.

1883   1881 Census.

Britain

House of Commons, Sessional Paper

1844   Aborigines (Australian Colonies). Return to an Address ... Copies or Extracts from the Despatches of the Governors of the Australian Colonies, with the Reports of the Protectors of Aborigines, and any other Correspondence to illustrate the Condition of the Aboriginal Population of the said Colonies ... vol. 34, no. 627.

OFFICIAL MANUSCRIPT SOURCES

Archives Office of New South Wales

Colonial Secretary's Correspondence, In Letters

Colonial Secretary's Special Bundles 4/7153, file 42/8829

Port Phillip Papers

1840   4/2510, 4/2511, 4/2512–1

1841   4/2547

1843   4/2626

1844 4/2665
1846 4/2741, 4/2742, 4/2743, 4/2744, 4/2745–1
1847 4/2748

Colonial Secretary, Commissioners of Crown Lands—Itineraries, microfilm roll no. 2748 (positive).

Australian Archives, Victoria

B312 Central Board appointed to Watch over the Interests of the Aborigines, correspondence files, 1860–1869.

B313 Board for the Protection of the Aborigines, correspondence files, 1869–1957.

B314 Minutes of BPA meetings, 1860–1967.

B330 Letter book of outward correspondence, Framlingham Station Manager, 1882–1889.

B335 Agenda items for BPA meetings, 1860–1968.

B337 Aboriginal case files

B2861 Register of inwards correspondence re financial and other matters.

B1272 Clothing book, Ramahyuck Mission Station, 1882–1907.

Public Record Office of Victoria

Aboriginal Protectorate Records

VPRS 10 Registered inward correspondence to the Superintendent Port Phillip District relating to Aboriginal Affairs.

VPRS 11 Unregistered inward correspondence to the Chief Protector of Aborigines.

VPRS 12 Aboriginal Protectorate returns.

VPRS 2893 Registered inward correspondence to the Superintendent Port Phillip District from W. Thomas and E. S. Parker.

VPRS 2895 Chief Protector of Aborigines outward letter book.

VPRS 2896 Registered inward correspondence to the Surveyor-General, Board of Land and Works.

VPRS 2897 Registered inward correspondence to the Land Branch, Superintendent of Port Phillip District relating to Aboriginal Stations.

VPRS 4397 Unregistered correspondence relating to the suspension of Charles Sievwright from the office of Assistant Protector of Aborigines, Western District.

VPRS 4399 Duplicate annual reports of the Chief Protector of Aborigines.

VPRS 4410 Aboriginal Protectorate weekly, monthly, quarterly and annual reports and journals.

VPRS 4414 Copy (abridged) of the Chief Protector's journal of an expedition to the Eastern Interior.

Other Series

VPRS 4 Police Magistrate Port Phillip District inward registered correspondence, 1836–39.

VPRS 19 Superintendent Port Phillip District registered inward correspondence, 1839–51.

VPRS 21 Crown Law Office, inward unregistered correspondence.

VPRS 24 Coroner's Court: inquest deposition files.

VPRS 30 Crown Solicitor's criminal trial briefs, 1841–1908.

VPRS 34 Police Magistrate, Portland, letter books.

VPRS 109 Geelong Police Office, deposition book.

VPRS 264   Capital case files, 1852–1925.

VPRS 515   Central Register of Male Prisoners.

VPRS 699   Warrnambool Petty Session Registers.

VPRS 626   Land selection files.

VPRS 937   Inwards correspondence to Chief Commissioner of Police.

VPRS 1095   Governor's Office, special files.

VPRS 1096   Governor's Office, inward correspondence.

VPRS 1189   Inward registered correspondence I (Chief Secretary's Office), 1851–63.

VPRS 1226   Chief Secretary, supplementary inward registered correspondence.

VPRS 1526   Belfast Petty Sessions Record Book, 1 August 1860–3 October 1863.

VPRS 1694   Board for the Protection of the Aborigines, correspondence files, 1889–1931.

VPRS 3991   Inward registered correspondence II (Chief Secretary's Department), 1864–84.

VPRS 3992   Inward registered correspondence III (Chief Secretary's Department), 1884–1959.

VPRS 7401   Case book of female patients, Ararat Asylum, Unit 7 (2 July 1906–19 December 1910), vol. G.

REGISTRY OF BIRTHS, DEATHS AND MARRIAGES, VICTORIA

Birth, Death and Marriage Certificates

OTHER MANUSCRIPT SOURCES

New South Wales

Dixson Library

Archival estrays. Official papers of New South Wales with individual items organised in lists: List 11, Protector and Assistant Protectors of Aborigines; List 20, Aborigines; List 30, Port Phillip District and Victoria.

Mitchell Library

Bayer, Louis to A. G. Stephens, 6 June 1903. Ab 120 Bayer L., catalogued under Dawson.

Orton, J. Journal 1832–39 (vol. 1) A1714; Journal 1840–41 (vol. 2) A1715; Letterbook 1836–42 (vol. 4) A1719; Letters 1826–41, MSS 942.

Robinson, George Augustus. Papers.

Vol. 17   Journals, Port Phillip Protectorate, 4 February–14 June 1841, parts 1–5, A7038.

Vol. 18   Journals, Port Phillip Protectorate, 8 June 1841–3 November 1842, parts 1–5, A7039. Field Journals, 3 November–2 December 1842, March–April 1843, October–November 1843, parts 7–9, A7039.

Vols 57, 57A   Correspondence and other papers, March 1839–49, A7078–A7078/2.

Vol. 59   Official reports, 1841, 1845–47, A7080.

Vol. 61   Annual reports, 1844–49, A7082.

Vols 62–3   Port Phillip Protectorate, miscellanea, includes sketches and Aboriginal vocabularies, A7083–4.

Vol. 65   Aboriginal vocabularies, South-east Australia, A7086.

Vol. 66   Miscellanea, A7087.

Vol. 67   Aboriginal vocabularies, South-east Australia, part 1, A7088.

Thomas, William. Papers, Uncatalogued MSS, Set 214, Items 1–24.

New South Wales Parliamentary Archives

New South Wales Legislative Council manuscript records. Copies of many documents concerning the Aborigines of the Port Phillip District, LA 35.

Victoria

La Trobe Library

Black, Niel. Journal of the first few months spent in Australia, 30 September 1839 to 8 May 1840, MS 11519.

Black, Niel. Outward Letterbook, January 1840 to October 1841, MS 8996.

Dawson, James. Scrapbook, MS 11514.

French, Acheson Jeremiah. Letterbook, 1 October 1841 to 10 October 1862, MS 10053.

Griffith, Charles James. Diary, 1840–41, MS 9393.

Henty, Edward. Daily Journal, Portland Bay, 19 November 1834 to 5 July 1839, 118A.

Henty, Francis. Diary, December 1834 to February 1838, H15592.

Howitt, Alfred William. Papers. Box 1053/1 (a), (b), (c), (d); Box 1053/5 (a), Box 1054/3 (b), MS 9356.

McKnight, Charles Hamilton. Journals (known as the Dunmore Journals), MS 8999.

Selby, Penelope. Letters, MS 9494.

Smyth, R. Brough. R. Brough Smyth Papers, MS 8781.

Tuckfield, Francis. The journal of Francis Tuckfield, missionary to Port Phillip, Southern Australia, 1839–42, MS 11341.

Wilson, Edward. Papers, MS 6369, Box 303/5 (b).

Winter Cooke family. Papers, MS 10840.

Museum of Victoria

Howitt, A. W. Papers, boxes 1–10.

Robinson, George Augustus. Robinson to La Trobe, 7 October 1842, Report of an expedition to the Aboriginal Tribes of the Western Interior during the months of March, April, May, June, July and August 1841, 42/1870.

University of Melbourne Archives

Ritchie, James. Diary for November and December 1841, 'Tour of the West', collection of R. B. Ritchie and Son.

Collections held locally in the Western District

Flower, Charles. Reminiscences, undated. Copy in possession of Mary Hamilton, Geelong.

Framlingham Manager's Letter Book. Copy of synopsis of the letter book and of the in-letters to the BPA from Framlingham made by the late Dr Diane Barwick. Copy given for personal use in the mid-1970s.

Lindsay, James. Aboriginal Language and Legends, Lake Condah, February 1892. Notes made by Lindsay when employed at Lake Condah, in possession of John Lindsay, Warrnambool.

McCann Papers. Port Fairy Historical Society.

MacKenzie, M. E. Early history of Peterborough. Paper in possession of Ann Wilkinson, Peterborough.

Merrang pastoral station records in possession of the Hood family, Merrang.

Pennycuick family. Newspaper cutting book. In possession of S. Pennycuick, Hamilton.

Register of Baptisms 1850–1908, Church of England, parish of Warrnambool. Held at Christ Church, Warrnambool.

Rutledge, Eliza. Letter to Martha Hamilton, 31 January 1885, in possession of David Hamilton, Geelong.

Warrnambool Cemetery Records.

NEWSPAPERS

Age
Argus
Camperdown Chronicle
Geelong Advertiser
Hamilton Spectator
Hampden Guardian
Portland Guardian and Normanby General Advertiser
Portland Mercury and Normanby Advertiser
Portland Mercury and Port Fairy Register
Port Phillip Gazette
Port Phillip Herald
Star (Melbourne)
Terang Express
Town and Country Journal
Warrnambool Examiner
Warrnambool Standard

THESES

Fels, Marie Hansen. Good Men and True: The Aboriginal Police of the Port Phillip District 1837–53. Ph.D, University of Melbourne, 1986.

Kerley, William D. In My Country: Race Relations in the Portland–Warrnambool District 1834–1886. MA, La Trobe University, 1981.

Lourandos, Harry. Forces of Change: Aboriginal Technology and Population in South Western Victoria. Ph.D, University of Sydney, 1980.

Wilkinson, Linda M. Aboriginality: The Framlingham Experience. Ph.D, La Trobe University, 1991.

Williams, Elizabeth. Wet Underfoot? Earth Mound Sites and the Recent Prehistory of Southwestern Victoria. Ph.D, Australian National University, 1985.

INTERVIEWS

Alberts, Henry. 20 June 1997.

Clarke, Banjo. 5 February 1996, 29 April 1996, 1 May 1996, 24 June 1996, 3 October 1996, 26 August 1997, 15 September 1997, 21 September 1997.

Clarke, Maisie. 8 July 1997.

Clarke, Mary. 23 April 1979.

Grauer, Reg. December 1996.

Hart, Connie. 26 June 1993.

Moloney, Robert. 8 September 1996.

Mathieson, Rex. 14 October 1996.

Rose, Mark. 22 August 1997.

PUBLISHED SOURCES

Allansford 125th Anniversary Celebrations Committee. *Allan's Ford: Allansford 1855–1981.* Warrnambool, n. d.

Attwood, Bain. *The Making of the Aborigines.* Allen & Unwin, Sydney, 1989.

Australian Archives and the Public Record Office of Victoria. *'My Heart is Breaking'. A Joint Guide to Records about Aboriginal People in the Public Record Office of Victoria and the Australian Archives, Victorian Regional Office.* Australian Government Publishing Service, Canberra, 1993.

Barwick, Diane. 'Changes in the Aboriginal Population of Victoria 1863–1966', in D. J. Mulvaney and J. Golson (eds), *Aboriginal Man and Environment in Australia.* ANU Press, Canberra, 1971, pp. 288–315.

—— 'Equity for Aborigines? The Framlingham Case', in Patrick N. Troy (ed.), *A Just Society? Essays in Equity in Australia.* Allen & Unwin, Sydney, 1981, pp. 173–218.

—— 'Mapping the past: an atlas of Victorian clans 1835–1904', *Aboriginal History*, vol. 8, part 2, 1984, pp. 100–31.

Bassett, Marnie. *The Hentys: An Australian Colonial Tapestry.* Melbourne University Press, Melbourne, 1962.

Billis, R. V. and Kenyon, A. S. (eds). *Pastoral Pioneers of Port Phillip.* Second edition, Stockland Press, Melbourne, 1974.

Blainey, Geoffrey. *Triumph of the Nomads: A History of Ancient Australia.* Sun Books, Melbourne, 1976.

Boldrewood, Rolf. *Old Melbourne Memories.* William Heinemann, Melbourne, 1969. First published 1884.

Bonwick, James. *Western Victoria: Its Geography, Geology and Social Condition: The Narrative of an Educational Tour in 1857.* William Heinemann, Melbourne, 1970. First published 1858.

Bride, Thomas Francis (ed.). *Letters from Victorian Pioneers.* Lloyd O'Neil, Melbourne, 1983. First published 1898.

Broome, Richard. *Aboriginal Australians: Black Response to White Dominance 1788–1980.* Allen & Unwin, Sydney, second edition, 1994.

—— 'Professional Aboriginal Boxers in Eastern Australia 1930–1979', *Aboriginal History*, vol. 4, June 1980, pp. 49–72.

Butler, Samuel. *The Handbook for Australian Emigrants.* Glasgow, 1839.

Campbell, Alastair (comp.). *Victorian Aborigines. John Bulmer's Recollections 1855–1908.* Occasional Papers, Anthropology and History, Museum of Victoria, no. 1, 1994.

Cannon, Michael (ed.). *Aborigines and Protectors 1838–1839.* (Historical Records of Victoria. Foundation Series, Volume 2B.) Victorian Government Printing Office, Melbourne, 1983.

—— (ed.). *The Aborigines of Port Phillip 1835–1839.* (Historical Records of Victoria. Foundation Series, Volume 2A.) Victorian Government Printing Office, Melbourne, 1982.

—— (ed.). *Beginnings of Permanent Government.* (Historical Records of Victoria. Foundation Series, Volume 1.) Victorian Government Printing Office, Melbourne, 1981.

—— *Who Killed The Koories?* William Heinemann Australia, Melbourne, 1990.

Carroll, J. R. *Harpoons to Harvest: The story of Charles and John Mills, pioneers of Port Fairy.* Warrnambool Institute Press, Warrnambool, 1989.

Cato, Nancy. *Mister Maloga.* University of Queensland Press, St Lucia, revised edition, 1993.

Chesterman, John and Galligan, Brian. *Citizens Without Rights. Aborigines and Australian Citizenship.* Cambridge University Press, Melbourne, 1997.

Christie, M. F. *Aborigines in Colonial Victoria 1835–86.* Sydney University Press, Sydney, 1979.

Clark, Ian D. *Aboriginal Languages and Clans: An Historical Atlas of Western and Central Victoria, 1800–1900.* Monash Publications in Geography, no. 37, Department of Geography and Environmental Science, Monash University, Melbourne, 1990.

—— (ed.). *The Port Phillip Journals of George Augustus Robinson: 8 March–7 April 1842 and 18 March–29 April 1843.* Department of Geography, Monash University, Melbourne, 1988.

—— *Scars in the Landscape: a register of massacre sites in western Victoria, 1803–1859.* Report series, Australian Institute of Aboriginal and Torres Strait Islander Studies, Canberra, 1995.

Cole, Keith. *The Aborigines of Victoria.* Keith Cole Publications, Bendigo, 1981.

—— *The Lake Condah Aboriginal Mission.* Keith Cole Publications, Bendigo, 1984.

Corris, Peter. *Aborigines and Europeans in Western Victoria.* Occasional Papers in Aboriginal Studies, no. 12, Ethnohistory Series 1, Australian Institute of Aboriginal Studies, Canberra, 1968.

Coutts, P. J. F. 'An archaeological perspective of the Western District, Victoria', in J. Sherwood, J. Critchett and K. O'Toole (eds), *Settlement of the Western District: From Prehistoric Times to the Present.* Warrnambool Institute Press, Warrnambool, 1985, pp. 21–67.

—— *Readings in Victorian Prehistory Volume 2: The Victorian Aboriginals 1800 to 1860.* Ministry for Conservation, Victoria, 1981.

Coutts, P. J. F. et al. 'The Mound People of Western Victoria: A Preliminary Statement', *Records of the Victorian Archaeological Survey*, no. 1, Ministry for Conservation, Victoria, 1976.

Coutts, P. J. F., Frank, R. K. and Hughes, P. J. 'Aboriginal Engineers of the Western District', *Records of the Victorian Archaeological Survey*, no. 7, Ministry for Conservation, Victoria, 1978.

Coutts, P. J. F., Witter, D. C. and Parsons, D. M. 'Impact of European Settlement on Aboriginal Society in Western Victoria', *Records of the Victorian Archaeological Survey*, no. 4, 1977, pp. 17–58.

Critchett, Jan. 'A closer look at cultural contact: some evidence from "Yambuck", Western Victoria', *Aboriginal History*, vol. 8, part 1, 1984, pp. 12–20.

—— *A distant field of murder: Western District frontiers 1834–1848.* Melbourne University Press, Melbourne, 1990. Paperback edition 1992.

—— *Our Land Till We Die: A History of the Framlingham Aborigines.* Revised edition, Deakin University Press, Australia Felix Series, Warrnambool, 1992. First published 1980.

—— (ed.). *Richard Bennett's Early Days of Port Fairy.* Warrnambool Institute Press, Warrnambool, 1984.

Davies, Suzanne. 'Aborigines, Murder and the Criminal Law in Early Port Phillip, 1841–1851', *Historical Studies*, vol. 22, no. 88, 1987, pp. 313–32.

Dawson, James. *Australian Aborigines: The Languages and Customs of Several Tribes of Aborigines in the Western District of Victoria, Australia.* Australian Institute of Aboriginal Studies, Canberra, 1981. First published 1881.

Duncan, J. S. (ed.). *Atlas of Victoria.* Victorian Government Printer, Melbourne, 1982.

Earle, William. *Earle's Port Fairy.* Olinda Public Relations Pty. Ltd., Olinda, 1973. First published 1896.

Eggleston, E. *Fear, Favour or Affection. Aborigines and the Criminal Law in Victoria, South Australia and Western Australia.* Australian National University Press, Canberra, 1976.

Fels, Marie Hansen. *Good Men and True: The Aboriginal Police of the Port Phillip District 1837–1853.* Melbourne University Press, Melbourne, 1988.

Fison, L. and Howitt, A. W. *Kamilaroi and Kurnai.* George Robertson, Melbourne, 1880.

Goldstraw, Alice. *The Border of the Heytesbury.* Terang Express Office, Terang, 1937.

Gott, Beth. 'Plants Mentioned in Dawson's *Australian Aborigines*', *The Artefact*, vol. 10, 1985, pp. 3–14.

Hall, Rodney. *J. S. Manifold. An introduction to the man and his work.* University of Queensland Press, St Lucia, 1978.

Henty, Richmond. *Australiana or My Early Life.* Sampson Low, Marston, Searle & Rivington, London, 1886.

Hood, Robert. *Merrang and the Hood Family.* Deakin University Press, Australia Felix Series, Warrnambool, 1991.

Howitt, A. W. *The Native Tribes of South East Australia.* Macmillan, London, 1904.

Jackomos, Alick and Fowell, Derek. *Forgotten Heroes. Aborigines at War from the Somme to Vietnam.* Victoria Press, Melbourne, 1993.

Jackomos, Alick and Fowell, Derek. *Living Aboriginal History of Victoria. Stories in the Oral Tradition.* Cambridge University Press, Melbourne, 1991.

Johnston, Commissioner Elliott. *Royal Commission into Aboriginal Deaths in Custody. National Report. Overview and Recommendations.* Australian Government Publishing Service, Canberra, 1991.

Kenyon, A. S. 'Aboriginal Protectorate of Port Phillip: Report of an Expedition to the Aboriginal Tribes of the Western Interior by the Chief Protector, George Augustus Robinson', *Victorian Historical Magazine*, vol. 12, no. 3, 1928, pp. 138–71.

Kiddle, Margaret. *Men of Yesterday: A Social History of the Western District of Victoria.* Melbourne University Press, Melbourne, 1962.

——— 'Vandiemonian Colonists in Port Phillip, 1834–50', *Tasmanian Historical Research Association Papers and Proceedings*, vol. 3, no. 9, 1954, pp. 37–45.

Leason, Percy. *The Last of the Victorian Aborigines.* Issued in conjunction with an exhibition of portraits at the Athenaeum Gallery, Melbourne, 1934.

Lourandos, Harry. 'Aboriginal Settlement and Land Use in South Western Victoria: A Report on Current Field Work', *The Artefact*, vol. 1, no. 4, 1976, pp. 174–93.

——— 'Aboriginal Spatial Organisation and Population: South Western Victoria Reconsidered', *Archaeology and Physical Anthropology in Oceania*, vol. 12, no. 3, 1977, pp. 202–25.

——— 'Change or stability?: hydraulics, hunter-gatherers and population in temperate Australia', *World Archaeology*, vol. 11, no. 3, 1980, pp. 245–64.

——— 'Swamp Managers of Southwestern Victoria', in D. J. Mulvaney and J. Peter White (eds), *Australians to 1788*, Fairfax, Syme & Weldon Associates, Sydney, 1987, pp. 292–307.

MacFarlane, Ian (comp.). *1842. The Public Executions at Melbourne.* Public Records Office of Victoria, Melbourne, 1984.

Manifold, W. G. *The Wished-for-Land. The Migration and Settlement of the Manifolds of Western Victoria.* Ausbooks, Camperdown, 1986.

Markus, Andrew. *Australian Race Relations 1788–1993.* Allen & Unwin, Sydney, 1994.

—— *From the Barrel of a Gun. The Oppression of the Aborigines, 1860–1900.* Victorian Historical Association, Melbourne, 1974.

Massola, Aldo. *The Aboriginal People.* Cypress Books, Clayton, Victoria, 1968.

—— *The Aborigines of South-Eastern Australia As They Were.* Heinemann, Melbourne, 1971.

—— *Journey to Aboriginal Victoria.* Rigby, Adelaide, 1969.

Memories Last Forever. Aboriginal History Programme, Abbotsford, Victoria, 1988.

Mortlake Historical Society. *Pastures of Peace: A Tapestry of Mortlake Shire.* Shire of Mortlake, Warrnambool, 1985.

Mulvaney, D. J. *Encounters in Place. Outsiders and Aboriginal Australians 1606–1985.* University of Queensland Press, St Lucia, 1989.

Mulvaney, D. J. and Harcourt, Rex. *Cricket Walkabout. The Australian Aborigines in England.* Macmillan, Melbourne, 1988.

Mulvaney, D. J. and White, J. Peter (eds). *Australians to 1788.* Fairfax, Syme and Weldon Associates, Sydney, 1987.

Nullawarre School Centenary and District History. 'Back To' Celebrations, Easter 1975. Souvenir booklet, no author, [1975].

Osburne, Richard. *The History of Warrnambool from 1847 up to the end of 1886.* Chronicle Printing and Publishing Company Ltd, Prahran, 1887.

Paton, Rev. James (ed.). *John G. Paton D.D., Missionary to the New Hebrides. An Autobiography.* Hodder & Stoughton, London, 1894.

Pepper, Phillip. *You Are What You Make Yourself To Be. The Story of a Victorian Aboriginal Family 1842–1980.* Hyland House, Melbourne, 1980.

Powling, J. W. *Port Fairy. The First Fifty Years.* William Heinemann Australia, Melbourne, 1980.

Presland, Gary (ed.). 'Journals of G. A. Robinson January 1840–March 1840', *Records of the Victorian Archaeological Survey,* no. 5, Ministry for Conservation, Victoria, 1977.

—— (ed.). 'Journals of G. A. Robinson March–May 1841', *Records of the Victoria Archaeological Survey,* no. 6, Ministry for Conservation, Melbourne, 1977.

—— (ed.). 'Journals of G. A. Robinson May–August 1841', *Records of the Victorian Archaeological Survey,* no. 11, Ministry for Conservation, Melbourne, 1980.

Reece, R. H. W. *Aborigines and Colonists: Aborigines and Colonial Society in New South Wales in the 1830s and 1840s.* Sydney University Press, Sydney, 1974.

Reynolds, Henry. *Frontier: Aborigines, Settlers and Land.* Allen & Unwin, Sydney, 1987.

—— *The Other Side of the Frontier: Aboriginal resistance to the European invasion of Australia.* Penguin, Ringwood, 1982.

Rintoul, Stuart. *The Wailing. A National Black Oral History.* Reed Books Australia, Melbourne, 1993.

Robson, Merryl K. *Keeping the Culture Alive.* Hamilton City Council, Hamilton, 1986.

Rose, Deborah Bird. *Nourishing Terrains. Australian Aboriginal Views of Landscape and Wilderness.* Australian Heritage Commission, Canberra, 1996.

Rowley, C. D. *Outcasts in White Australia.* Penguin Books, Ringwood, 1972.

Savill, Vanda. *Dear Friends, Lake Condah Mission, etc.* Kalprint Graphics, Hamilton, 1976.

Sayers, Andrew. *Aboriginal Artists of the Nineteenth Century.* Oxford University Press in conjunction with the National Gallery of Australia, Melbourne, 1994.

Shaw, A. G. L. and Clark, C. M. H. (eds). *Australian Dictionary of Biography 1788–1850.* Melbourne University Press, Melbourne, 1966–67.

Smyth, R. Brough. *The Aborigines of Victoria with Notes Relating to the Habits of the Natives of other parts of Australia and Tasmania.* 2 volumes, George Robertson, Melbourne, 1878.

Soilleux, G. 'Blackfellow's Mounds', in Robert T. Litton (ed.), *Transactions of the Historical Society of Australasia*, vol. 1, Historical Society of Australasia, Melbourne, 1891.

Special People. Aboriginal History Programme, Abbotsford, Melbourne, 1988.

Spreadborough, R. and Anderson, H. (eds). *Victorian Squatters.* Red Rooster Press, Ascot Vale, 1983.

Stanner, W. E. H. *After the Dreaming. Black and White Australians—An Anthropologist's View.* The Boyer Lectures 1968, Australian Broadcasting Commission, Sydney, 1969.

Tatz, Colin. *Obstacle Race. Aborigines in Sport.* University of New South Wales Press, Sydney, 1995.

Tindale, N. B. *Aboriginal Tribes of Australia. Their terrain, environmental controls, distribution, limits and proper names.* ANU Press, Canberra, 1974.

Turner, Sir William. *Report on the Scientific Results of the Voyage of H.M.S. Challenger during the years 1873–76.* Published by Order of Her Majesty's Government, London, vol. X, 1884.

West, Rosemary. 'The Killing Time', *Age Saturday Extra*, 5 March 1994.

Williams, Elizabeth. 'Complex hunter-gatherers: A view from Australia', *Antiquity*, vol. 61, no. 232, 1987, pp. 310–21.

—— 'Documentation and Archaeological Investigation of an Aboriginal "Village" Site in South Western Victoria', *Aboriginal History*, vol. 8, part 2, 1984, pp. 173–88.

—— 'Estimation of prehistoric populations of archaeological sites in southwestern Victoria: some problems', *Archaeology in Oceania*, vol. 20, 1985, pp. 73–80.

Index

Page references to illustrations are in *italics*.

Aboriginal languages, 2, 114, 125, 188–9, 194, 262
Aboriginal responses to European settlement: attacks on settlers and their property, 19, 21, 27, 41–2, 49–51, 119–20, 122–3; confinement to stations resisted, 14, 28, 39, 224–5; pacification in 1850s, 27–8; *see also* Port Phillip Protectorate
Aboriginal stations, *see* Board for the Protection of the Aborigines; Central Board to Watch over the Interests of the Aborigines; Port Phillip Protectorate. *See also* under names of individual stations: Coranderrk; Ebenezer; Framlingham; Lake Condah; Lake Tyers; Ramahyuck
Aboriginal traditional customs: basket-weaving, 39, 181–2, 184–5; belief in transcendental travel, 187; body markings, 115–16; corroborees, 133; 'country', 13–14, 25, 50–1, 57, 80–2, 95, 235, 237 (*see also* dispossession; land rights); doctors or sacred men, 83, 186–7; fish traps, 62–3, 72; food, 22, 39, 47, 62–3, 72, 116–17; handed down (or not), 187–90, 192, 193–4; housing and shelters, 9, 22, 26–7, 40, 45, 116–18, 192, 224–5; inter-clan suspicions lessen, 82–3; Isabella Dawson's study of, 125; James Dawson's study, *see* James Dawson; marriage, rules governing, 80, 109–10; meetings, 20–1, 53, 119, 127n; mounds, 116–18; movement within country, 15, 39, 45, 83, 225; numbers speaking language, 188–9, 194; polygamy, 26–7; punishment, 24, 66–7, 125–9, 190–1 (*see also* killing of Aboriginals); singing of a victim, 190; 'The Flatfish' story, 52–4; taking of kidney fat, 190–1; travelling through other clans' country, 25, 127, 128; tribal names, xviii, 124; widening of kinship links, 80–1
Aboriginality, *see* Koori identity
Aborigines Protection Law Amendment Act (1886) ('Half-Caste Act'): amendment, 1910 (assistance to half-castes), 222; child removals, 163–5, 198–9, 201–4, 234–5; definitions of 'half-caste' and 'white', 27n, 108, 109; rations refused to 'half-castes', 99, 108,

197–8; removal of 'half-castes' from stations, 108–9, 133, 150; restrictions on marriage of 'full-blood' Aboriginals, 109–10; *see also* Board for the Protection of the Aborigines (BPA); 'half-castes'
Abraham, William (Billy), 42–4
Abraham, Wilmot (Corwhorong), 33, *36*, 36–47, *40*, *44*, 140, 147; ancestry, 42–3; attitude to living at Framlingham, 39, 46; death, 46–7; drunkenness, 40–1; postcards of, *36*, 37; Koori memories of, 37–8; travelling around 'country', 39, 45–6
abuse and violence towards Aboriginals, 3–7, 33–4, 77, 81, 114, 120, 123, 228–30; *see also* dispossession; killing of Aboriginals
agricultural college and experimental farm, 108, 110
Akeroyd, Sergeant, 198
Alberts, Angus, 181; at Framlingham, 182, 188; wife, 189–90
Alberts, Beattie, 185
Alberts, Effie, 185
Albert(s), Henry, *48*, *79*, 145, 166–9, 173–4, 178, 181–5, 192–3, 195–7; and Maggie Mobourne, 166–9, 173–4; and Rachel Dawson, 195–7; at Framlingham, 197; at Lake Condah, 199; at Little Dunmore, 192–3; conducted church services, 182, 185; Connie Hart's memories of, 181–5; employment, 193, 197; marries Jessie Lancaster, 178, 183n; naming, 195
Alberts, Henry (grandson of Henry Albert(s)), 58, 201–2
Alberts, Jessie (née Blair, then Brown, then Lancaster), 17n, *79*, 178, 183–4, *184*, 185, 194
Alberts, Joseph (Jo), *184*
Alberts, Louie, 183, *184*
Alberts, Rachel (née Dawson), 195–9
Alberts, Roderick ('Mookeye'), 191, 193
Alberts, Sally, 185
Albion House, 164
alcohol: abstaining from, 60, 91, 133; effect on Aboriginals, 30–2, 40–1, 84–5, 90–1, 132–3, 228; supply to Aboriginals prohibited, 13, 30–1, 70, 72; *see also* prison
Alfred, Prince, Duke of Edinburgh, 28–9
Allan, John McMahon, 16, 21, 26, 38, 42–3